JL 709 JON

_____ The Jet Pioneers

The Jet Pioneers

The Birth of Jet-Powered Flight

Glyn Jones

Methuen

To Daphne, Nicholas,
Sarah and Gareth
– who waited

First published in Great Britain 1989
by Methuen London
Michelin House, 81 Fulham Road, London SW3 6RB
Copyright © Glyn Jones 1989

Printed and bound in Great Britain
by Richard Clay Ltd, Bungay, Suffolk

Cataloguing in Publication Data is available
on request from the British Library.

ISBN 0 413 50400 X

Contents

Jet propulsion is one of humanity's great adventures. The first flight of the first jet was aviation's most important event since the Wright brothers became airborne and the story will be told for as long as men and women are curious to know how the human species has developed on – or just above – this planet.

This book aims to tell for the first time the full story of the British, German and American strivings to invent, develop and fly the jet engine during the lowering peace of the 1930s and, after that, in the darkest war in human history. It was a close-run race, with the British indisputably first, the Germans starting later but overtaking the British because of wilful malice and inefficiency within the British civil service and industry, and then the Americans, invited into the club by the British but quickly starting to outplay them towards the end of the war.

The story is about much more than the hunks of inert metal which stand around the museums of the world today. It is about intangibles – the power of an idea to change the world, and the mysterious demon which drives inventors on, even to the edge of self-destruction, in their pursuit of a better way of doing things. Just as these forces pulse strongly in the arteries of our best engineers and scientists, so the dams of inertia stand solidly ahead of them. As Machiavelli noted, the old order will always have more defenders than the new, so there are always the makings of human drama, even tragedy, in the annals of invention. The jet pioneers were no exception to the rule, but when they succeeded they did so to glorious effect: once the war was over they shrank the world.

So close were the German and British efforts in the 1930s and 1940s that the chapters here cross-cut between events in each country, following the progress of an idea from concept to reality almost blow for blow. The problems that were met and had to be overcome were so similar that the British and German jet pioneers, working in secrecy from one another, jumped the same hurdles, often in the same way, because there was only one sure route to the jet engine.

But within that route there was a world of fascinating detailed differences. Who would have thought that at one moment the German Air Ministry was almost begging its manufacturers to take on the jet engine, while the British Air Ministry stood disdainfully by, waiting for our one serious competitor to fail?

Any author dealing with the jet revolution must owe a great deal to Sir Frank Whittle for writing his memoir of his struggles, and also to William Green, whose *Warplanes of the Third Reich* (Macdonald and Jane) is a monumental work of research and learning. My ideas were much influenced by both. My thanks to the following publishers for permission to quote passages from books they have published: HMSO and Longman, *Design and Development of Weapons* by M. M. Postan, D. Hay and J. D. Scott; Sir Henry Royce Memorial Foundation, *Hives, the Quiet Tiger* by Alec Harvey Bailey: Heinemann, *The Brabazon Story* by Lord Brabazon of Tara; Century Hutchinson, *Jet, the Story of a Pioneer* by Sir Frank Whittle and *He 1000* by Ernst Heinkel; Airlife Publishing, *Not Much of an Engineer* by Sir Stanley Hooker; Cassell, *With Prejudice* by Lord Tedder; Methuen, *Sir Henry Tizard* by Ronald W. Clark.

My thanks for help with this book, which has been six years, on and off, in the writing, go first to two members of my family – my wife Daphne who devotedly pulled me through three serious illnesses and kept me pegging away at it, and my son Nicholas, an historian by training, who first broached the enormous quantity of material, hitherto untapped, in the Public Record Office at Kew and discovered the remarkable history of British jet development, written from all the secret documents at the end of the war, by Miss Cynthia Keppel (Lady Cynthia Postan). I refer to Lady Cynthia as the official historian throughout: her narrative was invaluable.

The jet pioneers I approached all greeted me with warmth and helped me greatly. They were: Sir Frank Whittle OM and Lady Whittle; Dr Hans von Ohain and his wife; Lord Kings Norton; Sir William Hawthorne; the late Sir Stanley Hooker; Dr G. B. R. Feilden; Roy Fowkes; the late Raymond Holl and his wife Cynthia; Dr Anselm Franz and Dr Helmet Schelp. The staff of the National Air and Space Museum, Washington, gave valuable help in my early work.

The prize for patience and prodding goes to my agent, Murray Pollinger, and of course my thanks to the Methuen team, especially Ann Mansbridge and Ann Wilson; and thanks also to the excellent *New Scientist* magazine who started it all off by publishing two articles of mine on this theme.

Glyn Jones
April 1989

The Jet Pioneers

Prologue _____ 'It flies!'

Five am, Sunday, 27 August 1939: at Marienehe, a lonely airfield near the German Baltic port of Rostock. It is a brilliant dawn with a clear blue sky except for a thin haze a few hundred feet off the ground, highlighted by the rising sun. A German test pilot of great skill and almost reckless bravery, Eric Warsitz, climbs into the cockpit of a grey shoulder-wing monoplane, the Heinkel 178. It has no propeller. Warsitz has been loaned for the day by Wernher von Braun, who is busy developing rocket missiles down the coast at Peenemunde. He runs up the engine, watched by Ernst Heinkel, the small, plump, self-important but gifted planemaker, and a group of his senior staff. Among them is a tense young man, aged twenty-eight and more than six feet tall – Hans Joachim Pabst von Ohain, who only four years previously had completed his postgraduate studies; it is his engine that powers the plane – a jet engine. On test, some of the bearings have run hot and the plane's undercarriage will not retract: the flight should be postponed. But Heinkel insists. Von Ohain and Warsitz and their patron Heinkel are about to initiate the jet age. Germany is about to initiate the most cataclysmic war in history; the first shots will be fired five days later.

Warsitz opens the throttle and lifts off the runway, to disappear into the haze towards the sea. A few minutes later the new sound in the sky, a high-pitched, whistling whine, is heard by the group on the ground, who prepare for a landing. But Warsitz flies over, invisible, and goes out of earshot. He has been dazzled by the sun and cannot find the airfield. Flying inland he manages to pinpoint his position and brings his small plane in to land, sideslipping and putting his wheels on the runway to roll to a halt in front of Heinkel.

It has been, he tells the group, a perfect flight. His speed has not exceeded 200 mph because of the undercarriage problem and he has climbed no higher than 3,000 feet: a modest enough start for the jet engine, whose purpose is to drive aeroplanes to very high speeds at very high altitudes.

Heinkel telephones General Ernst Udet, director general of equipment at the German Air Ministry. Udet, roused from his sleep, is irritable. He has no real understanding of the implications of the flight. The coming war is his main concern. To Heinkel he says, 'Oh well, congratulations, but now let me get back to sleep,' and rings off. Later he will begin to understand the implications but in 1941, tormented and deranged by Hitler's Third Reich, he will shoot himself.

Also in 1941, on 15 May, almost twenty-one months after the German jet first flew, Jack Smedley, a labourer, was concreting runways at the Royal Air Force station at Cranwell, in Lincolnshire. 'I see an aeroplane coming out of a hangar with no propeller. That fascinated me as we were used to seeing aeroplanes with propellers. It turned into wind and runned along the ground just like a partridge and took off into the air and circled whistling all around and disappeared into the clouds.' A dark huddle of more anxious spectators beside the runway on that May evening included an RAF officer, Frank Whittle, who eleven years before was the first man to patent a proposal for the aircraft gas turbine – the jet engine.

At 7.40 pm Gerry Sayer, chief test pilot of the Gloster Aircraft Company, taxied his Gloster E 28/39 to the end of a runway and ran up Whittle's first flight engine before releasing the brakes and lifting off after a 600-yard run. The first British jet was airborne and quickly disappeared into cloud. For several minutes the group on the ground heard only the smooth roar of the engine. Then Sayer brought the plane in to land in a series of confident gliding turns. Someone slapped Whittle on the back and cried 'Frank, it flies!' Whittle responded curtly, 'That's what it was bloody well designed to do, wasn't it?'

Sayer reported a smooth flight, although he had had difficulty in lowering the undercarriage. Sayer and Warsitz recorded roughly the same figures for speed and height but within days the E 28/39 reached a top speed of 370 mph at 25,000 feet – well above the top speed of the Spitfire, the RAF's greatest fighter at that time. To the leaders of a nation locked in an apparently hopeless war with the Germans, the news of the Whittle/Gloster success was a shaft of hope. Only a very few knew that Britain had thrown away the lead that Whittle had given the nation and that further bungling would delay the proper exploitation of the jet engine in time to help the war effort.

In Germany, too, bureaucracy, resistance to change and the personal whims of Hitler were to delay and shorten the lead which von Ohain, Heinkel and his airframe designers had snatched, without knowing it, from Britain. Even so, the first operational jet aircraft, the Messerschmitt 262, a twin-engined fighter, was in service in 1944, beating its R A F counterpart, the Gloster Meteor, to which in other ways it was markedly superior, by some weeks. The first reported Allied encounter with an Me 262 was on 25 July 1944, although the Luftwaffe claimed 'kills' before this date. The first Meteor action was on 4 August 1944, when Flying Officer Dean used his wing tip to flip a V1 flying bomb on to its back so that it crashed harmlessly in Kent. There was no encounter between the rival jets during the war. The British Air Ministry forbade pilots to fly over German-occupied territory for fear of a Meteor falling into German hands.

These early encounters now seem as far away as the Spitfire, Messerschmitt Bf 109 and the Battle of Britain, telescoped by time into the blurred five years of World War Two. But the jet engine meant something quite different from all the other developments of that war, though some of them, like radar, were essential to the full realization of the jet's capabilities. The jet engine inaugurated a new era which was hardly glimpsed at the time the invention was first revealed. Its military possibilities have been lethally exploited in almost every war fought since 1945: the low-flying jet dispensing death over the rooftops of the Middle East and Far East has become a commonplace of television news bulletins. But the real jet revolution has been peaceful. It is the civil – benign – jet which has not changed the face of the earth so much as shown hundreds of millions of people for the first time just what that face looks like.

In the thirty years to 1980 more than 150 million passengers flew the Atlantic – 140 million of them by jet transport. The impact of this sort of mass travel is impossible to state simply in figures but new industries and new technologies have been born because of it. There is more leisure time – and incomparably more places to spend it. The transatlantic Concorde commuter and the holiday-packaged Huddersfield family reddening in the Florida sun are Whittle's and von Ohain's legacy. Social and business contacts are easier by huge factors, giving rise to new businesses and more jobs. The cost of air travel has been reduced to the level where an air fare to almost anywhere is within reach of hundreds of millions of workers in the industrialized world.

Against these gains, the jet engine has created noise and atmospheric pollution; it has guzzled fuel and land because of the ever-larger airfields it has demanded, and it has worsened the lives of those forced to live nearby. But these problems are to some extent yielding to treatment. Jet engines are becoming quieter and using less fuel. Short take-off and landing capabilities will halt the voracious demand for longer and longer runways. On balance, civil aviation has been a boon and its vast promise has been realized largely through the jet, which humbled the mighty passenger liners of the North Atlantic and brought the farthest habitable parts of the earth within reach in hours rather than weeks or months. The achievement was bought safely, too. No airline operator could face the loss of life and serious injury caused by that great peace-time predator, the motor vehicle. He would be driven out of business. And it has all happened in far less than a normal life span – one of the most rapid revolutions in man's history.

Whittle had his shattering idea of the jet engine in its definitive form in the autumn of 1929; von Ohain in the autumn of 1933. Both men arrived at broadly similar conclusions; neither knew of the other's work. Each had had his first vision of jet flight while he was a student, uncluttered by the traditional luggage of the aero engine manufacturers; and each rightly saw that those manufacturers would disdain their ideas. Both men realized that the piston engine and propeller were useless for high speed flight at high altitudes, and both were motivated by an almost aesthetic dislike of the reciprocating engine, in which thousands of mechanical parts moved to and fro in an over-complicated skein, to seek a simpler, more elegant answer. Both of them have spent their later years in the United States, where they have benefited that country's late but overwhelmingly successful entry into jet propulsion. Two men could hardly be more dissimilar in outlook, appearance and temperament, but each respects the other.

It is impossible to overstate the vision – and optimism – of either of the young men who pioneered the jet engine. They were thinking in terms of flight at 500 mph at heights of 30,000 feet and above, where the air density is around one quarter of its density at sea level. In those days the top speed of a fighter (a biplane) was about 150 mph and the world airspeed record was little more than 200 mph. Commercial flight with passengers and mail was still an uncertain adventure, and the men who started on the path which led to the Comet, Concorde and Boeing 747 Jumbo did so at a time when the airship was still regarded as the likely winner in the field of commercial civil aviation. The materials which they would need for their engines were scarce or non-existent: they were to demand operating temperatures and efficiencies which were at that time impossible, and the airframes into which their engines would be fitted were too advanced to be believed.

Yet they were not the only visionaries. In 1935 an international scientific congress in Rome was devoted to the possibilities of supersonic flight. One paper, given by a young German, Dr Adolf Büsemann, suggested the swept-back wing and showed how its properties might solve the aerodynamic problems which were known to arise with aircraft flying near the speed of sound at around 750 mph. A young Hungarian, Dr Theodore von Karman, who had emigrated to the USA in 1930, was also at the congress. Later dubbed the father of the supersonic age by the American press, he wrote subsequently of the Rome meeting:

> This meeting was historic because it marked the beginning of the supersonic age. It was the beginning in the sense that the conference opened the door to supersonics as a meaningful study ... and most developments in supersonics occurred rapidly from then on, culminating in 1947 – a mere twelve years later – in Captain Charles Yeager's piercing the sound barrier in level flight.

But however visionary the conference, it was not at all evident how the aeronautical world was to realize its vision. Just as the development of the balloon into the airship and aeroplane awaited the invention of the petrol engine, so the advance to high subsonic and supersonic flight awaited the invention of the jet engine. But in 1935 one of its inventors, Frank Whittle, had to let his jet patents lapse because he could not afford the £5 needed to renew them. He had also become convinced that he was too far ahead of his time, that the cost and effort needed were beyond his reach. In Germany, von Ohain had got a little further. He was about to receive a doctorate in physics at Gottingen University and was using his savings to build a small model of a jet engine with the help of the head mechanic of the garage where he had his car serviced. Neither Whittle nor von Ohain dreamt that within four years they would both have achieved one of the most brilliant successes in man's most spectacular technological achievement – powered flight – nor that their names would rank with the great engine inventors, Watt, Trevithick, Parsons, Benz and Diesel.

Why was the jet engine essential to high speed, high altitude flight? It was obvious in the 1920s that very fast speeds could be achieved where air resistance to the aeroplane was least – in the relatively thin air at 30,000 feet and above. But other factors begin to work against conventional aircraft at these heights. An aeroplane flies because the wing is so designed that there is more air pressure acting upwards on its underside than there is acting downwards on its top. This is called lift. At the same time an aeroplane encounters resistance from the air through which it is moving. This is called drag, and it is overcome by the thrust of the engines. The efficiency of an aeroplane is the ratio of lift to drag – the L/D ratio, as designers call it. Drag lessens as the air gets thinner, so an aeroplane should travel faster the higher it flies, but at great heights the power of the piston engine falls off severely because of the absence of the very air which a conventional engine must 'breathe' to go through its process of combustion. The boosting of power in a supercharged piston engine, where the exhaust gases are used to drive a turbine and compressor to supply still greater amounts of compressed air back to the engine, was not enough to overcome the innate problem that, at height, engine power falls off more rapidly than drag. So in the 1920s the ceiling for conventionally engined fighters was fixed at around 20,000 feet – too low for economic high speeds. The ceiling for passenger-carrying planes was much lower – under 12,000 feet; above that height it becomes necessary to breathe extra oxygen or fly in a suitably pressurized cabin.

At the speeds Whittle was contemplating (around 500 mph) the efficiency of the propeller falls off sharply, partly because the thin air at 30,000 feet and above does not enable it to bite off enough to drive the aircraft forward: the propeller and aeroplane begin to slither, as Battle of Britain pilots found when they were in combat at such height. Also, at high speeds the blade speed near the tip of the propeller leads to more problems. The air gets no warning to part smoothly ahead of the propeller, which builds up a bow wave of air like the bow wave of a ship as it cleaves the sea. This causes a steep rise in drag which offsets the advantage of flying in thin air. The designer is thus confronted with a loss of thrust from the engine together with a loss of lift and a rise in drag – all at the same time.

It was known in the 1920s that the gas turbine might be more efficient at height but the handful of engineers who were thinking in these terms coupled a turbine to a propeller, failing to see the enormous advantages of the 'straight through' jet engine. The gas turbine, or jet, is basically simple compared with the piston engine, though it works on the same principle. It is an internal combustion engine which, like the motor car engine, produces power by burning fuel. In the gas turbine, as in the car engine, air is compressed, fuel is injected into it and the mixture is burnt: the heat produced from this burning causes a rapid expansion of the gas. In the motor car engine the expanding gas pushes a piston to give power to a shaft which drives the car wheels. In the pure jet the expanding gas is simply

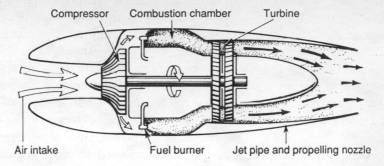

Fig. 1 The Whittle-type jet engine: air enters left to be compressed and channelled to combustion chambers (combustors); fuel is injected and the mixture ignited; hot gases pass through the turbine before being ejected at the rear.

used to push the aeroplane forward at high speed – no piston is needed.

The motor car engine works in a cycle – the burning of gas in the cylinders is intermittent and goes by turn in each cylinder. But in the jet engine the burning is continuous. Air enters the front of the engine, is compressed, mixed with fuel and ignited, and the expanding gas is forced out through a jet pipe at the back of the engine. Before reaching this nozzle, the hot gas expands through a many-bladed turbine (or turbines) which in turn drives the compressor on the same rotating shaft at the front of the engine. This continuous process is simple and extremely efficient, so much so that one wonders why nobody had thought of it before.

Many people had in fact thought of the jet – in different ways at different times – before von Ohain and Whittle in the 1930s. As long ago as the first century A D, Hero of Alexandria produced a practical example of jet propulsion – a machine which he called Aeolipile – in which steam from boiling water was fed into a hollow sphere, escaping through two nozzles and making the sphere rotate. The rocket, which is also a sort of jet propulsion, was first invented by the Chinese in medieval times and from then on inventors have developed rockets for peace and war. In 1687 Isaac Newton formulated his third law of motion, which states that for every action there is an equal and opposite reaction – the scientific principle on which jet and rocket propulsion is founded. The jet and rocket do *not* work by pushing the exhaust gas against the atmosphere: the reaction of the expanding gas is against the back of the engine itself – in the case of the jet, the combustion chamber and the cone in the tail of the engine. This reaction travels from engine to airframe and the thrust (as it is called) is measured in pounds or kilogrammes.

It is one thing to state the principle, as Newton did; but another to apply it. By the late nineteenth and early twentieth century scientists and engineers were toying with the possibilities of propelling aeroplanes by the jet reaction, either using it to drive a propeller or as a pure jet. Turbine technology made big advances through the work of Sir Charles Parsons and many outstanding engineers in Germany, France, Switzerland and Sweden. The Frenchman René Lorin proposed as long ago as 1908 a form of jet engine in which all the energy in a reciprocating (i.e. piston) engine was allowed to remain in the exhaust instead of supplying power to the piston and crankshaft. Dr J. S. Harris of Esher patented in 1917 a design in which a fan, driven by a piston engine, compressed air to which fuel was then added and burnt. Whittle considered this possibility on his way to the pure jet solution but rejected it because he thought it gave no real advantage over the piston engine and propeller. The Italian aircraft firm Caproni Campini persevered with the idea, flying (with much *élan*) an aircraft powered on this principle in August 1940. They found through hard experience what Whittle had seen theoretically: it gave little advantage over the piston engine. Meanwhile, in 1921 a Frenchman, M. Guillaume, had proposed using the exhaust of a gas turbine for jet propulsion.

The idea of the basic gas turbine has been around since the eighteenth century (there is an English patent in the name of John Barber, dated 1791) but its industrial use was delayed by a century while developments in engineering and materials grew. The first continuous fuel-burning gas turbines capable of running under their own power were developed in France in the early 1900s but their efficiency (the ratio of useful work done to the total energy expended) was very low – around 3 per cent compared with 30 per cent for the piston engine. One constant problem was that the materials available for the turbine blades could not stand up for long to the fierce temperatures of the gas flowing around them. Compressor and turbine efficiencies were also low.

The Swiss firm of Brown Boveri was a notable pioneer in the field of industrial gas turbines. One use for them was supplying compressed air to blast furnaces. Reaction propulsion of other kinds began to make faster strides because they were simpler. Paul Schmidt in Germany developed the pulse jet which powered the first of Hitler's notorious V weapons. This engine was a development of the ram jet, which is an open-ended duct, a metal funnel, in which fuel is burnt to produce a high velocity jet exhaust. The air is compressed by hurling the jet into it at high speed, so acceleration to such speed is essential before any thrust is produced. The pulse jet is a ram jet but it has a series of spring-loaded inlet valves which open inwards to take in air and slam shut when the mixture of fuel and air ignites in the combustion chamber. It was used in the unmanned V1, which during the onslaught against Britain in the closing stages of World War Two, killed 5,475 people, seriously injured another 16,000, and damaged 20,000 houses per day. Wernher von Braun's V2 – the first realization of the power of the guided rocket/missile – killed 2,724 people and injured another 6,000 despite the fact that only 518 V2s reached London.

It is no discredit to Whittle or von Ohain to see the jet, or gas turbine, as a slowly evolving power plant rather than the instant realization of a lone inventor. Even so, a mistaken estimate of the gas turbine's promise was to prove a serious obstacle to Whittle's earliest efforts. As long ago as 1920 the Royal Air Force had proved to its own satisfaction that the gas turbine could not power an aeroplane. This judgement was made by Dr W. J. Stern, of the Air Ministry's South Kensington laboratory, who examined the use of a turbine to drive a conventional aircraft propeller (the turbo-prop as it later successfully became, powering the famous Viscount airliner). His report, issued by the engine sub-committee of the Aeronautical Research Committee, said: 'In its present stage of development the internal combustion turbine is unsuitable for aircraft on account of weight and fuel consumption, the main difficulty in the case of aircraft being the design of a light, compact and efficient compressor.' Stern also pointed to the need for new materials to improve turbine blades.

Stern's starting point – his ideal engine – called for seven compressors staged through the engine, one after another, and a two-stage turbine. He assumed a very high efficiency for a 1,000 hp engine – ambitious for those days. But he found that the total weight of such an engine would be very high – 6,000 lb, giving a ratio of 6 lb for every horsepower produced. Aircraft piston engines of that day had a ratio of 2.5 lb per horsepower and their fuel consumption was half that of the proposed turbine, so Stern's conclusions were inescapably unfavourable.

Stern was working in 1920, immediately after World War One, when aeroplanes and their engines were still at a primitive stage in their evolution. His conclusions were understandable, but he lacked imagination and took the worst case to be the general rule. When he came to estimate the weight and size of his ideal engine he was wrong, and seriously so, because he looked at current designs of gas turbines for industry and not at what might be achieved by a designer of aero engines, who knows that weight is always a penalty and aims to make his design as light as possible. Stern did not take into account the possibilities of smaller size: his compressor worked out at six feet long and three feet in diameter, weighing 2,000 lb. That would be normal for ground-based industrial compressors for many years to come but lightweight compressors were produced for aeroplanes as soon as they became necessary – a point which Whittle was able to make years later with great effect. Stern's compressor chamber was made of cast iron, although stainless steel, which was in use at that time, would have been lighter and more durable.

Stern's shortcomings are the more frustrating because he recognized all the advantages a successful gas turbine would have over the piston engine: simplicity and reliability; perfect balance; a high power-producing engine on only one shaft (the jet engine can be thought of as just one moving part, compressor and turbine spinning together on one rotating shaft); the possibility of supplying a series of turbines with compressed air, and also supplying the aeroplane's cabin with air under pressure for high altitude flying, just as today's airliners do. Against these virtues he counted low efficiencies, high weight, the difficulty of starting and governing the engine, and the need for a heavy gear system to drive a propeller at the right speed because the turbine and compressor spun at much higher speeds than any propeller would need or could stand. Stern concluded his report: 'The internal combustion turbine (or jet engine) will not be rendered practical by a revolutionary design of some lucky inventor. The steam turbine engineer and the metallurgist of wide experience are the people with whom the future development must rest.'

What actually happened? The very opposite. The jet came to pass through the revolutionary designs of two young and lucky inventors, though Whittle at least might find 'lucky' a debatable description. The steam turbine engineers, full of the wisdom of doing what was done in their fathers' day, contributed hardly a jot to the first jets. The metallurgists did indeed provide the metals, but only when the inventors insisted on their doing so.

The hindrance to new development posed by such reports as Stern's is not so much that they are wrong – Stern was part-right for his day – but that they can later be quoted against anyone who proposes to do something radically different which will overleap the pessimism of the original forecast. If such reports are not treated conditionally, with enormous caution, the authorities are given an excellent excuse to ignore the difficult, even disagreeable, task of revising their judgements in the light of later knowledge. The British are far from being alone in possessing this fault – as this book will show – but it has been elevated almost to an art form among assessors of new ideas in technology. Innovators may thus face a challenge that only the most exceptional, given luck, overcome. As Sir Barnes Wallis once said: 'There is no greater joy in life than proving that something is totally impossible and then going away and showing exactly how it can be done.'

Although Frank Whittle and Hans von Ohain are rightly credited with the invention of the jet engine, there was another Englishman who came close to walking off with the entire credit only six years after Stern declared that the gas turbine was a non-starter. He was Dr Alan Arnold Griffith, nicked-named 'Soap-bubble' Griffith, a tall, slim, serious-minded man whose academic brilliance remains a byword in British aviation circles. The son of an explorer and journalist, he had got a first in mechanical engineering at Liverpool University and then his doctorate there.

One of his contemporaries, Lord Kings Norton (later to be a steadfast supporter of Whittle through some of the worst days), says that Griffith was a gifted applied mathematician with an intuitive grasp of the laws of nature which made him equally at home in the theories of materials structures, aerodynamics and heat engines – to all of which he made notable contributions. He was nicknamed Soap-bubble because of a paper he published in 1917 called 'The use of soap bubbles in solving torsion problems'. In it he showed that if a soap bubble is stretched in a film across a hole shaped like the cross-section of a bar of metal, and if the film is distorted, the contours seen in the bubble are like the stress lines in the metal bar when it is twisted – a demonstration which had valuable practical applications.

Griffith went to work for the Royal Aircraft Factory (now the Royal Aircraft Establishment, or RAE) at Farnborough in 1915 and it was there, in the 1920s, while he was studying propeller problems, that he made a fundamental discovery which was to revolutionize turbine design – a step in the direction of jet flight. He saw that the poor performance of turbines and compressors was due to the fact that they were normally run 'stalled' i.e., the flow of air around the blades was the same as the flow which would make an aircraft wing stall, making the aeroplane fall (until the pilot corrects the failure) out of the sky. He went on to remedy this by proposing that the flat blades should be designed like aerofoils – shaped, in other words, like an aeroplane wing in cross-section – so that the airflow would behave as it does around a wing in flight. The genius of this idea lay in Griffith's realization that the real job of the turbine blade was to transfer as much energy as possible between airflow and blade, but the blade was being designed in a way which was bound to lead to serious losses of energy just where they were least wanted. He brought an aeronautical scientist's vision to a problem which terrestrial blade designers had not realized, simply because they were terrestrial.

No doubt this idea had been germinating in the minds of some gas turbine engineers but Griffith got there first with his paper, 'An aerodynamic theory of turbine design', published in July 1926. The paper went further, by showing conclusively that the gas turbine would, one day, make an aero engine. Griffith saw this engine as a compressor and turbine working together to drive a conventional aeroplane propeller. It was to be designed on the axial flow principle, in which air is forced from the front to the back of the engine through row on row of blades, making up the compressor, and the turbine which drives them. Once air has been whipped to greater and greater pressures by the rows or stages of compressor blades, it is mixed with fuel and burnt in the combustion chamber (or combustor) between the compressor and turbine. Then the hot gas passes through the turbine blades, which can also be in rows, giving them the motion to drive the compressor at the front of the engine.

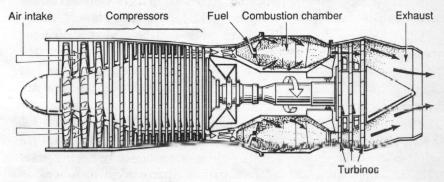

Fig. 2 The straight-through axial flow jet engine: air enters left and passes through a series of compressors into the combustion chambers; the hot gas mixture then expands through the turbine and ejects at right

   Both Whittle and von Ohain recognized that the axial flow compressor was ultimately the way ahead but for their earliest engines they chose the more simple centrifugal compressor, in which air is whirled and compressed outwards against the engine casing, compressing it by the action of centrifugal force. Both men wanted something simple at first to demonstrate conclusively that the basic idea of the jet engine was sound. In a different version, Griffith's idea of the axial engine coupled to a propeller was used twenty years later to power passenger planes such as the Viscount and the American Electra. Virtually all jet engines were to be designed on the axial flow principle.

   What separated Griffith from Whittle and von Ohain – and made him a loser, though an important one – was his failure to comprehend that the jet flow itself was all that was needed to push the aeroplane forward. Griffith, however, did make a fundamental discovery, and he interpreted his theory in scientific terms for use in designing compressors and turbine. He worked out formulae for calculating the efficiencies of his design, too, as a true pioneer must. That he did not sweep on to design the world's first working jet – or turbo-propeller – engine is perhaps partly due to the economic climate – in the 1920s to 1930s Britain was in a serious industrial slump – and to his complex intellect, more academic than practical in outlook.

   Griffith's treatment of each blade as an aerofoil, or wing, behaving as the laws of aerodynamics said it must, meant that he could define the design of blades scientifically. Limits, laid down by known laws of nature, could be set to the angle at which air could be deflected by a single row of blades without them stalling, and so losing energy. Limits could similarly be set to the number and size of blades in each row, and to the velocity of air through the blades, which was necessary because of the unpredictable (at that time) behaviour of wing-shaped aerofoils as they approached the speed of sound.

These criteria defined the engine layout. Because one row of rotating blades could deflect the air only to a limited extent, there had to be several rows of them to force air at each stage up to the compression needed; the same was true of the turbine if it was to provide maximum energy, so both compressor and turbine had to be multi-stage. By calculating the shape of blade best suited to the airflow, the aerodynamicist could work out the best blade size, its shape and position. And the speed of the air could be controlled by a row of stationary blades placed in front of each rotating row.

Griffith suggested that the compressor and turbine should drive a propeller, through gearing, on the same shaft, and he went on to propose that the turbine should be mounted within the compressor, so that two separate components become one. This, however, raised a problem about where to locate the combustion chamber – the middle stage where the fuel and air were to be burnt. The Griffith's layout generally was becoming extremely complex for an early proposal, which needed to be kept as simple as possible, but nevertheless this reserved and rather detached scientist had made the gas turbine grow several dimensions in a very short time.

However, at this point nobody proposed to build a complete engine. The Aeronautical Research Committee (ARC), which, with the Air Ministry, examined Griffith's proposal, recommended only that a simple rig should be built to test the theory. It would consist of a single compressor stage and a single turbine stage of aerofoil blades mounted on the same shaft. In fact, a cascade or series of aerofoil blades had already been built at RAE to Griffith's design and had been tested in a wind tunnel in 1927 – probably the first-ever test of aerofoil blades. In 1928 the test rig was also built.

Two sets of tests confirmed Griffith's theory, although the highest predicted efficiencies were not reached and a mechanical failure prevented Griffith from completing the full programme. But the results he did obtain enabled him to probe more deeply into the problems of the internal combustion turbine as an aero engine and he presented an ebullient report to the ARC in November 1929.

There was no doubt that the project was looking very promising and Griffith made detailed proposals for an engine of 500 horsepower, weighing about 1.05 to 1.30 lb per horsepower, and measuring 18 or 20 inches in diameter and 30 to 40 inches long. Part of his confidence stemmed from the knowledge that suitable materials were being developed and the National Physical Laboratory was able to confirm big improvements in the safe working stresses of various steels.

Griffith calculated that the increased efficiency of his compressor design would reduce the air consumption needed. This meant that the bulk and weight of the engine (taken together with advances in materials science and technology) would come down to about one-fifth of what Stern had calculated in 1920. Increases in thermal efficiency and the reduction in air consumption led Griffith to believe that the performance of his engine would be greatly improved at high altitude – exactly what was wanted. He admitted one problem: the engine would have to work over a range of conditions – starting up, take-off, climbing to height and so on – each of which meant a change in the operation of the engine and that, in turn, meant a change in the behaviour of the airflow through the engine. Griffith thought it impossible to design blades that would work efficiently through all the conditions an aeroplane would encounter through its flight cycle. One solution was to have a series of turbines to drive low-, medium- and high-pressure compressors. The problem was not insoluble, but this complication in design would enable many experts to shake their heads many times over many years when they considered the possibility of achieving high efficiencies with the jet engine. Griffith was also proposing to complicate his design still further by departing from the convention of having alternate stages of stationary blades, known as stators, and rotary blades, known as rotors. He replaced the stators with rows of blades rotating in the opposite direction from the rotors, a refinement associated with the airflow through his combined turbines and compressors.

Griffith summed up his position boldly and ticked off the benefits at the end of his 1929 paper:

The turbine is superior to existing service engines and to projected engines in every respect examined. The efficiency is higher and the weight and bulk less. No external cooling is required. At high altitudes there is an inherent supercharging effect, coupled with a substantial decrease in the specific [fuel] consumption. The use of a variable pitch airscrew is unnecessary. Starting presents no difficulty and control is simpler than in the case of existing engines. Any liquid fuel of suitable chemical composition may be used . . .

This paper was examined by a special panel of the ARC's engine sub-committee early in 1930. They concluded that the superiority of the turbine over the reciprocating engine had not been proved – it could not be predicted with absolute certainty – so they could not recommend the Air Ministry to develop a gas turbine as an aero engine. However, they thought that an efficient compressor was important, not least for its possible uses in industry, and that there should be a definite answer to the question of whether efficient compressors could be achieved by applying aerodynamics to the design of blades. They recommended that the multi-stage test rig now proposed by Griffith should be built because it would provide 'an unquestionable check on theory'.

The Committee noted (rightly) two other fundamental problems: the rapid consumption of fuel at constant pressure; and the behaviour of blade materials in a high temperature stream of oxydizing (corroding) gas. They thought that these problems should be investigated and that the National Physical Laboratory should continue metallurgical tests while the RAE explored the combustion problem. Although not sold on the complete engine, the ARC undoubtedly grasped the importance of Griffith's work and wanted it pursued so that there could be greater certainty one way or another over his claims. In the words of the official historian:

Although the ARC experts wanted further proof, the steps they recommended clearly indicate that they were extremely interested in the possibilities opened up by Dr Griffith's work and by no means considered his previous efforts wasted. Indeed they probably wished to sponsor the sole British exponent of internal combustion turbines in view of the practical work they knew was going on abroad . . .

Then the unbelievable happened. Nothing. For seven years no direct work was done at the RAE on gas turbines. Griffith, in the year of the ARC recommendation, was appointed head of the Air Ministry laboratory in South Kensington, where there were no facilities for him to do his work, but in 1932 he went back to the RAE to head the engine department. Though not ideally placed, the RAE was the one establishment that had the opportunities and facilities to carry on Griffith's work. Admittedly, money was short and his project would have had to compete with others for limited

funds. Priorities were decided on the basis of what was likely to
have practical application and what funds were available were spent
on other projects, such as supercharging piston engines. Griffith's
seniority put him in an influential position to press for funds and
people to continue the work in which he had placed his own rising
confidence, but there is no record that he did so. The begetter of the
multi-stage axial-flow gas turbine, the world leader in his field at that
moment, let his ideas languish. So did everyone else. The official
historian, and other specialists who have seen the papers or know of
the work, find this inexplicable. Even the supercharging work failed;
after many blade and bearing failures it was eventually dropped.

Griffith and others at Farnborough only became interested in the
gas turbine again in 1936 because they heard that Whittle was on the
verge of running one. The evidence for this harsh-sounding judgement
will be advanced later. There is another inexplicable factor which
must be examined first: Griffith's extraordinary treatment of Frank
Whittle when their paths first crossed in 1930.

In June 1986, as Sir Frank Whittle sat in his Piccadilly club, you could have walked straight past him – an unknown man, small, with a crisp, rather wary look. When his petite American wife, Tommy, came in from a shopping trip in the London rain, they exchanged quiet greetings, just two visitors to London. But this was the week in which the British Establishment made its *amende honorable* to Frank Whittle, first by a visit to the Prime Minister at 10 Downing Street, then to Buckingham Palace to receive from the Queen the highest honour in her gift, the Order of Merit. The following year, among other engagements, the eighty-year-old genius attended a dinner with the Duke of Edinburgh to mark the fiftieth anniversary of the first run of a Whittle jet engine. And he also attended a graduate parade of the officers initial training course at R A F Cranwell – a full circle from the days when he was a cadet and the first ideas for a jet engine buzzed in his head. Recognition is sweet, however belated, sweet enough for Sir Frank to say he feels no bitterness now towards his detractors, who are long since in limbo but who once provided formidable opposition to a young officer striving to make a great idea work. Half a century on, however, it is still possible to detect in his conversation the marks of a searing experience.

The most noticeable physical characteristic of Sir Frank Whittle is his smallness – the very smallness which almost cost him his place in the Royal Air Force, and also Britain's role in the invention and development of the jet engine. When he was fifteen, in 1922, he applied to join the R A F as a technical apprentice. He passed the written examination easily but was failed medically because he was only five feet tall. Whittle persisted. A friendly physical training instructor gave him a diet sheet and a list of exercises, and in six months he added three inches to his height and another three to his chest measurement. Still he was rejected. At last, in 1923, his persistence paid off: he received an apprenticeship to R A F Cranwell.

Whittle was born in 1907 on a housing estate in Coventry. His father had come south from the Lancashire cotton mills, where he went to work at eleven, and had found a job as a mechanic in a factory. Frank was an adventurous child – he says he was a combination of wiriness, strong nerves and good balance. By 1916 the Whittles had moved to Leamington Spa because Frank's father had managed to scrape together enough money to buy a one-man engineering business there. It is to his father that Frank modestly credits such engineering and inventive abilities as he has. His father was indeed an innovator but his main effort went into the design of a perpetual motion machine, which has defeated thousands of men for thousands of years. Whittle senior fared no better than any of his predecessors, although no doubt he demonstrated to his son the worth of challenging accepted beliefs, even if you are unsuccessful. Frank certainly picked up a lot of basic engineering knowledge from the age of ten, when he started to help his father on piece-work rates of pay. His early experience was in drilling valve stems for petrol engines of the kind he was so fruitfully to reject in his search for a power plant for a very high speed aircraft.

Although Frank Whittle won a scholarship to a secondary school in Leamington, his school performances were poor. He had made up his mind to get through the curriculum safely but with the minimum of work and had found for himself a secret world (not for the last time) in Leamington public library, where he spent hours reading up popular science and engineering. He was drawn towards aircraft – at that time a fairly miraculous new shape in the sky – and also towards turbines. He studied the theory and practice of flight until he felt competent to fly an aircraft, although he had yet to go anywhere near one. He had an inner confidence.

Once in the RAF he did not enjoy his apprenticeship, though he was working on metal aircraft, which were still a radical innovation. He disliked discipline and barrack-room life, and once more he found an alternative world, the model aircraft society, which he believes had a profound effect on his life and work. He led a team which designed and built a large monoplane with a ten-foot wingspan, powered by a two-stroke petrol engine. The idea was to fly it before a distinguished audience on passing-out day. The day came but the spark plugs (the only shop-bought bits of the plane) failed and the model never left the ground. Nevertheless, Whittle discovered many years later that it had helped him on his way from successful apprentice to a coveted RAF cadetship, which rarely came the way of working-class boys who made up the ranks of the apprentices. Only the top five of them each year were accepted as cadets. Whittle was number six on the passing-out list but even if there were a drop-out, he had the handicap of not having been a leading boy – up to that time no apprentice who had not been promoted leading boy had ever been made a cadet. Whittle recalls:

> Wing Commander Barton, the commanding officer, had seen this large model aircraft that we'd made, and other things, I suppose, must have impressed him, so that when the number one boy failed his eyesight test I became eligible and I was recommended by Barton. But there was another narrow escape because I've since read in Trenchard's biography [Marshal of the RAF Lord Trenchard, Chief of Air Staff – head of the Air Force] that he nearly stopped it because I hadn't been a leading boy and I hadn't made a name for myself in sport, on which a lot of weight was put in those days. He said to Barton, 'You're sure you're not making a mistake?' and Barton replied that he thought he'd got a mathematical genius. Trenchard then said: 'All right Barton, but if you've made a mistake with this young man I'll never forgive you.'

The RAF college at Cranwell was an elite; to join, meant officer rank and flying instruction. Whittle was to become a pilot (an outstanding one) but his first few weeks were spent parading in a dark lounge suit and a battered bowler hat while his uniform was being specially made because he was so small. Apart from learning how to fly, the cadets were taught physics, maths, the theory of flight, English literature and history. Whittle even then was regarded as exceptional. Years later another cadet with whom he shared quarters, R. Dudley Williams (later Sir Rolf and a Tory MP), recalled being immediately impressed on a first meeting by Whittle's self-confidence and judgement:

> I was attracted by the intensity of his eyes and the keen, crisp way he spoke. He was a great man for challenging accepted beliefs, religious, economic, whatever. He was a socialist, whereas I rather accepted matters as they stood. I found myself very attracted to this critical being. He forced me to think. During our time at Cranwell Frank Whittle quickly began to challenge the accepted things about aeroplanes as well.

Whittle's chance to do this came in his fourth term as a cadet. He was expected to write a thesis each term and this time around he chose as his subject future developments in aircraft design. It was the beginning of his invention of the jet engine. The thesis is now in the London Science Museum, written in a round, callow hand, but clearly expressed and confidently argued. Whittle noted that the latest achievement in aircraft performance, the flight of an aircraft called the Southern Cross from San Francisco across the Pacific to Sydney, had happened less than a score of years since the first uncertain crossing of the English Channel by Blériot: 'It is a hazardous business to forecast the future,' wrote Whittle. Dividing the future into three, the immediate, the middle and the far, he plumped for the middle future. He calculated that a 100 mph wind against a machine travelling at 600 mph at 120,000 feet would have less effect than a 20 mph head wind against the same machine at 1,000 feet. 'Thus everything indicates that designers should aim at altitude.' Whittle grasped the inefficiency of propellers and petrol engines at great heights but dismissed rocket propulsion as inefficient except for space travel. He then plumped for the turbine driven by a petrol engine and demonstrated its efficiency mathematically as height increases. He concluded his thesis by saying: 'The most important developments which will take place [in aircraft design] will follow as a result of the development of a more suitable prime mover, i.e. an air turbine.'

His tutor commented below: 'The thesis shows much careful and original thought, and also a good deal of private reading.' Whittle was contemplating an aircraft travelling at a speed of 500 mph at 60,000 feet. Remember, the top speed of RAF fighters in 1926 was 150 mph and their ceiling was little more than 10,000 feet. Whittle, at nineteen years old, had only one more intellectual step to take before he invented the jet.

Whittle's performance as a cadet was generally excellent. He flew solo after eight hours' instruction in the air, overcoming a temporary loss of confidence caused by a short-tempered instructor. The final entry in his log book, under special faults to be watched, read: 'over-confidence . . . he gives aerobatics too much value and has neglected accuracy . . . inclined to play to the gallery and flies too low.'

He then passed out second in his year and was posted to a fighter squadron at Hornchurch. In 1929 he was sent to the Central Flying School at Wittering as a pupil instructor. The problem of the engine which would power high flying, high speed aircraft continued to nag him and he continued to think in terms of creating the jet stream by a fan driven by a piston engine. At last he realized that this was really no better than the propeller-piston combination from which he was trying to escape. (The Italians were to spend some years and a lot of money discovering this through their experimental aircraft based on this principle.)

One day at Wittering it came to him in a flash that he could do away with the piston engine and use a turbine to drive the compressor. Air compressed by the compressor would be mixed with fuel and ignited: this expanding gas would flow through the turbine blades at high velocity and the turbine would then be used to drive the compressor. The jet stream produced would push the aircraft through the air at very high speeds. If compressor and turbine were mounted on the same shaft, you had, essentially, only one moving part compared with the hundreds in the reciprocating piston engine.

The elegance and simplicity of this solution were so obvious that Whittle wondered, like many inventors in other fields when they see a solution which has evaded them for some time, why he had taken so long to reach such an obvious conclusion. He was twenty-two.

He needed to sound off his ideas against someone with whom he could have a critical but creative discussion. He chose Flight Lieutenant W. E. P. Johnson, who was at that time lecturing to the Central Flying School trainee instructors on the theory of flight. Before joining the RAF, 'Johnny' Johnson had been a patent agent; though not an engineer, he had a deep interest in, and feeling for, technical innovation – much as a good literary or art critic can assess a book or a painting with discrimination and balance. Whittle, still a young pilot officer, saw in Johnson an intelligent sounding board, while Johnson came to regard the gifted pilot and inventor as his protégé. 'In a way I adopted Whittle,' he has said. It was an adoption which would lead to Johnson playing a major part in jet development. When Whittle unfolded the idea of the jet to him, Johnson saw its possibilities at once and introduced Whittle to the station commandant, Group Captain John Baldwin, who immediately passed on the idea to the Air Ministry in London.

Although so young, Whittle had captivated these two men by his intellectual audacity and by his ability to explain his ideas so lucidly. He radiated confidence and when he was summoned to the Air Ministry, within a few days of meeting Baldwin, his head was filled with hope. After showing his drawings and calculations to a technical officer, W. L. Tweedie, he was taken to the Air Ministry Laboratory in South Kensington to see its superintendent – none other than Dr A. A. Griffith, already supposed to be pioneering the propeller-jet. Griffith told him that he personally believed in the gas turbine as a way of driving a propeller – as indeed he had just shown in his optimistic paper to the Aeronautical Research Committee only weeks before. He told the pilot officer that his assumptions were over-optimistic and that there was a mistake in his calculations.

Tweedie pointed out that the Air Ministry's attitude to the gas turbine had been determined by an unfavourable report written some years before. This can only have been Stern's report, which had already been rocked, if not discredited, by Griffith's work from the mid-1920s onwards.

Whittle went back to Wittering with the ashes of disappointment in his mouth. His work had been challenged, his calculations found faulty, his confidence for the moment shaken; it was the common lot of inventors but a new experience for a young man who did not then know how the world treats its innovators. He was not aware, for Griffith did not tell him, of the Farnborough work; nor that Griffith himself was involved, for it was never hinted at. A few days later Tweedie wrote him a letter, dated 8 September 1929:

Dear Mr [sic] Whittle
There has now been an opportunity to examine in some detail the general description of your proposed constant pressure turbine, together with the relevant calculations which were left with me after your recent visit. After a careful study of all the papers it can be stated clearly that no reason has been found for any alteration of the preliminary comments on your suggestion which were made both by myself and also the Superintendent, Air Ministry Laboratories, nor of the criticism advanced against your various assumptions.

While there is of course a very definite lack of published information on the subject of the modern aircraft-type compressor, *it must be remembered that a tremendous amount of work is being done* and while it is not possible at present to publish any complete details of the results of this work *you may rest assured the criticisms of your scheme were made with the full knowledge of the results achieved by actual experiment.* [author's italics]

You are trying to obtain success with an engine embodying a turbine and compressor, both of which machines are at the present time relatively inefficient, and it must be remembered that with a small ratio of positive to negative work it is quite easy to obtain a negative overall mechanical efficiency, and thus a useless engine, however great the thermal efficiency of the cycle and however small the thermal losses incurred ... The internal combustion turbine, in spite of many past and present failures, will almost certainly one day be developed into a successful engine, but before this can be done the performance of both compressors and turbines will have to be greatly improved.

However, it has been a matter of real interest to investigate in detail your scheme and I can assure you that any suggestion, backed by careful and considered theory, that is submitted by people in the Service is always welcomed.

Your calculations are returned herewith and I will be obliged if you will kindly return the receipts for the documents now in your possession.

This extraordinary letter was presumably calculated to warn Whittle that others in the field, his superiors, were doing experimental work. The 'tremendous amount of work [which] is being done . . .' must refer to Griffith's work, and the 'criticisms of your scheme . . . made with the full knowledge of the results achieved by actual experiment' must be Griffith's criticisms, as the experiments must also be his. But Griffith's work had come to a full stop – where it was to remain until Whittle's efforts forced Farnborough to re-start their gas turbine work in 1936.

Was Griffith intent on forcing Whittle out of the field because of his own interest? The character of the man and his record as a scientist suggest that he be given the benefit of the doubt. But Griffith seems undoubtedly to have seriously underestimated Whittle's grasp and vision. Griffith was thirty-six years old when the two men met, so he was no elderly scientist with all the weight of years on him dismissing a green amateur and smiling indulgently on his optimism. Griffith's knowledge of the field must have told him that Whittle's concept was by no means out of court, for all his immaturity. He might have suggested that Whittle continue his theoretical work, but there is no hint of that in Tweedie's letter, which is a straightforward invitation to stop meddling in a field where others are already getting results. Nor would it have done Griffith any harm to take Whittle into limited confidence about his Farnborough work. Griffith, however, did nothing, despite the backing of the ARC for his project, which Whittle did not, of course, have.

What happened in all probability was that Griffith saw before him a young pilot without any academic qualification or experience in engineering science. He recognized that Whittle had the germ of an idea but thought his assumptions were over-optimistic – as indeed they were for the time. He would also have been aware that it was impossible for Whittle to pursue his project. He had no experimental experience and no laboratory in which to work, nor was any likely to be made available to him, yet the proof of the jet principle would have to come through extensive experiments by scientists and engineers with expensive laboratories and test facilities. The chance of a twenty-two-year-old pilot ever getting a team together and finding the laboratories in which to work was minimal.

This is the most generous judgement of Griffith's part in Whittle's rejection and it still leaves him guilty of failure to understand the genius of the proposal, and guilty too of the 'not invented here' syndrome – the tendency to believe that if a new idea has not been born within the creative ferment of one's own laboratory then it cannot be significant. At best the charge is intellectual snobbery and blindness; at worst, deceit. The truth will never be known, but it is significant that when the paths of the two men did cross again in the mid-thirties, Griffith was once again disdainful of the better man.

When Pilot Officer Whittle returned to Wittering dejected, Johnson quickly persuaded him to patent his proposals and helped him to draft the formal documents for the Patent Office. The provisional specification was filed on 16 January 1930 and the Air Ministry was formally told of the application. Indeed, the Air Ministry, the Army, and the Admiralty all examined the patent under service procedure; all declared that they were not interested. The President of the Air Council wrote that there was no need for secrecy. Eighteen months later, when the specifications had been completed, the patent was open in the usual way for inspection by anyone. In 1933 it was published worldwide.

Whittle qualified as a flying instructor and was posted to Digby in Lincolnshire, where he was promoted to Flying Officer rank. He went on developing his ideas, refining and discussing them with the other instructors and their pupils. Most were sceptical. He also kept in touch with Johnson at Wittering and they made one or two illicit flights in RAF aeroplanes around Britain to visit manufacturers whom Johnson thought might be useful to Whittle.

In October 1930 they flew to Brooklands, Weybridge, to see George Reid, of Reid and Sigrist, the aircraft instrument manufacturers. Reid was sympathetic but declared that building a jet engine would cost far more money than he could ever find. Johnson arranged a meeting with engineers at the British Thomson-Houston turbine factory at Rugby. They, too, were sympathetic but put development costs at about £60,000, which they could not contemplate at that time. It was the year in which Britain was in the depth of industrial depression, with three million unemployed and a government unable or unwilling to think of a way out of its problems.

In such a climate, ingenuity, innovation, invention, are among the first casualties: it is better not to risk anything at a time when you risk losing everything. There was no venture capital to be had. Whittle, now married with one son, was extremely hard up himself. But he had matured into a brilliant pilot. After Digby, he was posted to the Marine Aircraft Experimental Establishment at Felixstowe, where, as a test pilot, he showed great personal skill and courage in catapult launch tests and experimental ditching of landplanes in the sea.

From 1929 to the mid-1930s Whittle had nothing to show for his ideas but rejection. The fundamental engineering objections to his project were that he was expecting too much from his engine on the basis of contemporary knowledge and that the materials needed to work in the high temperatures essential to the jet engine were simply not in existence. This was the final verdict of the chief engineer of Armstrong Siddeley, an aero engine manufacturer approached by Whittle and Johnson. Whittle admitted the force of these arguments but he believed that the problems would be overcome if somebody insisted that they should be: efficiencies would improve and materials would become available if someone was bold enough to demand them. He was right, in the end; but the realization of his convictions was to bring him to the verge of collapse and turn his success to ashes.

While Whittle strove for support in Britain, it was dawning on Hans von Ohain, a more affluent student of physics and aerodynamics at Göttingen University, that the piston engine, with its hundreds of moving parts, was an ugly and inefficient way of powering an aeroplane. When flying in a Junkers 52 tri-motor passenger plane he experienced the same sort of aesthetic dislike which had occurred to Whittle. 'When I looked at flying I was appalled by the horrible noise and vibration, and its contrast with the elegance of flying, which I felt strongly as a young scientist interested in gliders.'

Von Ohain was the opposite of Whittle: tall, over six feet, compared to Whittle's five feet plus; inherently charming and modest, while Whittle can be astringent and proud; and most of all well-off, where Whittle was poor. He could beat the system; Whittle had to endure and fight within it. 'If I had had to undergo what Whittle had to undergo I would never have succeeded,' he says. 'I am a compromiser, whereas Whittle goes straight for the right solution against all opposition. I would, I think, have given up. But I often thought that a guardian angel stood beside me at the most critical moments of my life and saved me.'

Von Ohain's guardian angels included his grandparents, who were very rich, his parents, who were rich, his professor, R. W. Pohl, who was influential, and Ernst Heinkel, the maverick rich aircraft designer and manufacturer. Von Ohain was born in Dessau in 1911, the son of a career officer in the Germany Army, whose career vanished at the end of the 1914–18 War but who had backing enough as a civilian to survive the ravages of inflation and became a successful businessman. The grandparents gave von Ohain 'quite a bit on the side' and with some of this money he was able to run a small car, which he garaged at Bartels and Becker, a servicing and repair garage in Göttingen. This was to have much to do with putting a German jet in the air ahead of the British.

Although a young student reading for a rather abstract PhD, von Ohain was constantly on the lookout for practical applications of what he learnt in physics and aerodynamics. Late in 1933 he began to think of a way in which the energy needed to compress air could be extracted from hot exhaust gas as it expanded – a steady aeroflow process which is, of course, the basis of the jet engine. It never occurred to him that he was challenging any accepted beliefs – 'When you are a young student you think that you can do anything. Quite frequently inventions are made by people outside the mainstream altogether. Neither in Britain nor Germany did the aero engine companies think of the jet. They were too busy making piston engines to think about alternatives.'

He denies any prescience over the need for jet propulsion and high-speed flight. He did not know of Whittle's work but he thought intuitively that the jet engine would be inherently more powerful, smoother, lighter and more compatible with aeroplane design than the piston-propeller combination. After one false start his ideas crystallized on a compressor and turbine spinning together: lightweight, compact and simple. He chose a centrifugal compressor, in which air is compressed by centrifugal force, as did Whittle, but he made a mental note, as had Whittle, that the engine for the future should have an axial flow compressor of the kind which Griffith had favoured. For the moment though, in common with Whittle, he favoured a simple solution to demonstrate the principle.

By 1934 von Ohain had done some rudimentary design and weight studies, from which it seemed to him that speeds around 500 mph would be possible. The high fuel consumption which his figures indicated troubled him but this might be offset by the lighter weight of the jet, which should be only one quarter of the piston-propeller combintion. He began patent procedures and while he was thinking of the best way to develop his ideas he decided to build a model of the system he proposed. In his efforts to do this von Ohain found another of his guardian angels, Max Hahn, the head mechanic at Bartels and Becker. Hahn was ten years von Ohain's senior, a dour man of poor health who had been an apprentice on the German railways before working in the garage. He was an expert machinist and during their frequent discussions of cars, von Ohain came to realize that Hahn was an outstanding natural engineer, with considerable knowledge of manufacturing methods. Hahn agreed to work with von Ohain and this collaboration of ideas and experience proved invaluable. 'Hahn's ingenuity and practical mind brought creation of my model within my financial means,' says von Ohain. It cost him around £5,000 at today's prices and although von Ohain continued to run his car – given to him by his father – he had to sell off some of his collection of optical instruments and use up all his savings to complete the job.

Von Ohain was still a PhD student in the Institute of Physics at Göttingen. His professor, R. W. Pohl, had an open-minded and generous view of his student's extra-curricular activities, and he lent him instruments and equipment for the trials of the model. The tests in the garage were, to say the least, eventful. The combustion chamber in which air and fuel were mixed and burnt did not work properly, a problem faced by all the jet pioneers. Combustion obstinately refused to take place in the chamber designed for it, but in the turbine at the rear instead. Long yellow flames streaked from the model. Von Ohain says that 'it looked more like a flame-thrower than a gas turbine. The metal glowed red hot and we could not get a self-sustaining operation.' This meant that the engine would not work on its own, but could only be driven by its starter motor. If the outcome for von Ohain was disappointing, it did reveal a rare glimpse of Hahn's sense of humour. At least, he pointed out, the starter motor was fully used up and the flames came out at roughly the right place with seemingly great speed.

Von Ohain and Hahn realized that there would have to be much more fundamental work on almost every aspect of the engine, especially on combustion, and a long development programme would be needed. Professor Pohl came to the rescue. He had been convinced by his student of the possibilities of jet propulsion and he suggested to von Ohain that he should take his idea to industry, offering to give him a letter of recommendation to any company of his choice. The young student thought carefully and decided against an approach to any of the aero-engine companies, reasoning that their attitude would at best be negative – and so it turned out to be in 1938, when even the German Air Ministry could not persuade the engine manufacturers to work on the jet, although the offer was backed by large sums of government money and meant little risk for the companies involved.

In the end von Ohain plumped for the planemaker Ernst Heinkel, 'because he was a crazy fellow'. Professor Pohl would have preferred Willy Messerschmitt among airframe manufacturers – a sounder, safer man with good university qualifications, including a professorship – but von Ohain insisted on the unorthodox Heinkel, who had already shown, with a succession of successful high-speed aeroplanes, that he could design for speed, was indeed obsessed by it. Heinkel, von Ohain felt, must be waiting for the engine which would match the grace of his airframes; he was a man who could take risks and, moreover, he was the sole owner of his company, his own man, able to work fast.

Pohl wrote to Heinkel in February 1936, saying that von Ohain's ideas were scientifically sound but he had reached the end of his personal resources. He described the engine as a new power unit that did not need a propeller. Von Ohain's choice proved to be prescient (another guardian angel stood beside him). Heinkel was disillusioned with the German aero-engine manufacturers and their products. He had to use Rolls-Royce engines to power one of his aircraft and he believed that the British and Americans were far ahead of the Germans. This was true, and was mainly caused by the ban imposed on the Germans after World War One, which forbade them a military air force. Although the ban was now being freely broken, Heinkel felt that he did not have enough influence with the engine makers; he was frustrated and someone offering a revolutionary alternative was just what he wanted – provided the man was talking sense.

Von Ohain was summoned immediately to Heinkel's private house at Warnemünde, on the Baltic coast. The inexperienced twenty-five-year-old student found himself confronted by some of the most formidable brains in the German aircraft industry. Among them were the twin brothers Siegfried and Walter Gunter, the former an expert mathematician and the latter a brilliant airframe designer. Von Ohain recalled that there was a thermodynamicist in the group; as the specialist in the study of the relationship between heat and other forms of energy, including mechanical energy – the theoretical basis of jet engine work – the thermodynamicist challenged some of von Ohain's calculations, but the young PhD was able tactfully to refute him. The crucial meeting wore on for almost the whole day, during which Heinkel became convinced that von Ohain was brilliant and had a burning faith in his project. The other engineers appeared to von Ohain to be undecided, and he did his utmost to make his point. 'So many people will not look at what might be, only at what is,' as von Ohain says. The Gunter twins were, he thought, captivated by the idea that their graceful shapes, the need for speed and the abolition of the propeller, all added up to his new engine – if it would work. One of them told von Ohain some years later that the group thought his ideas were risky and did not look as though they had a future; on the other hand nobody wanted to say no to Heinkel and they were all worried lest the young man should go off to someone like Messerschmitt, who would develop the engine success-fully, leaving them looking like fools. Faced with this sort of agnosticism, von Ohain's conviction and sincerity told. One idea, though, was ruled out of court: a vertical take-off plane with engines mounted pancake-like in the wings. It was an idea that would have to await perfection of an engine which would also give fast forward motion: the Harrier – an invention of genius – did not emerge until more than twenty years later.

Von Ohain won. Heinkel engaged him immediately, giving him an employment contract dated 15 April 1936. The young scientist insisted on a royalty contract and asked that Max Hahn should join him. The personnel department objected to this, not on the grounds of intellectual snobbery, but because Hahn was a family man: they could not offer him a permanent contract and felt that the insecurity of the project was such that he should not be coaxed away from his safe job as head mechanic at Bartels and Becker. Heinkel brushed the objection aside. If the project failed they would still have a first-class mechanic who could be found work elsewhere in the company.

Heinkel had a special hut built at his plant in Marienehe, near Rostock. Into this primitive building he put von Ohain and Hahn, with instructions to go ahead as quickly as possible – instructions which were to be ruthlessly pressed almost from the first day. Nobody was allowed in the hut unless they were working directly on the project. Heinkel kept the work secret from the German Air Ministry and the Luftwaffe, and, of course, from the engine manufacturers. In the end his fine contempt for officialdom would bedevil the project. But the jet engine was on its way.

In England, too, the jet engine was on its way, but in very different circumstances which very nearly aborted the idea completely. While stationed at Felixstowe, Whittle continued to refine his ideas and argue them through with his brother officers, one of whom uncharitably dubbed the jet 'Whittle's flaming touch hole'. But Flying Officer Dudley Williams, who had shared quarters with Whittle at Cranwell, turned up at Felixstowe as a pilot in a flying boat squadron, and he took Whittle very seriously indeed. Learning that Whittle had only applied for British patents, he tried unsuccessfully to borrow money from his sister to apply for patents worldwide. All the same Dudley Williams was to play a key role in financing the jet.

While at Felixstowe Whittle made other, comparatively minor inventions and wrote a paper called 'The Case for the Gas Turbine', which he did not publish, although the calculations he made showed that the jet conferred large increases in efficiency at high altitude. The RAF respected Whittle at this time – within their limited terms of reference. His annual report for 1932 read: 'A very keen young officer and useful test pilot. He shows considerable ability in aircraft engineering.'

In August he was posted to an officers' engineering course at RAF Henlow in Bedfordshire, where he proved so able that he was allowed to do the course in eighteen months rather than the usual two years. Reinforced by excellent exam results, he applied to take the Mechanical Sciences Tripos at Cambridge University. The RAF had just discontinued a scheme under which a small number of exceptional officers were sent to Cambridge but in view of Whittle's record they made an exception. He arrived in Cambridge in 1934, a flight lieutenant, married, with one son and his wife expecting another child. On his junior officer's salary with a growing family to support Whittle had no means to pay the £5 fee for his original 1930 jet engine patent when it came up for renewal in January 1935; nor would the Air Ministry pay, and so his patent lapsed.

In Germany a student was spending his savings on the model jet engine he was building in his local garage, while in England a student had resigned himself to the fact that his jet engine was too far ahead of its time. He was immersed in his studies, through which he was successfully learning, as mature students often do, the theory behind what he had practised for some years. While Whittle was resigned, and von Ohain was just beginning to see his problems, two other young men treated themselves to an expansive lunch at the Café Royal in London. They were Rolf Dudley Williams, now retired from the R A F because of ill health, and Collingwood Tinling, who had been invalided out of the service after a plane crash. The two were in business together looking for an engineering project to promote. Tinling had never met Whittle and when Dudley Williams raised Whittle's idea of the jet engine, Tinling's interest grew. After lunch Dudley Williams went to the R A F Club and wrote to Whittle:

> Dear Frank,
> This is just a hurried note to tell you that I have just met a man who is a bit of a big noise in an engineering concern and to whom I mentioned your invention of an aeroplane, sans propeller as it were, and who is very interested. You told me some time ago that Armstrongs had, or were taking it up and if they have broken down or you don't like them he would, I think, like to handle it. I wonder if you could write and let me know.

Whittle rammed the note in his pocket, re-read it several hours later and decided to reply that the idea was too far ahead of its time. Then he reconsidered and decided to meet the two men because he had other inventions in mind with which they might be able to help. In the end he wrote to say that the jet patent had lapsed, the work needed would be very expensive, but he still had enough faith in the idea because it was the only way to fly fast and high.

The following Sunday Dudley Williams and Tinling went to see Whittle at his home in Trumpington. Dudley Williams recalled years later that Whittle discussed the idea of the jet engine, then poked about at the back of his desk and produced the expired patent. He explained that, although it had lapsed, he thought that the lost ground could be reclaimed by patenting improvements on the engine which he had been working out over the previous few years. Whittle wrote later of the meeting: 'I did not feel the confidence I was showing. I did not really feel that the time was ripe for an attempt on the turbojet engine itself, but I felt that if they were encouraged to believe it was worthwhile, something would come of our joint activities.'

Whatever Whittle's doubts, he had cast the spell of his idea. Over dinner on the train back to London, the usually quite sceptical Tinling told Dudley Williams that he had never met such a man before and that he was absolutely convinced that his idea would succeed. Both he and Dudley Williams were still in their twenties, with little experience of inventors or inventions, but in all their greenness they proceeded to become company promoters. They undertook to act as Whittle's agents, negotiating a deal with a financier or financial group for money, in return for a share in the rights of the invention. The two agents agreed to cover the cost of further patents, and each was to receive a quarter share in the commercial rights. Their aim was to raise £50,000 which, in their innocence, they supposed would cover the costs of developing a complete jet-propelled aeroplane.

The two promoters toiled unsuccessfully for some months to raise what would now be termed venture capital – money injected without immediate hope of return into a promising but high-risk project. The British investment scene, always hyper-conservative, was particularly dull in the early thirties. Investors did not want to back innovation; they wanted security in their investments, an attitude which has done much down the years to ensure that, while Britain could undoubtedly invent things, financial backers would much prefer to see someone else make them – at their own risk. At last, late in 1935, Williams and Tinling found an aeronautical consulting engineer, M. L. Bramson, who *was* interested. Whittle was at first resistant to oulining the project to anyone with links to the aero industry but once he had overcome his reluctance, Bramson introduced the trio to a firm of merchant bankers, O. T. Falk and Partners.

The Falk partnership, seeing the dangers of no-risk investment policies for the nation, took on business which was not suitable, for one reason or another, for their parent company, O. T. Falk Ltd, and not only made investments themselves but also raised further capital from outside sources for some projects. One of the partners, L. Lance Whyte, had already proposed that a large development corporation should be created to spread the risk of financing new technical developments over a large number of investors. Whittle and his promoters had struck exactly the right company at exactly the right moment. Falk had great faith in Bramson's knowledge and judgement and they hired him to advise them on the soundness – or otherwise – of Whittle's proposals. Bramson became so interested in the project that he voluntarily gave up any share in the profits he might expect from having advised Falk on the jet engine's feasibility.

Whittle, Williams and Tinling met Lance Whyte and another director, Sir Maurice Bonham Carter. Whyte, a Cambridge-educated physicist who had become a banker, was an outstandingly gifted man. His diary entry for 11 September 1935, the day he first met Frank Whittle, read simply, 'Stratosphere plane?' Of this meeting Whyte wrote:

It was like love at first sight: the impression he [Whittle] made was overwhelming. I have never been so quickly convinced, nor so happy to find one's highest standards met. Whittle had all the winning cards: imagination, ability, enthusiasm, determination, respect for science and practical experience – all at the service of a stunningly simple idea: 2,000 hp with one moving part. This was genius, not talent. Though I have known a number of the greatest living scientists and thinkers, this meeting with Frank Whittle gave me a thrill I have never experienced otherwise, partly because he was younger and I was discovering him for myself, and partly because abstract intellectual activity lacks the concrete reality of practical invention. An Einstein does his work in an intellectual dream; Whittle would have to do his in the harsh world of human conflict and his aeroplane would have to fly – or crash. That stern challenge appealed to me, and I believed that Whittle was equal to it.

That night I told my wife that I had met one of the great inventive engineers of our time. To explain my excitement I said that it was like what I imagine was the experience of meeting a saint in an earlier religious epoch: one surrendered to the enchantment of a single-minded personality born to a great task ... Whittle explained his idea with superb conciseness: 'reciprocating engines are exhausted. They have hundreds of parts jerking to and fro and they cannot become more powerful without becoming too complicated. The engine of the future must produce 2,000 hp with one moving part: a spinning turbine and compressor.' ... The elegance of this idea won me. Every great advance replaces traditional complexities by a new simplicity ... Whittle was on a winner.

As it turned out, Whyte's euphoria was well placed. But everything now hinged on Bramson's engineering report: if it was negative, Falk would withdraw. Bramson's report of 8 October 1935 (now in the Public Record Office files, though Whittle wrote in his book 'I have been unable to trace this important document') gave the project almost unstinted support. He wrote that Whittle's calculations and deductions were 'substantially correct' and that he had made a fundamental discovery that the gas turbine could power a jet aircraft which, 'if all were successful', would do 500 mph over a 5,000-mile range, making less noise and vibration than contemporary or future piston-engined aircraft. Bramson accepted Whittle's optimistic views on the efficiency of compressor and turbine for his design – the only technically qualified man to do so at this stage – and while he pointed to certain design difficulties which would have to be overcome, he concluded: 'The proposed development, though necessarily speculative as regards time and money required, is so important that it should, if possible, be undertaken. I recommend the adoption . . . with the proviso that all designs shall be submitted to an independent authority on turbine and compressor design before actual construction is undertaken.'

In giving his support, Bramson was among the very few that at least kept Britain level-pegging with Germany in jet development. (It would be four months later that von Ohain was recommended by his professor to Ernst Heinkel.) Bramson's witness was certainly lucky for Whittle. Here was an inventor of twenty-eight years old, a junior RAF officer albeit an excellent pilot, without at this point even a formal engineering degree and with no experience of research and development, who was proposing to challenge the aviation world in the teeth of vastly experienced engineers who maintained that the things that Whittle was claiming for his engine were quite impossible. Nor did anyone know if there was a market for the jet engine in the unlikely event of its success. Whittle himself had only a limited vision of its uses: his sole suggestion was that the jet should be the engine for a high-altitude, long-distance (transatlantic) mail plane. He seems to have discounted any military use in fighter aircraft because current tactics did not call for such an engine. Whittle and his sponsors simplistically believed that, once called into existence, the jet engine would generate its own market and create a new industry – and how many modern business schools would teach, how many great corporations would invest in, so slender a set of assumptions? Whatever the market forces of 1935, none pulled the way of the jet engine: for the market was ignorant. The fact that there was no conception in the Britain of that time of market research as it is understood today was probably another stroke of good fortune for Flight Lieutenant Whittle.

Within a month of Bramson's report, Whittle, hope renewed, had a draft agreement with Falk and a small company was set up to make the engine, called Power Jets. The name was chosen to indicate purpose without giving the project away. Whittle was able to take out new patents on specific parts of the design but even so he felt himself unprotected against any major company which wanted to steal his concept; it could afford patent litigation, which he could not. There was also the question of Air Ministry conditions, to which Whittle, a serving officer of the RAF, was subject. Government practice was that where its employees made inventions which had to be kept secret for military purposes, government itself would retain all rights. If there was no secrecy involved, the inventor was given commercial and overseas rights after payment of part of the royalties to the government; and the government retained the right of 'free user' of the invention. Whittle accurately foresaw that if the government had free user rights, it would be a severe handicap should the government become the chief customer, user and paymaster, but there was nothing that could be done about it. He resubmitted his proposals for secrecy tests and after they had been vetted by all three services, the Air Ministry ruled that it was unlikely that the jet engine would ever be of military use and therefore there was no need for secrecy. Commercial and overseas rights were given to Whittle and he transferred them to Power Jets.

Whittle was allocated shares in the company instead of royalties on his invention, and the Air Ministry agreed to take 25 per cent of these shares instead of its slice of commercial and overseas royalties. This was not an unfavourable situation for the inventor. The shareholding was of two types: class A shares, totalling ninety-eight, of which Whittle received forty-two while Williams and Tinling received twenty-one each and the Crown received fourteen; and class B shares, worth £1 each. Class A shareholders had 49 per cent, and class B shareholders 51 per cent, of the voting power, profits and proceeds of liquidation. Once 50,000 class B shares had been issued it was expected that the company would be reorganized to provide for further expansion. Falk were to subscribe £2,000 at once, with an option to put in a further £18,000 within eighteen months.

One point recognized all round was that the entire enterprise centred on Whittle. He was the inventor, chief engineer without salary, the sole begetter of the jet in the UK. Lance Whyte was chairman and managing director. With working capital of £2,000, the team, if it can be graced with that term, set out to make the jet engine – but with one or two reservations.

Whittle was now in the final year of his engineering degree course at Cambridge. At the same time he was negotiating with manufacturers, setting up his company and beginning the serious design of a working jet engine for bench tests, if not yet for flight. The Air Ministry stipulated that the inventor should not, save with the permission of the President of the Air Council, work more than six hours a week on his invention. Thus Britain approached the jet age.

Power Jets was incorporated in March 1936. A month later von Ohain joined Heinkel with a royalty contract and, in Heinkel's terms, limitless hours of work on the jet engine. In 1939 Whittle's patent drawings were published in the German aviation journal *Flugsport*. There was no reason they should not be, for they were not secret; in any case the Germans by then had little need of them.

When Heinkel gave orders to build the shed that was to house von Ohain and Max Hahn, he stipulated that, although it was to be sited at Marienehe, it must be as far as possible away from the main complex. This was not only done for secrecy; it was also to insulate the jet designers from the sceptics in the factory who would express their lack of belief in von Ohain's idea. A clause in the young scientist's contract laid down that he was to report to Heinkel alone on progress in the project, which was called *Sonder-Entwicklung* – special development – rather than jet engine. The senior person assigned by Heinkel to work in the small team to back up the two pioneers was Wilhelm Gundermann, a stress analyst and engineering designer, and under him were six to eight draughtsmen and stress analysts, mostly newly recruited. Each man focussed on his particular interest, with Max Hahn working on manufacturing and combustion experiments. Von Ohain directed the project and, when asked to estimate time and cost to a complete test engine, told Heinkel with the optimism of youth that it would be a matter of months and 50,000 marks. It was to take years and a lot more money.

This was not Heinkel's only high-speed project. A few months before meeting von Ohain, he had met another young man just out of university, Wernher von Braun, who was building his first primitive rocket engine, the precursor of the notorious V2 used to bombard London, and was later to found the United States' post-war rocket programme. Von Braun convinced Heinkel that his rockets could be used to propel aeroplanes, and Heinkel promptly gave him one of his new high-speed fighters, the He 112, as a test bed. Von Braun found a test pilot, Erich Warsitz, who was brave enough to fly it. After many terrifying adventures, Warsitz flew Heinkel's rocket plane in 1937, though not before the first He 112 had blown to pieces on the ground, luckily hurling Warsitz clear in a miraculous escape.

While all this was happening in great secrecy, von Ohain was facing his first crisis. He had been over-optimistic about the time needed for his programme, and Heinkel, wanting quick results, stipulated that ground testing of the jet should begin in one year – June 1937. Jet development was to be Heinkel's personal enterprise: he wanted no help from the German Air Ministry or the engine manufacturers – which meant that the almost absurdly young inventor could draw on no outside assistance.

Von Ohain wanted first to design a sound combustion chamber and then design the rest of the engine around it. The reason for this was simple: combustors had been the main barrier to successful gas turbine development for many years, because the section in which the compressed air-fuel mixture is burnt becomes immensely hot and in the mid-1930s – as Whittle was also to discover – the materials which could withstand constant running in such infernal heat did not seem to exist. Yet without a successful combustor to drive the turbine, which in turn drives the compressor, there would be no jet engine. Von Ohain visited the Leipzig Trade Fair to try to find a manufacturer who could match his needs, but nobody would commit himself. (Whittle, some months earlier, visited the British Trade Fair on the same mission. He found just one manufacturer willing to try.)

As well as the relentless pressure from Heinkel, von Ohain had the additional problem of the political climate at the factory, where the 'secret' project was viewed with scepticism. Von Ohain knew from his Göttingen model that a poor combustor would mean the end of the jet project and, realizing how critical the issue was, he decided on a dual approach. He would build very quickly a simple demonstration jet with minimum risk, which would prove the principle to the doubters and to Heinkel, and he would simultaneously start serious fuel-air combustor development as a separate project. In his demonstration he would get round the combustion problems by burning hydrogen, which was much easier to handle and burn in a low-risk combustor, although hydrogen could never be used in a true jet engine. Von Ohain denies great prescience in this decision: 'I was between the devil and the deep blue sea. Heinkel wanted results, he pushed me very hard, but I realized that if you do not do combustor developments separately you face absolute catastrophe. The idea of the hydrogen combustor was, if you like, my good luck – my guardian angel was there again.'

Wilhelm Gundermann proved another, tangible guardian angel. Knowing Heinkel's ways and his organization inside out, he was able to guide von Ohain through the intricacies and the politics. Von Ohain thought he was an excellent engineer, but more: 'He was the fixer. He knew the ins and outs of the factory. He could get unbelievable things passed through. If I said to him "How do we get this done?" he would say "I know old so-and-so in that department, leave it to me." ' Meanwhile, to the fury of the works superintendents, Max Hahn had creamed the best eight fitters and mechanics from the factory to help him, and it was Hahn who played a major part in the design. The combustion chamber was almost entirely his work, and its development took two years.

Progress with this combustor was slow throughout 1936, mainly because work was focussed on the hydrogen demonstrator, called the He S1, which had to have a successful run before Heinkel would commit himself to making the first jet engine proper. The demonstrator was completed and installed in its test bed around the end of February 1937 according to von Ohain, who is uncertain about the exact date of its first run but believes that it was probably in the following month. Heinkel was more confident, but probably wrong, when he asserted in his autobiography:

It was started up for the first time one September night in 1937. I shall never forget how Hahn, who, like von Ohain, was on the job almost day and night, jubilantly called me about one o'clock in the morning. The unit had functioned for the first time – as fuel for the combustion chamber we used hydrogen and not, as later, petrol or crude oil. A quarter of an hour later I heard with my own ears that remarkable howling and whistling noise which made the whole workshop shudder, and which today is for all of us a commonplace when a jet passes over.

Whatever the date, there is no doubt about the impact of this successful first run. From being treated as a gifted but probably wrong-headed young amateur enthusiast, von Ohain suddenly became, within the organization, an inventor of genius: 'Heinkel and his engineers suddenly believed firmly in the feasibility of the engine and my position in the company was now very firm. It was a considerable morale boost to my co-workers and myself.'

Heinkel sent von Ohain a letter of congratulation and gave him an increase in salary. Nowhere in the letter did he mention the jet engine, only the *Sonder-Entwicklung*. Heinkel went on to say in his book:

After six months' difficult work, the He S3 gas turbine was born: its running no longer a matter of chance, but scientifically controllable, and it burnt petrol instead of hydrogen. Even this very primitive apparatus developed approximately 1,100 lb of thrust. Now the only thing that mattered to me was that the engine should fly. I planned the building of a test unit, to be called the He 178, and which, for the first time, was to be equipped with the jet engine.

This rather airy, inaccurate account concealed a mountain of hard, tense work and some major achievements by von Ohain and his sweating team. Once the hydrogen engine ran, Heinkel certainly pressed still more relentlessly for a flight engine which he could put in an aeroplane. His ambition was to fly the world's first jet plane before an audience consisting of Hitler, Goering and such members of the German Air Ministry and Luftwaffe as would wish to crowd to applaud his genius. A demonstration of this kind would indeed show his foresight, the brilliance of his judgement of new ideas and the remarkable capabilities of his staff. He was certain that once he could demonstrate a successful world's first he would be given the money and facilities and, most gratifying of all for his exhibitionist character, the recognition, which would enable him to found an engine division of his company with exclusive right to the jet engine. Thus he would outsmart the established German engine companies of which he was so contemptuous. Unfortunately for Heinkel, it would not work out that way. In Berlin, two outstanding young engineers were planning an altogether different future for the industry, and to them Heinkel was to become a nuisance, an irritant who might upset the delicate relationship they were trying to establish with the manufacturers.

At Marienehe, however, none of this was known to von Ohain's team now working on the flight engine. Their job was to make something which worked and which would power a propellerless aeroplane into the sky over the Baltic and bring its pilot safely back to earth. It would be the most formidable achievement since the Wright brothers first took off from Kittyhawk, for the jet would be opening the skies not just to a few professionals but to the millions who would fly for the price of an airline ticket. This was not, of course, thought of at the time. If Whittle's first use for the jet engine was to power a small mail plane, von Ohain looked at speed purely as an end in itself; only at the end of the thirties did Heinkel think in terms of a jet fighter.

The demonstration jet had produced about 550 lb of thrust, but the first flight engine was intended to have a thrust of between 1,760 and 1,980 lb – very ambitious for a true 'first'. Von Ohain's visit to the Leipzig Trade Fair to try to interest industrial companies working in the boiler field in the expected problem of the combustion chamber had met with no success: none of them believed that the required intensity of combustion was possible. Von Ohain's own staff, especially Max Hahn, would have to solve it themselves. However, by 1938 von Ohain's team believed that they had a satisfactory combustor, and work on the engine, the Heinkel S3, was progressing well. Meanwhile, another team, led by Dr Heinrich Hertel and chief designer Schwartzler, together with the Gunter twins, had begun design work on the airframe of the world's first jet plane. The first run of the engine was almost certainly later than Heinkel stated in his book, and certainly later than the first run of Whittle's engine – thus establishing Whittle's as the first true experimental engine, liquid fuelled, to run. Von Ohain himself says that comparisons with the hydrogen-fuelled demonstrator are not meaningful.

By 1938 tests of the first flight-engine showed that it was falling far short of its designed thrust. The engine was later flown attached to a Heinkel 118, a prototype single-engined dive bomber which had lost a Luftwaffe contract in favour of the Junkers 87 Stuka. Heinkel states:

> This machine stood high enough to give sufficient ground clearance (so the jet could be slung under the fuselage). Warsitz flew with Kunzel (another test pilot). Test flights took place each day at dawn while the factory was empty and deserted to prevent us having any audience. After the He 118 took off with its normal engine, Kunzel would switch in the jet unit. All this would take place at about four o'clock in the morning. At six o'clock we had to finish the test flights, for soon after that the normal work day began. It was a brief but indescribable performance that we saw. We used to watch how first the bluish jet stream shot into the air, then almost at once the plane was forced up to an enormous speed. These air tests were repeated day by day until the turbine burnt out one day on landing. This was a stroke of bad luck and made us decide to build the second unit into the He 178, which in the meantime had been completed as the first purely jet driven plane ... The major constructional problem was its equipment, for the first time, with a jet unit behind the pilot's seat, with a jet exhaust, and a forward intake for the air, which entered through a huge opening in the nose and led beneath the pilot's seat.

The reason for the He S3's poor performance was that its designers had made its compressor and combustor too small. This was due to an attempt to keep down air resistance (drag) by reducing the diameter of the engine beyond its feasible limits. Many modifications were made, to which Max Hahn and Gundermann made great contributions, but von Ohain's role, though constantly underplayed in his own account, was crucial despite his youth and inexperience. The He S3b was eventually persuaded to give 1,100 lb of thrust, a figure reached in early 1939, and in mid-1939 the airframe of the He 178 was ready. It was a shoulder-wing monoplane, metallic grey and simple in design, although the designers had faced fundamentally new problems. The size and shape of the air intake to the engine, the position of the engine and the shape of the jet outlet at the back of the plane were all entirely new considerations for an entirely new type of aircraft.

In-flight performance showed that the Heinkel–von Ohain team had got the design substantially right, but before the He 178 flew, Ernst Heinkel attended another demonstration which should have warned him that he was innovating in a climate where innovation on this fundamental scale was not wanted by those to whom he had to sell the results of the company's pioneering work. This was a demonstration of the He 176 rocket plane, which Erich Warsitz flew in a startling fifty-second flip on 30 June 1939. Ernst Udet, the unstable and sceptical head of equipment and development at the Air Ministry, was then invited to watch a longer test flight, together with Colonel-General Milch, Goering's deputy. After seeing one short flight Milch congratulated Warsitz but then, according to Heinkel, Udet refused to allow any more flights because he considered the aeroplane unsafe. He later relented under persistent pressure and on 3 July Warsitz demonstrated the plane before Hitler at a display of new weapons. Goering and other members of the German general staff were present.

On seeing the rocket plane in flight, Hitler gave Warsitz an immediate pay rise – at Heinkel's expense – but there the interest seemed to end. Heinkel came away believing that Goering had been condescending and had failed to understand the significance of rocket-powered flight. Warsitz was summoned to Berlin to a twenty-minute interview with the Führer about rocket-powered aeroplanes, during which Hitler asked perceptive questions and was polite, but Warsitz told Heinkel afterwards that he had the impression that the whole enterprise was regarded in Berlin as a diversion or, worse still, a *folie* without any practical value in the near future. Heinkel began to suspect that there was a plot to rob him of the development of new types of engine because of the interests of the traditional manufacturers. Something like this was indeed going on, but not for the reasons Heinkel suspected.

Heinkel's reaction to the damp reception of his enterprise was to press forward with work on von Ohain's engine and the airframe which would be powered into the skies by it. And on 27 August 1939, the world's first jet was flown by Warsitz. The group that assembled at Marienehe at about 4 am included Heinkel, von Ohain, Max Hahn and Gundermann – who was almost barred because meticulous security men could not find his name on their list. Heinkel fully understood the significance of the day: he saw that the jet must be pre-eminent over the rocket, which could burn only for a few seconds or minutes. He wrote: 'This was not simply a new aircraft, but a completely new source of power which could start us off on a new path.' The group watching experienced intense strain, as even Heinkel admitted. Von Ohain was particularly nervous.

Twenty years afterwards Eric Warsitz gave this account of the flight:

The machine was towed to take-off point. Since Heinkel had built it off his own bat and without telling the Air Ministry, we weren't allowed to be seen with it out on the factory site, since that would have breached secrecy. Heinkel wanted to present the Air Ministry with an aircraft that was ready and working and for this reason I was obliged to dispense with the taxiing trials that are normally required.

I tested that all the ailerons were working, checked the turbine at different revs, checked the pump pressures, temperatures and lots of other things, and gave the mechanics the signal to close the cockpit. After a take-off run of about 300 metres I quickly built up speed. I could hold the direction marvellously with the brakes and then I got her up. I kept trying to retract the landing gear, but something wasn't right. The main thing was, she was flying. My airspeed indicator was registering 600 km per hour and Herr Schwarzler had told me that on no account was I to go any faster. So I had to throttle back.

I'd now been in the air for six minutes and had to prepare for landing. The turbine reacted obediently to my throttle lever, even though a fuel pump had broken down, as I could see from my instruments. As I flattened out I went too far, but for fuel reasons I couldn't fly another circuit and so I had to side-slip, otherwise I would have run into the River Warnow. I wasn't at all happy sideslipping with a new aircraft, especially very close to the ground. The machine touched down smoothly, without bumping. She ran on in exactly the right direction and I brought her to a halt right in front of Dr Heinkel and his party.

The riggers had cheered when the jet took off; now they shouldered Heinkel and Warsitz. Then Heinkel made for the nearest telephone to call Udet in Berlin. Warsitz had told him that apart from the undercarriage and the fuel pump the flight had been perfect, with those pleasing characteristics that other jet pioneers would report in the future: the ample surge of power, the lack of noise and vibration, the general sense of confidence that the jet engine generated. Although the ecstatic planemaker did not receive a jubilant response from Udet, who after congratulating Heinkel announced with some asperity that he was going back to sleep, he soon forgot his sense of disappointment as, in the next few days, he turned his whole attention to the development programme for the jet engine and a new airframe for a revolutionary fighter.

Each day Heinkel phoned Udet, or his deputies, to try to force them into a definite date on which the Luftwaffe's equipment and technical development controller would come to see for himself the company's latest wonder – and the future of aviation. He hoped that Udet would also coax Hitler, Goering and Milch from Berlin. But Udet was always evasive and Heinkel finally had to beard him in his favourite Berlin restaurant, Horcher's, where he plied him with champagne, for which Udet had a powerful thirst, to try to find out what the Luftwaffe's plans for new engines and airframes really were. Udet was preoccupied, unforthcoming. They drove to his flat early in the morning – 1 September – where Udet indulged in a favourite game of his: dressed as a redskin, he fired pistols at a target over Heinkel's head. Towards dawn, Heinkel turned the radio on, to hear the newsreader giving the first news of Germany's invasion of Poland. 'Well, there you are,' said Udet, sweeping his head-dress off in a weary gesture. The Luftwaffe was about to go to the kind of war for which its planes had been mainly designed – as a support to the army's blitzkreig armoured columns.

Heinkel recalled long afterwards that he drove back to Warnemünde to receive orders the same day that he was to cease all research and development work and concentrate on war production for what was to be, in the high command's view, a short war. Rockets and jets could be contemplated when Poland was German and the

British and French had abandoned their absurd declaration of war. So for the moment Heinkel was to set aside his jet programme, though he kept von Ohain's team at work developing the engine, paid for by himself.

In Britain, the Air Ministry made it clear to Whittle that they regarded his jet engine project as a spare-time job. Lance Whyte later recalled the opinion of a senior Air Ministry official (unnamed): 'This is an unexplored world: we don't even know which way Whittle's engine will turn round.'

Air Ministry collective thinking was summed up by Whyte: 'It is up to you City people to gamble on Whittle. We can't give you money but we will help by lending you Whittle's services as chief engineer of your company because we expect to get valuable scientific information from your failure.' In fact, it is now known that the official view was that Whittle's data, if at all useful, would be fed to Griffith at the Royal Aircraft Establishment to help with his gas turbine work, now resurrected because of the stimulus that Whittle's activities were giving to the Farnborough scientists.

Of these years of often bitter struggle, the official historian of the project wrote:

> Whittle only received recognition for jet propulsion from the Air Ministry at the moment when he actually demonstrated mechanical success and had compiled scientific data to support his claim for the efficiencies of his compressor and turbine. It was these efficiencies which were to prove that the gas turbine was superior to the reciprocating engine in certain conditions of flight. Thereby he convinced the Air Ministry, his only customer, that flight by jet propulsion was possible and even an urgent necessity. This was in 1939, but he had been at work for eleven years, and the story of these years is a record of his engineering genius and enthusiasm.
>
> His busiest years were from 1935 onwards, when with the assistance of a handful of engineers, technicians and draughtsmen, he designed his experimental unit, superintended the construction and himself conducted most of the tests. But during this period frequent breakdowns and the necessity for altering and re-designing parts deferred his success and led the Air Ministry to withhold

their approval. There were indeed moments when the uncertain prospects were nearly fatal to the work, for the Air Ministry's moral support was always doubtful and private financial support was once or twice on the point of disintegration.

Whittle, as chief engineer of Power Jets, had not waited for the formal incorporation of his company to get on with the job. Early in 1936 Falk and Partners placed the first design contracts for a test engine with British Thomson-Houston and the company got the construction order in June that year. Like von Ohain, Whittle wanted to build and test engine components separately, mainly because he was ahead of all previous engineering experience and to try to build a complete engine straight off seemed to him too great a gamble. He quickly found, however, that this approach would be too expensive – a separate compressor test plant alone would cost £27,000, and Power Jets had an authorized capital of only £20,000. Whittle accepted the inevitable when faced with the figures and set out to design and build the complete engine.

It was a leap into almost complete darkness. The young designer expected far greater efficiencies from his compressor and turbine than had ever been achieved before, while the combustion chamber was to burn with an intensity twenty-four times greater than any known boiler furnace. And all this was to happen in a very small space with materials as yet untested in such a hostile environment. Whittle was confident – too confident – that he could get high efficiencies for the compressor and turbine but, like von Ohain, he was worried about his combustor. Just as von Ohain visited the Leipzig Trade Fair at about this time, Whittle went to the British Industries Fair at Castle Bromwich in February 1936. Most of the companies he approached thought he was mad or joking when he put to them his combustor requirements – a chamber which would burn almost 200 gallons of fuel per hour in a space of six cubic feet. Luckier than von Ohain, however, Whittle found one small Scottish firm, Laidlaw Drew, whose director, A. B. S. Laidlaw, was willing to try. Laidlaw guessed that Whittle was working on a gas turbine but Whittle refused to confirm his supposition.

In the first half of 1936 Whittle travelled the country for meetings with backers and engineering companies. Barely five weeks before his final examinations he settled down to study for his engineering tripos – the reason he was in Cambridge at all. The stress of all his work was making him physically ill but he had set his heart on getting a first class honours degree and, to his surprise, he did. He

should now have returned immediately to engineering duties in the
RAF but his tutor managed to persuade the Air Ministry's director
of education to allow him a year's post-graduate research. This
enabled him to spend most of his time on the jet engine, the
components for which were now taking shape at various engineering
companies. Crude combustor experiments started in the autumn and
they quickly established that Whittle could get the high intensities
that were essential to the engine, still designed to power a 500 mph
small mail plane. These experiments were made at British Thomson-
Houston at Rugby and they produced deafening noise and thick
clouds of fuel vapour and smoke, which penetrated the company's
nearby planning office. Fuel would drip from the leaking apparatus
to form fiery pools on the ground beneath. Power Jets drawings, it
was said, were recognizable by the smell of the fuel oil with which
they became impregnated.

There was, however, no doubt about the progress. Steels were
being developed by British manufacturers which were resistant to
creep – the tendency of materials to expand at high running temperatures – and the combustor experiments, while alarming, were not
unpromising. Whittle was proved right in foreseeing that materials
of the right strength would be available when they were wanted by
the designers. All the same, there were problems lying just over the
horizon – caused not by materials but by men.

Whittle was lucky enough to have made a friend of Sir Henry
Tizard, rector of Imperial College and chairman of the Aeronautical
Research Committee (ARC) which advised the Air Ministry on what
research it should pursue. The two men met at a Cambridge dinner
in March 1936, and Lance Whyte sent Tizard a copy of Bramson's
favourable report on Whittle's project a few days later. Tizard was
progressive and influential, a champion of new ideas. It was he who
saw to it that the country was able to use radar in time for the Battle
of Britain – the nick of time – and his rows with Lord Cherwell,
Churchill's taciturn scientific adviser, would become a Whitehall
legend during the Second World War. While Whittle was unable to
arouse anything more than passing interest at the Air Ministry,
Tizard admired the young man and held that the work he was doing
would at the very least yield valuable scientific results. He insisted on
an orderly programme of tests worked out with the Air Ministry and
he also persuaded the research directorate to get the Royal Aircraft
Establishment at Farnborough to study Whittle's project and report
on it to the ARC.

It thus came about that on 31 October 1936 Power Jets handed over the full theoretical and engineering details of Whittle's invention to, of all people, Dr A. A. Griffith, who had already brushed Whittle aside in 1930. Griffith reported in March 1937 – just as Whittle was about to do the first test run of his engine. This time round Griffith was warmer towards the project. He conceded the advantages of a pure jet over the gas turbine driving a propeller (his own idea) and said that Whittle's engine had the advantage of great mechanical simplicity. It did away with the weight of the propeller and the gearing needed to drive it, and it also overcame the problems of designing a propeller that would work efficiently at around the speed of sound.

But Griffith was critical of Whittle's forecasts about the efficiencies of his compressor, and he calculated that fuel consumption was very high compared with conventional engines, although there were weight reductions to compensate for that. He also pointed out that take-off performance for a pure jet was low because of the absence of a propeller slipstream over the wing to give lift. Given the way in which he had shifted his ground, his concluding paragraph was all the more astonishing:

> In its present form the proposed jet propulsion system *cannot* compete with the conventional power plant in any case where economical flight is demanded (e.g. the transport of the maximum percentage of useful load over given distance). It is of value only for special purposes such as the attainment of high speed or high altitude for short times in cases where take-off requirements are not stringent.

Whittle and his small Power Jets team at once pointed out that Griffith had not reported on the engine's predicted performance at high altitude, thus ignoring the whole purpose of the design. Griffith retorted that, while he believed that high speed and economic flight would ultimately be attained by jet propulsion in the stratosphere, he was satisfied that Whittle's expectations were much too optimistic. He was to be proved wrong once again – and once again in circumstances which put his motives in doubt.

Tizard went on backing Whittle, believing that the gas turbine promised great advantages. He now also had before him Griffith's proposals for a gas turbine driving a propeller, which had suddenly reappeared after a gap of seven years. There is little room for doubt – and the official historian thinks it most probable – that these plans were resurrected by the Farnborough scientists because they realized that Power Jets were intent on a gas turbine and they could not afford to be caught lagging – which was what they had been doing since 1930 when the ARC told them to get on with the work. Tizard, with the backing of the ARC, made it known in Whitehall that the time was ripe for new departures in aero-engine design and urged the Air Ministry to foster development work quickly on both the Power Jets and Farnborough projects.

To make matters worse for Power Jets, the Griffith report coincided with another cash crisis. Lance Whyte described the situation in early 1937 as 'desperate'. The need for absolute secrecy – it was now clear that German rearmament was a threat to peace – made it impossible to raise money through the usual City sources. When Whyte approached rich investors they all said: 'If it is so secret it must be a matter for the government.' Yet the Air Ministry's support remained trivial. Early in 1937 Whyte appealed to Tizard – 'the one independent person in Britain with the highest expert knowledge and authority' – who replied on 22 June 1937:

You ask for my opinion about Flight Lieutenant Whittle's scheme. I think there is nothing inherently unsound in his ideas. He may possibly be optimistic in some of his predictions, but even allowing for that I think it highly probable that, if he has the necessary financial support and encouragement, he will succeed in producing a new type of power plant for aircraft. I am particularly interested in this work because I think that if we are to provide the high powers which will be necessary for aircraft of the future we must develop some type of turbine. Further, the fact that such an engine would use heavy oil is of great importance from the point of view of defence and of commerce.

I have a very high opinion of Flight Lieutenant Whittle. He has the ability, the energy and the enthusiasm for work of this nature. He has also an intimate knowledge of practical conditions. This combination of qualities is rare and deserves the utmost encouragement. I sincerely hope that you will get the necessary finance because I think that you will have to make up your mind that a large expenditure will be necessary before final success is reached.

Of course, I do not mean to imply that success is certain. All new schemes of this kind must be regarded as 'gambles' in the initial stages. I do think, however, that this is a better gamble than many I know of, on which much money has been spent!

This recommendation from Tizard enabled Whyte to approach some of the engineering companies already involved in the project.

They gave some modest financial help, together with technical assistance, and so staved off complete collapse.

On 12 April 1937 Whittle ordered the first test run of the jet engine. He wrote in his diary:

> ... jet successfully ignited at 1,000 revolutions per minute (rpm). Speed raised to 2,000 rpm ... requested further raising of speed to 2,500 rpm and during this process opened valve B and the unit suddenly ran away. Probably started at about 2,300 rpm ... flame tube red-hot at inner radius; combustion very bad ...

High drama lies behind this bald narrative. As Whittle opened the main control valve, the engine note rose to a nerve-racking shriek. The combustor casing glowed red and the jet ran out of control. The engineers ran for cover while Whittle tried to screw down the control valve as fast as he could. Still the revolution counter rose until it reached 8,000 rpm, then the engine slowly subsided like a spent banshee. After making some adjustments to the fuel system, Whittle tried a second run on the following evening. This time the jet's behaviour was even more alarming, running out of control from 1,500 rpm, and the speed continued to rise after Whittle had shut down the fuel supply completely. Streams of flame roared from the jet pipe, fuel vapour poured aflame from leaking joints and an aura of fire danced in the air. Once more everyone took to their heels while Whittle, terrified though he was, tried to regain control. Eventually, after touching 8,000 rpm, the engine subsided.

An inquest into these runaways discovered that the fault was simple. The faulty fuel control system was leaking unburnt fuel into the combustor before the engine was ignited, and a small reservoir of this fuel built up between tests. This pool caught fire on ignition so that the engine developed a wildfire life of its own. The third test also ran away, this time because of a simple mechanical fault. The fourth test ran under control, but Whittle shut down at 7,500 rpm because the combustor was glowing red and had set fire to the ignition cables.

Further test runs through April showed that the combustor and compressor were a long way short of Whittle's estimates, and the overall condition of the engine was deteriorating. By August the Power Jets team realized that major alterations would be needed, but now a new complication arose. The jet engine was mounted on a test bed in the gallery of British Thomson-Houston's turbine factory, with the jet pipe pouring out into the open air through a window. Sheets of steel plate one inch thick were built around and over the engine to contain the pieces should it explode at high speed, but BT-H decided that the risks were nevertheless too dangerous. Whittle and Power Jets were politely moved to a disused foundry at the company's Ladywood works at Lutterworth.

These dangerous early tests took place against a background of continual cash problems. New parts were often needed to replace those which had failed or burnt out and at one stage even these modest needs were threatened. By 1937, Falk, who had raised some £7,000, were having trouble in raising more venture capital and there was no sign that the company would take up the option to increase their Power Jets holding up to £20,000. The option expired on 20 July. Earlier in the month Falk said that this method of finance must stop, but the company continued to keep Power Jets operating by small loans, almost on a weekly basis.

Meanwhile the Air Ministry was considering whether to chip in with some money. Scepticism about the project, particularly from Dr (later Sir) David Pye, Deputy Director of Scientific Research, prolonged Whittle's agony, and civil servants were not slow to point out that if the private backers were not willing to put up any more finance, should good public money be thrown after bad? The Air Ministry had been thinking of a contract worth £10,000, but they reduced it to £5,000 and continued to prevaricate even about that. The Catch 22 lay in the fact that Falk found it difficult to raise money on the market because the need for secrecy scared away possible investors, while the Air Ministry held that if there were no private investors willing to back the company it must mean that the venture was even more speculative and risky than they thought.

While Whittle and his tiny team sweated on what little money they had in their disused foundry in the soggy Midlands, von Ohain had no financial worries. The vast resources of a successful and internationally known company, Heinkel, were at his disposal. The British official historian points out that it has not been possible to calculate what costs von Ohain and his team were incurring, but there was little doubt that they had far more money and security than the Power Jets team. It was Whittle's darkest hour: it seemed that Britain was on the verge of abandoning one of the great inventions of the modern world. But in Germany, too, the young visionaries outside Heinkel's charmed circle were running into troubles of their own.

In Heinkel's version of events, German jet development was stalled
by the outbreak of war in September 1939. However, although he
may have been ordered to concentrate on producing the Heinkel 111
bomber for the Luftwaffe, he continued von Ohain's work at Marienehe and fought the bureaucrats hard to become a jet engine
manufacturer in his own right. During 1938 and 1939 engineers in
another major airframe company, Junkers, just as disillusioned as
Heinkel with the traditional aero-engine manufacturers, were making
their own bid to design and build a range of jet engines. At the same
time, Air Ministry officials in Berlin, remarkable for their insight
and foresight, were laying the foundations of a jet engine industry.

Unknown to Heinkel, in the two years up to the outbreak of war,
Germany was put into the forefront of jet invention and development
due to the engineering skills and managerial flair of a handful of
young engineers whose achievements had virtually no post-war recognition in Britain. Had these Germans held on to their lead,
Britain, the USA and Russia would have been confronted in 1943
with a jet fighter-bomber which was more than two years ahead of
anything that the Allies could have put into the air. A high-altitude
bomber virtually unassailable by Allied fighters would have been in
service by 1944. The consequences of these developments would
have been profound. The German bombardment of London by V2
rockets would have been extended by at least one year, and the
aerial destruction of German communications in 1944–5 might have
been impossible. Any operation which required Allied air superiority,
including D-Day, would have been seriously delayed and, if not
frustrated, bought at a price which must have prolonged the war,
with unknowable consequences, particularly for a war-weary Britain.

Although the atmosphere in German jet engine circles was rich
with rancour and suspicion, the jet effort was never so poised on a
knife's edge as it was for Power Jets and Whittle. In 1936 work had
begun in the Junkers Aeroplane Company (*not* the Junkers Aero-
Engine Company) on a gas turbine to drive a propeller – much like

Griffith's idea in Britain. The man behind Junkers' initiative was Herbert Wagner, recognized by his colleagues as one of the most brilliant engineers in Germany, and of equal stature with the best aeronautical designers in the world. Wagner was interested in jet propulsion because, like the other jet pioneers, he saw that the piston engine was nearing its limits and something had to be developed to propel his airframes to faster speeds and greater heights.

Wagner was an unlikely product of the Austro-Hungarian empire, who served in its navy but by 1918 was seeing far beyond the derelict empire's pretensions to sea power. When a naval ensign he read an article in a technical journal about steam turbines which so fascinated him that he decided to become an engineer. He studied at the technical universities of Graz and Berlin, where he became assistant to the professor of steam turbines after graduating in 1922, and was soon doing important work on aircraft structures which contributed to the revolution in this field in the 1930s.

Wagner's starting point in the jet revolution was his belief that the modern airframe, on which he was an authority by the time he joined Junkers in 1935, was capable of greater speeds than the piston engine could ever provide. He was also versed in turbine design and high-altitude flight. Inevitably he was led to speculate about new forms of propulsion, though at first he concentrated on the possibilities of the turbine driving a propeller. He quickly saw that the surplus jet thrust from this type of engine might be used to help propel the aircraft, and the greater the speed the more efficient the thrust would be.

Wagner's brief was to make Junkers the leading aircraft company in Germany – better still, the world. With his chairman, Heinrich Koppenberg, he believed that the head of aero-engine development, Otto Mader, was too conservative in his attitude towards aero-engine development. Mader had already burned his fingers by unsuccessful innovations, and his hands were full making Junkers piston engines equal to or better in their performance than those of prospective enemy air forces. Wagner was able to get permission from Koppenberg to start research into unorthodox engine designs and he brought his assistant, Max Adolf Mueller, from Berlin to run the work, instructing him to investigate the broad field of turboprops, jets and ducted fans. Like Heinkel, these two men had neither the experience, staff nor facilities for their task, and they kept their work secret from everyone except Koppenberg, who supplied the finance. Mader was kept in the dark even after the airframe and engine companies were merged in 1936 and Wagner became head of development.

The secret jet team were housed in an engine production plant at Magdeburg, while engine development was based thirty-five miles away at Dessau. By 1937 Wagner and Mueller were convinced that the pure jet was the shortest way to high aircraft speeds. By 1938 they had a staff of about thirty designers and draughtsmen working on a project which became an axial flow engine of considerable ingenuity. It had a five-stage axial compressor, a single combustor and a two-stage turbine. The engine was only two feet in diameter and it was ready for testing by mid-1938; the turboprop was ready a year later. The project was funded entirely by Junkers until, in 1938, Wagner heard that German Air Ministry officials were themselves thinking of jet propulsion as the answer to the high-speed, high-altitude flight problem. He approached the Air Ministry for financial backing but he was firmly told that his business was airframes, not engines. It was the Heinkel problem all over again.

The Air Ministry itself was in some confusion. Many senior staff considered that rockets and jets were the schemes of dreamers who were very properly kept lean and well away from serious mainstream engineering. But soon after his first rebuff Wagner heard that Hans Mauch, head of rocket development in the Ministry, was also interested in jet propulsion. Mauch was already sponsoring the pulse jet (which powered the V1 missile and might be regarded as the 'Puffing Billy' of jet engines) and the ram jet, in which air is compressed simply by the high forward speed of the plane, which is accelerated to that speed by rockets. Mauch himself had heard, apparently by accident, of von Ohain's work at Heinkel and he went to Marienehe in mid-1938, where Heinkel showed him the engine and partly built airframe of the He 178. Back in Berlin at the ministry, Mauch concluded that speeds were approaching the point where this new form of propulsion was essential.

In another chance encounter Mauch met a young engineer named Helmut Schelp. Today, Dr Schelp has a lavish aerospace consultancy on Sepulveda Boulevard, Los Angeles. 'I was regarded as a brash little upstart,' is his explanation of why German aero-engine manufacturers looked on him with disdain in 1938–9. Indeed, Schelp was only twenty-six in 1938 when he set out to sell the manufacturers the idea of the jet engine. His engineering education had been in Germany and the USA, and in 1936 he was one of a small group chosen for an advanced course in the German Research Institute for Aeronautics in Berlin. Speed was the watchword: aircraft designers were showing what streamlining could do for the performance of aircraft like the Messerschmitt 109. If better airframes could do so much for speed, what could better engine developments achieve?

Schelp was given this problem to study at the Research Institute and he began by believing that speeds of around Mach 0.82, or 620 mph, could be achieved before stability trouble was encountered at around the speed of sound – the so-called sound barrier. (Mach 1 is the speed of sound at sea level – approximately 760 mph.) Schelp saw quickly the limits that were being reached with the piston engine. To attain really high speeds, piston-driven aircraft would be so heavy and so complex that they could carry almost no fuel, no weapons and preferably no pilot! He then made a study of the alternatives and concluded that some form of jet propulsion would be essential. He knew a little about turbine design and eventually decided that this type of engine offered the best solution. He found no takers at the Institute:

> It caused a furore, but in the end my views prevailed and I was able to define and describe a family of jet engines, including turboprops and pure jets. Some distinguished engineers thought my ideas were pure fantasy and my professors and examiners were very doubtful. All this time I was working entirely on my own and knew nothing of Heinkel, Junkers or the British work in this field.

In 1937 Schelp was sent to the research division of the Air Ministry, taking his heretical baggage with him. Even there he could arouse little interest in the turbo jet. 'Maybe I made myself unpopular by pushing too hard,' he says now. However, the head of the division, doubtless with mixed motives, suggested to him that he should transfer to the development division to get a fair hearing. Here, Schelp met Mauch. Both men were outstanding and precocious. Mauch, with his brief to sponsor special propulsion devices, was very interested indeed in the language which Schelp was talking, especially after Schelp laid before him his range of possibilities and the theoretical studies which underpinned them.

Schelp then had another stroke of luck at the best possible moment for his career. Opposition to his ideas up to this time was not simply obscurantist. Many of his older colleagues could not believe – as British engineers could not believe – that the compressor and combustor for a jet engine could reach the efficiencies that Schelp knew to be essential. Like Whittle, Schelp persisted. In his case, manna came in the form of three leading compressor engineers, Professors Prandtl, Betz and Encke of the Aerodynamic Research Establishment at Göttingen. They announced that they had succeeded in getting just the compressor efficiencies that Schelp needed. They, too, found that the key was to design the blades as aerofoils, that is, shaped like a wing in cross-section, and to use them in cascades – or row on row behind one another – just as A. A. Griffith had suggested years before.

By the late summer of 1938, Mauch had been convinced by Schelp that the time was ripe to develop jet engines. But Mauch was also convinced that the work must be done by the best and most experienced engineers in the aero-engine industry. He refused to support Heinkel and Junkers for this very reason: he held that airframe designers should design airframes. In autumn 1938, Mauch and Schelp set out on a tour of the four main manufacturers, Junkers Aero-Engine, Daimler Benz, BMW and Bramo.

Daimler Benz (ironically the strongest backers of the Nazi regime) refused point blank to have anything to do with such madcap schemes. The head of Junkers Aero-Engine, Otto Mader, accepted a small development contract, saying nonetheless that the day of the jet engine, though it would come, was still very distant. Even now he did not know what his colleagues at Junkers Aeroplane were up to. BMW engine company of Munich accepted a study contract because they had developed an advanced water-cooled turbine and were looking around for something to use it on. Bramo of Berlin were a little better disposed. It was not that the boss, Professor Bruno Bruckmann, and the head of research, Herman Oestrich, were more far-sighted than the rest. Their enthusiasm was born of a fear that they were shortly going to lose all their piston engine contracts because the government was rationalizing the industry. This pruning was being pushed through by Udet, who felt that Bramo could not compete with its main rival, BMW.

Each of the manufacturers was obsessed with designing better piston engines because they wished to reach the standards of companies like Rolls-Royce. All the same, by the end of 1938 a mole who was privy to the secrets of the British and the Germans would find it astonishing that the German Air Ministry was trying to persuade the engine companies to take money to design the jet, while the British Air Ministry was refusing the money to the only British company – Power Jets – which could provide it with the jet. The comparison is even more stark when one considers what was on offer in Germany. Schelp says he was in a position to offer the companies all the money they would need. 'I never had to fight for money. When I signed something, I got more money,' he says. To the end of 1939 the British effort had cost £20,000, grudgingly given over four hard years. At the outbreak of war there were still only ten people on Power Jets' payroll. In the time it took Whittle to convince his peers of the jet's potential, Germany had built a complete modern air force and taken the first steps into the jet age.

However, during the first six months of 1939, Schelp was hampered by the helter-skelter progress of the Luftwaffe; manufacturers were working towards present, not future needs, for what they believed would be a short war. Early in 1939 he paid several visits to each manufacturer, trying with some desperation to play them off against each other. He would tell X of the brilliant work being done by Y, and Y of the huge strides being made by Z. Still, they would not play wholeheartedly. On the third or fourth visit to Junkers Engine, Schelp was told by Otto Mader that, even if there was something in the jet idea, he had nobody to put in charge of so complex and advanced a project. Schelp recalls that he retorted, 'Yes you have – Anselm Franz.' At that time Dr Franz was in charge of supercharger work at Junkers and was highly respected by Schelp. Mader subsequently ordered Franz to do a study for a jet engine, which won Mader's approval. Franz was an inspired suggestion of Schelp's: he went on to produce the engine which powered the Messerschmitt 262 – the world's first production jet engine for the world's first jet fighter. However, it is likely that Mader never forgave Schelp for being both young and right at the same time.

Schelp was getting nearer his objective: two manufacturers working on two different types of jet engine; in the early stages of the programme he thought it too risky to entrust just one company with one type. That was not his only achievement. Around autumn 1938 another young engineer, named Hans Antz, joined the Air Ministry and set about doing for airframes what Schelp was trying to do for aero engines. While Schelp prescribed the engine – its thrust, weight and dimensions – Antz began work on the airframe to match. Equipped with the basic data, Antz went to see Professor Willy Messerschmitt, another designer of genius. Together they turned to Robert Lusser, Messerschmitt's chief of development, and put him in charge of design work.

Schelp and Antz spent many hours discussing all the problems they would have to overcome. Their goal now was to double the performance of the Luftwaffe's front-line fighters, virtually at a stroke. Knowing the Heinkel team's problems with von Ohain's early engine, the two engineers decided that the fighter should be twin-engined and that the engine should be an axial flow design rather than von Ohain's centrifugal flow, which needed a large diameter compressor and had other disadvantages, among them the sheer frontal size of the engine. Around October 1938 Antz placed an order with Messerschmitt for a jet-propelled fighter capable of one hour's flying time with a top speed of 528 mph. Given the engine weight and dimensions, Messerschmitt's staff studied a range of possible airframe designs. They settled for two wing-mounted engines, each of which was to have a thrust of 1,320 lb – a serious underestimate.

By May 1939 Mauch and Schelp were on their way to winning their battles with the companies and could feel some satisfaction when they surveyed the beginnings of a formidable jet engine programme. BMW, Bramo and Junkers Engine were now willing to work on jet engines, while Heinkel and Junkers Airframe went on with jets at their own expense. At the Air Ministry, Wolfram Eisenlohr, Mauch's boss, was fighting something of a rearguard action against the jet concept, but his attitude probably stemmed from a personal dislike of Mauch, who promptly went to see his friend Ernst Udet to persuade him to back the complete plan. The Luftwaffe's Director General of Equipment assented.

BMW had now bought up Bramo and, while BMW of Munich went ahead with one (centrifugal) type of engine, BMW Bramo had a contract for axial flow types, called 002 and 003. Engine 004, eventually the winner, was being designed by Anselm Franz at Junkers, while Daimler Benz were persuaded to take a contract numbered 007 for another kind of engine, a turbine-driven fan in a duct, which was to become popular again many years later in a different form. Engine 005 in the sequence does not appear to have had a maker. Engines 001 and 006 in the official sequence were in the hands of – of all people – Ernst Heinkel, who had managed to stay in the jet race by stratagem.

Although Schelp had come round to the view that airframe designers *could* also be engine developers, he had stopped short at Heinkel, because he believed, as Mauch had, that Heinkel's shortage of skilled engineers would hamper any progress he wished to make. Nobody criticized von Ohain's work – by now he was acknowledged in Germany as a man of genius – but Mauch wanted Heinkel's work, together with von Ohain, to be taken over by Daimler Benz. When Heinkel heard of the projected division of responsibilities, he was furious. He regarded himself (with just a few of his team) as an innovator with a three-year lead over everyone else due to his own foresight as a jet pioneer. Heinkel, like Mauch before him, went to see his friend Ernst Udet, and Schelp suddenly found himself under orders to finance all Heinkel's work without delay. 001 was to be a new centrifugal engine designed by von Ohain, while 006, an advanced axial flow engine, also became Heinkel's.

The tangled web now being woven by the German manufacturers resembled the synopsis of an extravagant television soap opera. Wagner, of Junkers Airframe, agreed to hand over their jet engine work to Junkers Engine. Dr Otto Mader of the engine division agreed to examine the airframe company's (until now) secret work. Dr Max Mueller, leader of the airframe company's jet engine studies, was forced to negotiate with Otto Mader (somewhat to Mauch's pleasure). Mueller disliked Mader's plans and did not see why he should give up complete control of his engine. He continued to talk to Mader while he made a secret approach to Heinkel: the delighted, turbulent planemaker offered Mueller *carte blanche*, and suggested that he should bring his whole team, who would all get salary increases, to work at Marienehe. In May 1939 Mueller and nearly all of his staff resigned to go to Heinkel. The chairman of Junkers invoked German labour laws to delay the move for one month and in the end only half Mueller's team finished up with Heinkel. The rest went elsewhere – but not to Junkers.

Meanwhile Dr Anselm Franz had arrived at Junkers to survey Mueller's work. Franz declared that the engine was not worth taking over, which enraged Mauch because he refused to believe that all Mueller's work should be thrown away. However, once Mueller was ensconced with Heinkel and the 006, the way was clear to give Junkers and Anselm Franz a contract for the completely new axial flow engine, 004, which became, many storms and a few years later, the only German jet engine to see sustained service with the Luft-waffe.

Among scientists and engineers as much as other mortals, embitterment and memories die hard. Heinkel wrote after the war:

Until 1938 only a small special branch at the Air Ministry, under Mauch, had been concerned with jet problems. This department had been formed primarily to deal with rocket research and the question of jet propulsion had been handed over to a young colleague of Mauch's named Schelp. The latter, with insufficient knowledge and only poorly supported by the really important men in the Air Ministry, was trying to control the entire field of jet development. Once he heard of the work being carried out by Junkers and me, he tried to get to know all about it and then, very ineptly, to take over its direction.

Forty years later Schelp told me that this was a travesty:

We did not try to stop Heinkel at all. In our philosophy such a complex engine could not be developed without knowledge and experience, especially in the field of materials. I wanted to consolidate the work of von Ohain and Heinkel, and later on in the war I managed this: I did not want to kill his engine at all.

Half a century on, memories falter. On balance, it would seem from interrogations immediately after the war, together with captured documents, that Schelp's is the truer version of the two.

Schelp's fortunes improved further towards the end of 1939 when Mauch left the Air Ministry to be replaced by Ernst Beck, a colourless administrator. This left Schelp with enhanced authority and he began to try to consolidate jet engine and airframe work in one or at the most two companies. He had now become convinced that delays in developing the jet were caused by a diffusion of effort and a climate in which status and jealousy were allowed too much rein. By Christmas 1939 he could look with some satisfaction on a more or less integrated programme of research, development and construction of jet engines, one or two of which were fairly certain to succeed.

By that time Whittle, too, discovered that he was all of a sudden wanted by his own Air Ministry: but he also was to run into a bitter struggle with the manufacturer of his engine, and Britain was almost to lose her way yet again.

Life at Ladywood Works, Lutterworth, the disused plant to which BT-H had banished Whittle and his tiny team because of the distraction and danger of their experiments at Rugby, was not all exalted thought and zeal. One day in 1940 Whittle learnt that the stark little plant with walls of bare brick and floors of bare boards had been dubbed by visitors the Cherry Orchard. One minute a small boy would come through the door carrying a cup of tea and the next moment Whittle would jump up and fire his .22 rifle through the window at a rabbit. When steam trains drew up alongside and blew off steam a few yards from the window, Whittle would pick up his telephone and by comic mime suggest that the driver should move on so he could get on with his calls. Some of them did. A Power Jets director would appear to ask whether they had enough money to order some three-inch pipe. Then the office boy would appear with more tea. One day a designer burst into a meeting shouting 'rocking blotters!', holding aloft a curved blotter, triumphant that the system had at last managed to provide this innocent piece of office equipment. The office furniture came second-hand from a Lutterworth shop.

Two night watchmen could be afforded by 1938, and Whittle gained a secretary, Mary Phillips, who relieved him of the need to type his own letters and keep his own diary. More importantly, Ms Phillips was able to make much more detailed readings while Whittle made his engine test runs. A watch dog (50p from the Battersea Dogs' Home in London) was added to the strength, although when Whittle fired his .22, the dog would disappear and had to be hunted down by the office boy. After a successful interview for the job of stress calculator, Cynthia Holl recalled that Whittle had to organize a whip-round to pay her travelling expenses. At the centre of this whirligig, Whittle charmed, cajoled and conjured work from a devoted team who, forty years on, still recall his gifts for getting the impossible, or at least the unlikely, out of people. 'He just sparkled,' said Cynthia Holl. 'He gave you all his attention and charm.'

Whittle must also have been expert in concealment. While he was driving his team with all his virtues of energy, charm and original thought, the vulnerability of his position was causing him anxiety and he was suffering under the stress from headaches and indigestion. Without Whittle there would be no jet, no company, and the shareholders would lose everything. He knew of the risks, and he had to contend with four main worries: how to keep contractors paid, honest and up to the mark; how to convert the sceptics; how to keep the lukewarm interest of the Air Ministry; and how to protect his career as an RAF officer. In forming Power Jets he had hopped sideways off the promotion ladder and was afraid of missing out in rank. Many years later Whittle admitted ruefully that he had often wondered whether a career in the highest ranks of the RAF would have been preferable to inventing the jet and securing a place in history. He had no doubt that he would have reached Air Marshal rank as a career officer.

Whittle's worries about status were assuaged at the end of 1937, when he was promoted to squadron leader from flight lieutenant, and he managed to move his family to Rugby, which eased his domestic life and cut down on travelling time. Other things were less secure: by 1937 it was essential to rebuild the test engine – an absorbing challenge which would mean designing and making new parts – but expenditure was rising again and the money worry was insistent. Whittle now knew how to check costs in some detail and he introduced some savings by preventing interested onlookers from BT-H booking their time down to the jet project. By October more combustor tests were run again and early in the new year the move to Lutterworth was made. The buildings were semi-derelict and Lutterworth police became intrigued by the comings and goings of the mysterious newcomers, suspecting for a time that Whittle and his band were an IRA bomb squad.

When it came to designing compressor and turbine, Whittle was unaware of Griffith's work on aerofoils and when he *was* aware of it he disagreed with Griffith's results, preferring to put all the weight on designing the channels between blades more carefully. But at the other, unsophisticated, end, he discovered that BT-H's engineers were doing work which was fundamentally flawed. This led to a row with some of the company's most experienced engineers, who were convinced that their designs were right; they had been done that way for fifty years. Times had changed, minds had not. Whittle explained:

I'd left the design to them until one day I went to a meeting in the deputy chief engineer's office where they were discussing a change in blade design. They were saying that one of the consequences of that change would be to increase the load on the engine bearing from 180 lb to about 1,800 lb, quite unacceptable if it were true because you would be putting ten times the strain on it. I went away and thought about it and then I asked one of the engineers what they assumed to be the difference between pressure at the root of the blade and at the tip, as the hot gases hit them leaving the combustor nozzles.

He said, 'What pressure difference?' To my astonishment I discovered that they didn't assume that the air coming out of the nozzles was whirling, but the jets were straight. I pointed out that the gas would come out in a vortex and that centrifugal force would mean there would be differences in velocity along the blade. The smaller the diameter of the vortex (i.e. at the root) the faster it is moving – much faster than it is at the tip. You can see the same thing in water running out of a bath tub. As the water moves nearer and nearer the centre of the vortex it flows faster and faster. That's what happens in the flow out of a set of turbine nozzle rings. To allow for that you have to put a good deal of extra twist on the blades – double the twist the BT-H people were putting. If you do that you have no trouble with the bearing.

This finding aroused strong opposition and resentment among some – though not all – BT-H engineers. Whittle made a test using compressed air in his engine instead of gas, and later the BT-H engineers made their own tests. Both experiments bore out Whittle's expectations. The process could be studied clearly because of the use of compressed air, which was much easier than trying to study the hot gas flow. The Power Jets team urged Whittle to patent his idea, which he did. BT-H engineers were irritated by this and Whittle felt that his relationship with them was never quite the same again. They were designing more primitive types of steam turbine, for which the calculations worked; they had not allowed for the fact that as design became more sophisticated in different running conditions, Whittle's calculations became valid. But, like Schelp with the German manufacturers, Whittle was now regarded as an upstart, or at the most polite, a precocious young man. Whittle, with the naivety of youth, was hurt by this attitude: he thought he had done his collaborators a service and instead found himself treated as though he had done them harm – even to the extent of being kept from their own findings.

The rebuilt engine ran in 1938, but there were various delays caused by snags in development. On 6 May it ran for 1 hour and 45 minutes, at which moment the turbine failed at 13,000 revolutions per minute because the whirling wheel came into contact with the nozzle – almost certainly the consequence of using old parts long after their proper life was over – and the intense chafing at high speed caused severe overheating. Nine turbine blades shattered, causing extensive damage to the engine as a whole. Although failures of this kind were not fundamental – none of the laws of nature had been broken, the jet idea was still wholly feasible – the morale of the Power Jets team plunged and Whittle confessed to intense depression. He was still suffering from severe headaches and other stress symptoms, and he felt certain that Lance Whyte and the other financial backers would join forces with sceptics in the Air Ministry and withdraw support. He was also suspicious of some of the BT-H engineering and workmanship.

By June 1938 Power Jets had run down to its last £1,000, and Whittle told Lance Whyte that he would return to active service in the RAF if Power Jets could not be put on a more certain footing. Whyte again pointed out that a secret project would not attract private investors. Whittle, Dudley Williams and Tinling stressed that Power Jets' liabilities must not exceed the cash available and that, rather than see any attempt to alter the company's structure to their disfavour, they would go into liquidation. This would mean that the patent rights would revert to them and they would be free to start another company – however difficult it might be to raise more capital. Lance Whyte replied that he would try to improve matters and that Falk and Partners would not let the company get into such acute difficulties.

Rumours of this rift reached the Air Ministry, where the new Director of Scientific Research, Dr David Pye, arranged a meeting with Whittle. He told him that it was disturbing that Whittle was losing faith in the project – an ironical point, since most of the main factors in Whittle's crisis of confidence stemmed from the attitude of the Air Ministry and officials like Pye. Whittle replied that he was sure that he would ultimately be successful, but that it would be a long job; he was worried about mechanical failures and finance, and his service career might be suffering to such an extent that if he did not receive assurances he would choose to return to the life of a serving officer with the RAF with good career prospects.

By now everyone was playing poker. Pye's deputy, William Farren, said that the Air Ministry would only continue support if Whittle was willing to go on; their interest in Power Jets would continue only if they could vest confidence in him and, if he were not confident, the work would cease and there would be no successor. Whittle was now in a double trap: Whyte assured him that he would not be able to raise private money, while Pye and Farren were firm that there would be no more public money if he resigned. The inventor in Whittle clamoured to continue, but the prudent family man and career officer insisted that he must at least make sure that his time with Power Jets should count in his years of R A F service.

While this struggle ground on, Whittle tried to get BT-H to invest more money. The general feeling in the company was that, having got this far, it would be senseless to stop. However, encouragement did not go so far as investment. BT-H took the orthodox view that the Air Ministry should finance the company if they thought so highly of Whittle and his project. At this critical moment it was, once more, Sir Henry Tizard, busy in the Whitehall burrows, who saved the day. He never gave up his conviction and he hinted strongly to Whyte that the Air Ministry would put in more money if Whittle went on. There was also support from another friend, the engineering consultant, M. L. Bramson, whom Whyte asked for another assessment. Bramson, always convinced of the feasibility of the jet, summarized the position in four main points:

Work so far done verified the principle of jet propulsion.

At three-quarters of the design speed, 'quantitive verification' had been obtained and there was a strong possibility of obtaining verification soon at full speed.

Experimental evidence made it practically certain that thermal efficiency could not be so far below estimates as to nullify the results.

The feasibility of jet propulsion for aircraft had, for the first time, been experimentally established.

By October 1938 testing of the second rebuild of the engine began. A new Air Ministry contract paid for most of the rebuild and the testing. In the new engine, ten small combustors replaced one large one, making for a more compact and lighter engine, and there were many other technical changes. However, these tests were going slowly in the early days of 1939 and Whittle heard once more that the Air Ministry was worried about lack of progress. In February Farren told the inventor that he would be hard put to defend his position with the other service departments unless Power Jets produced more results than they had done so far. True or not, Whittle interpreted the remark to mean that he should try to step up the programme of tests.

Whittle recognized that yet another critical point had been reached in his jet propulsion work. If the Air Ministry had to withdraw him (and with him their financial help), the whole venture must fail. By March, spurred by the sense of urgency, he managed to push engine test speeds up to 14,000 rpm. Combustion problems put a temporary stop to any higher speeds, and then cracks appeared in the blade tips of the compressor, forcing two months' delay. Nevertheless, by 26 June engine speeds reached 16,000 rpm. Then there were more compressor troubles and the entire team, including the two night watchmen, were thrown into making engine modifications round the clock. The material used for the turbine blades was found to be unsuitable, and temperatures around the turbine were higher than those provided for in the design.

In early 1939 an endorsement of the future of jet propulsion came from an unexpected source, the Royal Aircraft Establishment at Farnborough. In the person of A. A. Griffith, the RAE had been lethargic in following up its promising work of the late 1920s. Griffith had been quick enough to criticize Whittle's early, admittedly crude, initiatives, and he would continue to be a critic of the entire Whittle enterprise, but he did nothing throughout the first half of the 1930s to advance his own project, which he had apparently dropped altogether despite the urgings of the Aeronautical Research Committee. Griffith's tardiness remains a mystery. Sir William Hawthorne, an RAE scientist of great distinction who contributed much from 1940 onwards to the theory of jet engines, believes that Griffith was simply discouraged by the ARC's decision in 1930 not to go the whole hog and order a complete engine. This argues a faint-heartedness on the part of Griffith and does not explain his attitude towards Whittle. It seems likelier that the answer lies in Griffith's complex and somewhat academic character. He was not a man to pursue a line of enquiry relentlessly, nor did his later work show much determination to follow through marketable ideas in an entre-preneurial spirit. He was a researcher; he was no Whittle.

Neither was his new lieutenant at the RAE, Dr Hayne Constant, who from 1937 *did* advance the development and understanding of jet engines very considerably. On the face of it he was no more likely to succeed than Griffith. A withdrawn bachelor, much given to pacing his room in complete silence when he was thinking through a problem, he was regarded as supercilious and was known for his sharp, one-word retort to any fellow scientist putting forward an opinion as a statement of fact: 'Why?' This did nothing to soften his reputation for austerity and coldness, although, on a personal level, he was a profoundly polite man. His austerity went with decisiveness and single-mindedness, and he gave his staff great intellectual freedom, providing a climate for free discussion in which they could do their best work.

Constant may not have been a Whittle, but at least each man knew the other's grain. 'They were civil to one another,' as Sir William Hawthorne put it cautiously half a century later. Constant, the son of a Folkestone dentist, had been educated at Canterbury, Folkestone Technical Institute and Queen's College, Cambridge, where he was an outstanding student, taking the mathematical and mechanical sciences tripos and gaining a first class honours degree. He had arrived at Farnborough in 1928, leaving in 1934 to lecture at Imperial College, of which he tired because he found it repetitive and ultimately boring. His return to the RAE in 1936 may have been prompted by a conversation with Sir Henry Tizard, the rector of Imperial College, who told Constant that a great future for aircraft propulsion might lie in the gas turbine. If Constant interpreted this to mean *his* great personal future, he was right, for he and his team laid the foundations of the British axial flow jet engine, the design that would eventually triumph – as Whittle knew it would – over the centrifugal compressor engine.

On his return to Farnborough Constant was put in charge of superchargers by Griffith, who was head of the engine department. Griffith's work was obviously known to Constant, who saw the possibilities and in 1936–7 he set about designing a small axial compressor together with some turbine schemes. How far Griffith and Constant were spurred by Whittle's work is arguable, but knowledge of Power Jets' progress almost certainly gave them the reason for taking another, more determined, look at gas turbines generally. Constant submitted a report to the engine sub-committee of the ARC in March 1937 that was remarkably optimistic in its tone:

In the light of existing knowledge an internal combustion turbine could be constructed using only types of component which have been proved by past experience. The performance of such a turbine, on the basis of specific weight and economy, would be better than or substantially equal to that of the best modern water-cooled petrol engine, except when cruising at comparatively low altitudes.

Under take-off conditions both its specific weight and specific fuel consumption would be less than that of the petrol engine. At an altitude of some 20,000 feet its specific weight and specific consumption would be similar to that of a petrol engine operating under economical cruising conditions. Above this altitude both its specific weight and specific fuel consumption would be less than that of the petrol engine . . .

In this paper Constant recognized that the terms of trade were moving in favour of the gas turbine. Materials and compressor design developments were favourable: it could use lower grade fuel, its design was simpler as the power produced rose, and so on. Constant's beliefs (they can have been little more at that time) were no doubt underpinned by Griffith's earlier work. He accepted Griffith's figures for an axial flow design and he concluded:

The simplicity of the internal combustion turbine . . . has made it the dream of many engineers. The very magnitude of the advantages which it has to offer, associated with the repeated failures to achieve a practicable design, have given the impression that the ICT is merely a convenient medium on which to work off the surplus energy of imaginative inventors. In fact, however, the same principles and the same practical experience as have in the past predicted the performance of machines of far more novel design can be applied to determine the probable success or failure of the ICT.

Constant's project was intended, of course, to drive a propeller. Not until 1939 would the inherent superiority of Whittle's propelling jet be conceded by Farnborough. The virtue of RAE's proposal was that the axial flow compressor enshrined in it would be the ultimate design both for turbo jet and turbo propeller engines.

Constant's proposal to build an axial compressor gas turbine landed before the ARC sub-committee on exactly the same day as they were presented with Whittle's proposals: 16 March 1937. Coincidence? If so, it was a remarkable one. Did Tizard tell Constant to get a move on with a proposal because he and his colleagues would also be dealing with one from Whittle? Did Griffith, with foreknowledge of Whittle's work – after all, the first run of his engine would take place the following month, April – spur Constant into action? Whatever the truth, the simultaneous presentation of the two proposals signified the rivalry that developed between Farnborough and Power Jets.

The chairman of the March meeting was the indefatigable Sir Henry Tizard, who once more championed the gas turbine with great vigour. Soon after the meeting he wrote to the Air Ministry to recommend 'a concentration of effort and large-scale expenditure on an engine which would be a pure jet or preferably a jet and airscrew combination' – he, too, was not wholly convinced of Whittle's pure jet contentions. Tizard urged that the Air Ministry 'should take up the question and the development . . . as a matter of urgency and make all possible arrangements for its production at the earliest possible moment . . . this will probably require the co-operation of turbine builders and we recommend that possibilities in this direction be explored without delay'.

The Air Ministry was not to be so easily parted with its money or its attitudes: it still possessed the 'six hours per week' mentality and the response to the large-scale expenditure conceived by Tizard can be gauged by the miserly attitude towards Whittle's project up to 1940. However, Farnborough was instructed to start work on the layout of a gas turbine. Authority had already been given to build a small axial flow compressor, named Anne, for a supercharger for a piston engine. It was designed by Hayne Constant and had eight stages (or rows) of blades. It was completed in 1938, but thirty seconds into its first run it stripped all the blading because faulty design of an oil seal caused overheating of one of the discs holding the blades. It was rebuilt and run again towards the end of the year, and gave insight into many of the problems of multi-stage compressors until it was blown up by a German bomb in August 1940.

Various gas turbine schemes were thought up during 1936–7 by Constant, who was still working virtually on his own at Farnborough, although the ARC recommendations were to enable him to build up a small team throughout the years to 1940. The ARC recommendation to seek collaboration with established turbine manufacturers went badly: four firms refused to undertake the work – an echo of the treatment meted out to Helmut Schelp by German aero-engine manufacturers. However, by 1939 Metropolitan Vickers and C. A. Parsons were working on the construction of rotors and compressors, and Metro Vick were contracted to make a gas turbine for bench testing to demonstrate the possibilities (or otherwise) of this type of engine being used for aircraft.

At this distance Farnborough's work might seem little more than high-technology tinkering. Apologists for the RAE would say that this is grossly unfair: the establishment's role was to carry out experimental testing for the Air Ministry and RAF, not to build jet engines to fit into aeroplanes. As Sir William Hawthorne put it, 'We were inventing a profession.' His point is that in a major invention like the jet engine real understanding of the underlying reasons why the technology works successfully may lag far behind the advance itself – which has been made by engineers working empirically and driven forward by the urge to be first. The scientific knowledge to underpin the invention may seem frighteningly inadequate. That was the situation which faced Constant and his tiny team, and they did heroic work in filling in the enormous gaps in knowledge – gaps which had to be filled in if the invention was to be developed and exploited properly.

It is nevertheless hard not to see the spirit in which the RAE's work was carried out as markedly different from the spirit at Power Jets – admittedly a much different organization. Constant was making parts for hypothetical jets and building them as isolated components, a luxury denied to Whittle, who had built and was testing a complete unit designed to deliver useful thrust and lead to an engine which would fly in an aeroplane. Although much of the work at Farnborough was done in wooden huts, there was no real comparison with the stark atmosphere forced on Power Jets, which was constantly under suspicion from the sceptics at the Air Ministry, and starved of funds to an absurd extent. Constant was able to buy a large terrestrial gas turbine from Brown Boveri with which to experiment, and he was able as he went along to thank God – as he did to his assistants – that they had not had to build a complete engine from the start.

Constant first met Whittle in 1937, when he watched an engine run at BT-H. Sir William Hawthorne commented: 'From then on there was close collaboration between Whittle and Constant. They did not always agree on the best solutions to various problems but they held one another in high respect. Such rivalry as existed was not between their personalities but between the centrifugal and axial teams and supporters.'

What was Constant's programme? The RAE men who went to see Metro Vick on 3 June 1937 had three schemes: first a two-stage centrifugal compressor driven by a high pressure turbine, with a low pressure turbine to drive an airscrew; second, a low pressure axial compressor driven by a low pressure turbine, with a high pressure axial compressor driven by a high pressure turbine; and third, a contraflow turbo compressor with a separate parallel gas flow to power the turbine.

The first scheme was dropped almost immediately. This proposal for a centrifugal compressor had been made because of early fears that an axial flow compressor might prove too difficult to start up, but Brown Boveri proved to be operating an axial flow device satisfactorily and the Farnborough team concluded that they could at least do as well. Between 1937 and the outbreak of war in 1939 six axial compressors were designed and built. They had names like Anne, Alice and Ruth, and were built by Parsons and Fraser and Chalmers, another turbine firm. Metro Vick built a project called B10 under RAE supervision. This scheme embodied a multi-stage axial compressor and turbine, which ran in 1939. The machine was apparently unsuccessful and Constant wrote of it: 'We thanked God that we had not built the complete plant.'

There is no doubt that these designs progressed towards a technically successful conclusion in the 1940s, but they all assumed at first that the engine would drive a propeller. Not until September 1939 did Constant propose to Whittle that they should colloborate on an axial flow compressor and jet propulsion turbine. A design proposal called the F1 was sent to Power Jets with the suggestion that Farnborough should design and build the compressor while Power Jets should build the combustion chamber and turbine. By this time Power Jets were already far too busy with their own programme for the flight engines for the E28/39, and the RAE passed their proposal to Metro Vick to build, designating it F2. Work on this engine began in December 1940 and the unit was built by November 1941. This engine became the first British axial flow jet propulsion engine: it led to an engine which flew successfully and forms part of Constant's claim for a place in history as one of the inventors of this type of engine. The Germans were well on the way with their designs when Constant was starting his but, like Whittle, he was not to know of the German work any more than they knew of his.

If it had been possible to fuse the Farnborough designs with the vision and drive of the Power Jets' team, something a lot better might have happened than the fumble and confusion which resulted from the industrial efforts of Power Jets and Rover during what were to be the disastrous years of 1941–1942. If all had gone smoothly, a British axial flow engine would have been tried and tested around the same time as the German 004 engine – and it would have been a better engine if only because better materials were available to the British team. However, co-operation with Power Jets was impossible because their die was by now cast. Moreover, the two organizations were very different in their outlooks and their poeple, and a joint project might well have foundered on the yawning personal differences of the people involved.

The Power Jets' set-up was to be an increasing headache to the Air Ministry and the wartime Ministry of Aircraft Production. The collaborative work of the R A E and private industry was of a kind with which Whitehall was more familiar and more comfortable. The official historian was, however, unsparing in her verdict on the pioneering work of the British to the year 1940:

> The pioneer stage owed a little to private enterprise and a little to the Air Ministry and R A E. *Both private enterprise and the state did much less than they could or should have done had the possibilities of the gas turbine been fully appreciated.* [author's italics] In fact both private enterprise and the state failed more or less and no historian can allocate to either their rightful share in the failure.

She went on to note that because of their positions at the R A E, both Griffith and Constant had access to the facilities necessary to perfect the theories and basic calculations on which the design of their components developed. But their intimate involvement with the R A E was also a disadvantage and

> ... largely explains why the work proceeded so slowly and for a time was shelved altogether (the period 1930–35). The gas turbine was only one of many projects competing for time, finance and facilities at R A E. Moreover the building of so elaborate a piece of machinery was a task for which R A E were not equipped; more especially, they had none of the necessary testing equipment. This put them at a disadvantage from which they could only be rescued by the co-operation of turbine or aero engine firms. And unfortunately the co-operation of private firms was small in scale and late in coming.

Whittle remarked in his memoirs that Constant told him in April 1939 that he thought Power Jets had the basis of a successful aero engine. None the less, the official historian recorded that in May 1939 Griffith and Constant told Dr Pye, as Director of Scientific Research, that no further useful results could be gained from Whittle's work. Perhaps they genuinely believed that their superior axial flow approach should have pride of place over Whittle's centrifugal compressor. But clearly they would have stood to gain if Power Jets and its work were put at their disposal, even though such a bare-faced proposal was apparently never made. The verdict on Whittle's work was a travesty, but it also constituted a potentially powerful body blow because it hit at the one area where the Air Ministry felt there was any justification for supporting Whittle at all: the usefulness of his results. Dr Pye had made it clear to Lance Whyte in July 1938 that they were only interested in Whittle's unit because of the data from properly planned and controlled experiments – 'not because we expect to see the present apparatus take its place as a practical power plant in competition with the normal type . . . I still feel that the ultimate form of power plant in which jet propulsion is made use of may be along different lines.'

Those 'different lines' can only have been Farnborough's. The sympathetic attitude towards Farnborough is always immanent in Air Ministry attitudes. The RAE was there: it was official; it was what Whitehall understood. Rules existed for it, wheareas Power Jets was a strange hybrid, with a serving RAF officer mixed up with a band of civilians on an enterprise whose outcome looked very dubious indeed. But the political atmosphere which enveloped Hayne Constant's work, and that of his colleagues, should not obscure the fact that the work was outstandingly good and a major part of the jet propulsion story. It led to an axial flow engine, flown in 1943, which was a prototype of the modern jet engine. And so, it could be added, it should have done, and sooner than it did, for Farnborough had much on its side that was denied to Frank Whittle.

To return, however, to the position on the eve of war: the advice given by Griffith and Constant in 1939 was strongly resisted by Tizard, who continued to argue that Whittle was, at the very least, doing important applied research. Farnborough was doing little enough integrated work on jet propulsion even though they were trying to pull the rug from under Power Jets. Whittle's work had the attraction that it was both practical and cheap, far cheaper than the Air Ministry financing a complete project at Farnborough. At about this time Whittle's team was trying to measure the thrust their engine was giving with an ordinary spring balance: the observer had to lean over to take the readings, getting his hair singed by a red-hot exhaust pipe.

The Air Ministry were always uncomfortable about their relationship with Power Jets because the company had no track record, was not set up to manufacture, and had none of the technical and financial security which the traditional manufacturers could offer for government projects. The civil service mind was discomforted when it looked ahead: if Power Jets were successful, the company – in this case Whittle himself – would hold all the patents. Would it be possible to cut the traditional manufacturers in, or were Power Jets going to claim a monopoly position? How was the public money spent to be accounted for if Power Jets claimed a private monopoly position? On that question Power Jets' fate would eventually be determined.

Whittle meanwhile clearly believed that work should be intensified and Power Jets should be financed to develop several engines at once rather than continue with the piecemeal approach which parsimony forced upon them. About this time Tizard told Lance Whyte that he would back further attempts to wring money from the Air Ministry and Whyte himself fought off suggestions that Whittle should be posted back to active service in the RAF. He told Farren and Pye that a watershed had been reached in the previous weeks and they should go and see for themselves.

Pye arrived at Lutterworth on 30 June 1939 and watched a twenty-minute engine test run in which a maximum speed of 16,000 rpm was achieved. It was the day on which Whittle's secondment to Power Jets ran out, the day when he should have been posted back to the RAF. Pye studied Whittle's results of recent test runs. They showed that the engine did not meet its predicted performance at low speeds, but as speed was increased the gap between actual and predicted performance narrowed. Pye told Whittle that although he had asked for an extension of his secondment, he could not predict what might happen. The Treasury was objecting to costs, while the RAF, short of good squadron leaders, wanted Whittle back on active service. He warned Whittle that there might now be some damage to his career if he stayed with Power Jets. Whittle said he would take that risk.

At the end of the day Pye admitted that he was now convinced. It was Whittle's moment of victory. Career prospects could be put aside. As he drove Pye to Rugby station to put him on a train to London, Whittle had the ironic experience of listening to the Director of Research at the Air Ministry reel off all the advantages of the jet engine, advantages of which Whittle had been trying to convince his superiors, Pye included, for almost ten years. Pye said that the time had come to expand the effort and to place a contract for an aeroplane in which a flight engine could be tested in its proper environment – the upper air above the earth. The Air Ministry would pay for the engine and leave development in the hands of Power Jets. Whittle's recollection of the drive is that he managed to remain tactful throughout.

By mid-1939 the Germans were ahead, though they could not be sure of winning, in the race for a jet engine which could be mass-produced for war planes. The lead could have been made decisive, with immense consequences for aerial warfare, but luckily for the Allies the Germans were to waste their advantage in the pressures of war. In 1939, however, the designers of the chosen jet engine were about to perform one of the most effective examples of making-do known in aviation history. The Germans had ability, impetus and money but they lacked strategy, skilled manpower and raw materials such as cobalt and nickel – indeed, Germany was short of almost every raw material needed for aircraft and their engines, and the search for effective substitutes was now part of the national production programme. It was apparent that the jet engine would need some of the very scarcest metals for its hottest running parts – and German designers conquered this problem with something like genius.

Whittle, on the other hand, had the materials he needed and, at last, the promise of money and impetus. His problem was to be his chosen manufacturer, whereas in Germany, as was seen earlier, Schelp and Mauch had managed to corral manufacturers into working on several jet engine projects, which were intended to be further narrowed down to two. As well as the materials problem, German progress was also baulked by very severe shortages of skilled engineers. It was only by 1937–8 that Germany had an aero engine industry comparable in size to that of Britain, and even by 1939 they did not have an aero engine which could beat the Rolls-Royce Merlin. Planemakers like Heinkel were often privately scornful of the engine manufacturers, although ironically when Rolls-Royce wanted a really clean airframe to test air intakes in 1936 they bought a Heinkel 170 because it was the best off-the-shelf aircraft they could find.

The problems of the German manufacturers stemmed from the Versailles peace treaty following the First World War, under Article

198 of which Germany was forbidden to have an air force at all. In 1920, under Article 202, Germany was forced to destroy or disgorge 15,000 aircraft, 16 airships, 28,000 aero engines and one million square metres of hangar space; the aero industry was dismantled. Between 1926 and 1932 some covert military flying did take place, but the scale was puny. There was a secret German air base in the Soviet Union and some commercial flying schools and clubs in Germany, but by 1932 there were only 550 pilots, 180 other aircrew and 250 indifferent aircraft. Seven years later there were 20,000 aircrew and 3,500 front-line aircraft, many of formidable quality. The German air force had gone from being Europe's tyro to being its titan – and terror. In this giddying process, however, some fundamental mistakes were made and some of the wrong people got key jobs, which helped to delay and in the end vitiate Germany's jet effort.

Once Hitler had stripped the cosmetic democracy from a largely acquiescent nation, he appointed his political henchman Herman Goering (the Iron Man) Commissioner for Civil Aviation (January 1933), then Minister for Aviation (March 1933) with overlordship of the Air Ministry (May 1933) thrown in. The Luftwaffe which now grew with overwhelming speed at the behest of Hitler and Goering numbered among its hierarchy able men who were misfits and mutual antagonists. None was more able than Erhard Milch, Goering's Air Ministry deputy, who so impressed Goering with his intelligence and ruthlessness that he got Hitler to name him as his successor should he die. Later, Milch was to earn Goering's hatred, partly because he recognized the Iron Man's real failings as an indolent sybarite, and exploited them. Milch could not fly, nor was he a Nazi, but he was an effective toady of Hitler: he removed Professor Hugo Junkers from control of his own firm in 1933 because Junkers was not only anti-Nazi but opposed to German rearmament.

If Milch had the ability to create the Luftwaffe single-handed, Ernst Udet could hardly have been more ill-fitted for his job. Brave, open-hearted and rather stupid, he was a World War One fighter ace second only to Richthoven. Hitler saw him, rightly, as a brilliant pilot and, wrongly, as the man to be head of the Luftwaffe's technical office. Udet had little technical judgement, yet his decisions were to influence crucially the type of aircraft that pilots and crews would be flying in a few years' time. He was wholly out of his depth in the unscrupulous military-industrial complex of the Third Reich.

Such were the men who were to shape the German air force at breakneck pace during the 1930s. They were not necessarily best fitted to make judgements about the aerial equipment needed to fulfil

Hitler's plans to conquer the world. After Udet shot himself in 1941 (or, in the Goebbels' version, was killed testing secret apparatus), Goering said publicly: 'As Chief of Supply and Procurement he looked after the development of equipment which the German Luftwaffe has forged into a mighty shield to protect the homeland and a powerful sword to smite the enemy.' He knew that Udet had scrawled in red crayon on his bedroom wall the words: 'Iron Man, you left me.' Two years later Goering said privately to an aide: 'If only I could understand what Udet was thinking of. He made a complete chaos of our Luftwaffe programme. If he were alive today I would have no choice but to say to him "You are responsible for the destruction of the German air force".' In fact, Goering was as much or more to blame: he kept Udet in office long after even Udet himself had come to realize that he was unfit for the job.

The men who made the Luftwaffe made mistakes, but the manner and time in which they had to do the job would have taxed people of the greatest ability working harmoniously together. From 1933 onwards complex assumptions had to be made, and decisions taken, about the composition of the Luftwaffe and the aircraft it needed. What was its job? What types of planes would it need to do it? The Luftwaffe's role was defined as to give support to the German army but also to act to some extent as a strategic force in its own right. What should be the proportions of bombers, dive bombers (much loved by Udet because they needed flying flair and frightened the enemy, as well as being accurate in the hands of pilots as good as he was) and fighters. By 1935–6 Udet's understanding from Goering (who had it from Hitler) was that if war came it would be in 1941–2 in Poland or Czechoslovakia; there was no question of war with England and little need for a long-range, heavy bomber. (When the Germans realized they would need one, they turned to Heinkel for it, but the He 177 was a disastrous failure, mainly because of inadequate engines.)

The types standardized in the mid-1930s were medium bombers – the Dornier 17, Heinkel 111; dive bombers – the Junkers 87 and later the 88; and fighter escort and defence planes, allocated to the Messerschmitt Bf 109 and 110. Later the Focke-Wulf 190 fighter was ordered, an outstanding aircraft chosen partly because it had an air-cooled radial engine; liquid-cooled engines were wanted for all the other types. By 1937 replacements for the 109 included the Me 209, with a new Heinkel type as the alternative. These aircraft were, of course, all conventionally engined and were intended to last into the 1940s for short wars fought at close range. Thus the crucial decisions were all taken well before the advent of the jet – even before von Ohain's pre-flight engine, which was then underway at Marienehe, and still a step into the unknown. The nearest Hitler came to seeing a jet was in July 1939 when, in a display of the latest weapons at Rechlin flight research test centre, he was shown a mock-up of the Messerschmitt 262. Goering believed that Hitler based his decision to risk war in the west on seeing this display but there is no other evidence that this was so.

The Luftwaffe believed that the aircraft it had would last into the 1940s. They were in volume production and gifted planemakers like Heinkel were discouraged from rocking the boat – at about this time Heinkel had the He 111 bomber in mass production and no less than eleven other types in production or at the prototype stage. In July 1938 Goering had pointedly told a meeting of the major manufacturers that he wanted mass production of fewer models; yet Messerschmitt and Heinkel went on making aeroplanes that pleased them intellectually, and they were rich enough and secure enough to do so with impunity.

However, the pace of rearmament in the 1930s was so tumultuous that by the eve of war most manufacturers were gasping for the relative calm of standardized production. Plan had succeeded plan, year after year, sometimes with the interval between one plan and the next measured only in months. The plan of January 1934 envisaged 3,700 aircraft by the end of 1935; by July 1934 the number was increased to more than 4,000 in the same period. The 1935 plan called for 9,800 planes by the end of 1936, but a later 1935 plan called for 11,000 by 1 April 1936; further production plans came teeming forth in March, July and October 1936. Many new types of aircraft were to be made by March 1938, and by that time the manufacturers were expected to have delivered to the Luftwaffe 18,000 aircraft of eighty types and marks.

Many of the targets were unrealistic. On the day war broke out there were 3,374 combat aircraft, nearly all ready for action, of which more than 1,000 were medium bombers and about 1,000 were fighters – mostly the superb Bf 109. But this was a mere one-sixth of the target total due to be reached in 1943, when the Luftwaffe would have more up-to-date aircraft – 7,700 long- and medium-range heavy and medium bombers and 7,500 fighters. By that time war against Britain was to be considered a possibility, hence the long-range bombers. Goering had also sworn that the air defences would be so strong that not a single enemy bomb would ever fall on the Ruhr.

Under-strength it might be, but the Luftwaffe that went to war in 1939 was a very dangerous force which came within an ace of dominating the European skies. To achieve this force had meant the creation of millions of square metres of factory space, and the recruiting and training of thousands of engineers and skilled workers. The manufacturers had to cope with constant changes of specifications, which meant constant plant changes, new jigs and tools, new techniques. Every new aircraft had to go through the prototype stage, then through complex evaluation and flight tests, meaning yet more modifications for the factories to cope with. There had to be parallel production of aircraft and engines, down to the smallest component and including rivets and guns, armour and cannon, radios and bombs; even in the 1930s an aeroplane was a highly complex machine with many thousands of different parts. By mid-decade serious shortages of almost everything needed for the new Luftwaffe were slowing the pace of rearmament. Every plant manager was under intense strain; hierarchies in each company were grappling with urgent present problems, and hoping that future plans laid until 1943 would not be torn up many more times.

On to this seething deck stepped men like Mauch and Schelp with ideas which would not only rock the boat but were likely to sink it altogether. Their notions of an entirely new type of aero engine seemed designed to usurp all the work of the last decade – and that at the start of a war! The wonder is that any of the hard-pressed manufacturers listened to two such fantasts at all: Mauch and Schelp knew nothing of the piercing realities of providing proven engines for the Luftwaffe; they had never worked in industry; they had cooked up some theoretical calculations in Berlin and were now trying, in all arrogance, to teach hardened, experienced manufacturers where the future lay.

Even so, as was seen previously, by 1938 the most sceptical of the manufacturers had accepted contracts after intensive courtship by Schelp and Mauch. Junkers and B M W had study contracts. Bramo were willing, and by the end of 1938 had an axial flow engine on the drawing board. When Bramo merged with B M W, the child of the liason was to be a Bramo axial jet engine driven by a B M W turbine wheel. It was Junkers, however, that would pull ahead of everyone in the field, given their momentous lead by Anselm Franz.

Franz was born in Schladming, near Salzburg, in 1900, the son of a forestery engineer. He was lazy at school (his description) but at Graz University his interest was kindled in physics and maths and he did some good work in the turbo machinery department. He fell out with his professor for being too independent minded, but – as he tells it – the professor later apologized, telling him that some heresy he had proposed was in fact a correct alternative to current thinking. Franz stayed on after graduation, becoming an assistant lecturer. He later worked in Switzerland, and in Berlin on hydraulic transmissions, designing on the way a machine to make puzzles. He had always had a passion for aviation and the German rearmament programme gave him his chance. He applied to Junkers for a job in 1935. He was summoned by Dr Otto Mader to Dessau for an interview with a board which included Mader and several senior engineers, one of whom objected to Franz because he could not see how he could fit into the organization. Mader replied that he had more projects than he had men to manage them, and Franz was put in charge of the supercharger team, finding ways of boosting the company's line of piston engines.

Franz, in common with Mader and the rest of the team, did not immediately know of Herbert Wagner's initiative in the airframe division to design a pure jet engine. In Franz's opinion, Wagner 'was a very aggressive man, going, as Mader saw it, beyond what we can do this day. He was a briliant man, but he did not have a feel for the realities.' In 1939 Wagner left Junkers – the year that Mueller went to Heinkel, taking his jet engine expertise to a more receptive climate. However, the jet engine Mueller was working on for Junkers was complex and could not run under its own power, and once the secret of the work was out, Franz – who was now put in charge of jet engine design and development – inspected it and insisted that the project be scrapped and that he should start again from scratch on the design of a new engine. The Air Ministry gave this engine the series number 004, and it was to become the cornerstone of the German efforts to power a fighter which would sweep the Allies' piston-engine planes from the skies.

The 004 was a mundane engine, deliberately so. Having dismissed Mueller's efforts, Franz settled down to do what he felt was possible – to design the most conservative jet that he could. It would still be far ahead of anything else in its time, but Franz knew better than to try an over-complicated design which would prove hard to manufacture, even if it was technically brilliant. He had worked already on multi-stage axial compressors, so the idea of an axial flow jet caused him no difficulties. 'Schelp helped us a lot. He was a brilliant organizer and an aggressive engineer. He really managed to win round the Air Ministry people, who were tied to piston engines and didn't want to see too much effort diverted from them.'

Schelp certainly got Franz the support he needed, although when he saw that the 004 was so conservative in approach, he was led once to say, according to Franz, that

... if we couldn't do better than that we might as well stop the Junkers development. He looked into the future, but at the time he did not have, as Mader said of Wagner, a feel for what can be done and what can not. I believe that my success was that I set the goal at the level where I felt we could succeed. These other fellows all the time went for goals that were too high – one of the major reasons why some of them didn't really succeed.

Within Junkers Franz was answerable to Otto Mader, whom he described as a gentle man with exceptional qualities as an engineer and a human being – a great leader. Mader, however, had a problem common to all those who had to keep one eye on current piston-engine production while not frustrating the efforts of the innovators. He said to Franz at the outset: 'Some day in the future the jet engine will power planes, but we are under such pressure to produce piston engines, do me one favour: nobody can be transferred from that area to your project.'

Franz promised. He was allowed three people from the conventional engine group to start off with, and he then set about recruiting young men direct from the universities. They were inexperienced, but at least they were not blinkered by conventional engine attitudes. The group soon grew to thirty engineers and draughtsmen, and by 1943 about 500 people were working for Franz. Of two things he was never short: money and facilities. He had a department for materials research as well as design development, and test stands for individual components and complete engines. Later in the war, when Germany was desperate, the value of the work was rewarded by the German authorities giving the team double ration books, in return for which they worked a seventy- to eighty-hour week.

Like all other jet pioneers Franz had to have very high efficiencies for the components – compressor, combustor, turbine – of the 004. Some of his work was commissioned from outside Junkers: compressor blade design came from Dr W. Encke, of the Aerodynamic Research Institute at Göttingen, who was acknowledged as the leading engineer in his field; for turbine blading Franz relied on the steam turbine manufacturer AEG, of Berlin. The first engine the team built, the 004A, was purely experimental and unsuitable as a flight engine. It was heavy and contained heat-resistant materials such as nickel, cobalt and molybdenum which were simply not going to be available in Germany in sufficient quantities to produce the engine in any significant numbers. The team knew that, once this engine had proved their point, they would have to redesign the production engine using metals and alloys which *were* available.

The Air Ministry specification for the 004 called for a thrust of 1,320 lb at 560 mph at sea level. The design work, which began in the autumn of 1939, was guided by the overall principle that every decision taken must lead with the greatest certainty to an operational engine. Application of this principle meant that in some ways the 004 would be a lesser engine than the one which Mueller had started but Franz had scrapped. On the other hand, it led to an engine which ran – more than could be said for its erstwhile rival. Despite Schelp's reservations, Franz was given an entirely free hand. He chose an eight-stage compressor, a six-chamber combustor and a single-stage turbine. Although Franz had been more familiar with centrifugal compressors from his supercharger work, he chose an axial system for the 004, because of its smaller diameter and his conviction that a straight-through air flow would prove more efficient. The design was complete by spring 1940 and the first test run was on 11 October of that year. Two months later the full engine speed of 9,000 rpm was achieved and by January 1941 a thrust just short of 1,000 lb was reached; full thrust was achieved in August.

The 004 was living up to its expectations, conservative though they were, helping to allay the fear haunting Anselm Franz that failure would mean the end of all jet engine research and development, certainly in Junkers and possibly in Germany as a whole. One of the interesting innovations Franz conceived was the use of after-burning: after the compressed air is ignited in the combustor there remains a very useful amount of gas which is not burnt up; if it is mixed with fuel and ignited again in the tail of the engine it gives an extra kick to the thrust. (Whittle also spotted this useful increment of power and incorporated it in his designs.)

While development of the 004A was going on at full speed, design of the first pre-production engines was also going ahead, and it was here that Franz faced and solved his major problem – the shortage of exotic metals for the hottest parts of his engine. In the redesign Franz and his team also had to reduce engine weight from the prototype's 1,870 lb to 1,650 lb. Design of the 004B-o, as the early production model was known, was pushed along in parallel with the A engine. The most serious materials problem was in the turbine blades, which receive the full blast of scorching gas directly from the combustion chambers. The Junkers team made the turbine blades hollow, so that cold air channelled from the compressors could run up inside them. The fixed vanes in the engine were also hollow and air-blown. Two different types of hollow blade were developed in collaboration with the great armament company, Krupp. One used the alloy Tinidur, which contained 30 per cent nickel; ideally it should have contained 60 per cent nickel to give it the appropriate resistance to creep at high temperatures, but it was recognized that the nickel was just not available. Later on in the war nickel, even in the reduced amounts, could not be spared and another alloy, Cromadur, was developed, in which the nickel was replaced by manganese. Mild sheet steel was used in other hot parts of the engine and it was aluminium-coated to give it protection. The weight of scarce materials was more than halved. The production engine, designated 004B-1, with a thrust of around 2,000 lb was first delivered in June 1943. Its length was $12\frac{3}{4}$ feet and its diameter only $2\frac{1}{2}$ feet – a conclusive demonstration of the virtues of the axial flow compressor over the radial compressor, with its larger frontal diameter, which presented designers with increased drag penalties when it was used.

The 004 encountered many difficulties and its life in action was nothing like as long as that of the British engines which were eventually developed. The British could afford a relatively slow progress towards engines of great reliability and low fuel consumption, whereas the Germans were faced by the desperate need to develop fast fighters to counteract the shattering Allied bombing campaigns. The historic achievement of Franz and his team was to conceive and build the world's first production jet to be used in service flying – 6,000 had been produced by the end of the war, an astonishing achievement in the face of acute shortages and the disruption of Germany by bombing. The engine was brought into service in less than four years from the first designs to a production model. Yet there are few thrilling events about the design and development of the 004. Franz and his team did what they knew was possible, and such empiricism does not breed great drama. Patience and application brought rewards, not romance. There were no moments of blazing insight in which the human mind made some quantum leap. But there were some moments of quiet humour. During the summer of 1943, for instance, test engines suffered vibration failures of the turbine blades. They happened at high speed when blades of rather low natural frequency began to resonate (respond to vibration) with the combustion chambers and broke. Franz hired a professional musician to strike the blades with his violin bow. As with a tuning fork, he found exactly what frequency the individual blades had, and the engineers used the artist's skill to cut out blades with too low frequency and increase the taper of the substitutes, so increasing their frequency.

In 1945, from being vice-president, engineering, at Junkers, Dessau, Franz performed a trajectory which landed him finally as vice-president Avco Lycoming, the American jet engine company based at Stratford, Connecticut. He retired in 1968 but remained a consultant to Avco Lycoming for many years. In somewhat bent old age in the 1980s Franz remained a voluble champion of his cause: on one of the walls of his luxurious home near Stratford hung a signed commendation from Hitler for his wartime work on the jet. He confided that he felt that apart from his excesses the Führer had done 'much good'. An American intelligence report written in 1945 noted that Franz was unpopular with his staff at the Junkers plant; he had certainly driven them hard and produced remarkable results at a desperate time, when the Third Reich was crumbling around them.

Franz and his team were indeed responsible for a great engineering achievement, but they had one enormous advantage over Whittle, as Franz said: 'We never got stuck for money. There was always more when we needed it.'

Another German jet pioneer who was never stuck for money, once Udet was persuaded (fairly easily) to part with it, was Ernst Heinkel. His story runs in parallel with Franz and Messerschmitt, and he emerges as amazingly gifted, persistent and persuasive – but one of the nearly men, whose concepts never quite came off until too late in the war. His fine contempt for the Berlin bureaucrats partly accounts for his failure to become a maker of jet engines and aircraft, for Berlin responded in kind, even if with rather more restraint. Heinkel was a Nazi party member, but not an active one; his membership was an insurance policy rather than a battle banner. Heinkel was in fact rather better than the puffed-up omniscient which he portrays in his autobiography (*Stormy Life*). He was a considerable forward thinker and doer who believed he could change the face of aviation by his own genius and the work of his engineers around him. He was also willing to meet any and every specification put out by the Air Ministry in its often fumbled search for the right aircraft for the Luftwaffe. Perhaps his ardent willingness ('I gave them no peace') was responsible for some of the disdain from Berlin; but the bureaucrats could not deny that he had been successful up to 1939.

During the First World War Heinkel designed fighter floatplanes, setting up his own company, Ernst Heinkel A G, at Warnemünde, in

1922. He developed military aircraft in spite of the Versailles agreement and by 1937, when Germany's rearmament was a fact for all the world to see, he had factories at Rostock and Oranienburg, outside Berlin. Speed was his passion and his aircraft both broke and set records in the 1930s. Despite its shortcomings, his Heinkel 111 was a medium bomber and transport mainstay which bore the brunt of action in almost every theatre of war. His Heinkel 112 only just lost out to the Bf 109 in a competition for the standard front-line fighter, and many believed that his aircraft had the edge on the Messerschmitt. There was always a touch of genius in his megalomania; and he never gave up.

Once Warsitz had flown the He 178, Heinkel pestered Goering, Milch, Udet and even Schelp to venture north to the Baltic shores at Marienehe so that he could demonstrate the promise of the jet age as exemplified by the world's first jet-propelled aircraft. Not until 1 November 1939, two months after the first flight, could he persuade a party led by Milch, Udet and Schelp (Hitler and Goering pleaded other engagements) to come. Heinkel said of the demonstration: 'When I greeted Milch I saw that his face was cold and unfriendly. The others looked the same, as if they had only come with great reservations . . . The atmosphere was somewhat frosty during my explanation . . . Udet made a few facetious remarks.'

Standing in the raw of an early November morning on the Baltic coast might have accounted for some of the lacklustre response of the spectators. But Heinkel was to face an even worse challenge. Test pilot Warsitz began his take-off run but the moment before lift-off the engine cut out and the plane rolled to a stop. 'I sensed a catastrophe which would destroy all my hopes. I jumped into my Mercedes, leaving the rest of them behind unheeded, and dashed to Warsitz . . . "Hell!" he said furiously between his teeth. "The damn' petrol pump seized up."' Warsitz reckoned that they would need a couple of hours; he went across to the party from Berlin and explained that he had aborted take-off because of a burst tyre.

Heinkel took the party to the airfield club for a champagne breakfast. Two and a half hours later Milch announced coldly that he was returning to Berlin, while Udet made supercilious remarks about needing danger money. 'Surely you will wait for the flight?' said Heinkel. At that moment Warsitz burst in saying that he was ready for take-off. In the end he gave a perfect demonstration, diving low over the heads of the spectators. 'Warsitz made such a perfect landing that the machine rolled to a stop in front of the group. I felt we had won. My disillusionment came when the visitors, without any further remark, took their leave.'

Heinkel could only explain this coolness in terms of blind obfuscation, although the reaction was in fact more a reflection of the perpetual antagonisms within the group, and Milch's determination not to appear overimpressed by anything at all. However, Heinkel was not downcast for long. With his acquisition in 1939 of Max Adolf Mueller and part of his team from Junkers, he could now boast of 120 people working on jet engines, with von Ohain in overall charge, designing a production engine with a centrifugal compressor, while Mueller's group worked on an axial flow engine. Heinkel built new plant and test facilities, and seemed to be fulfilling his reputation for high performance more than ever. His designers were working on what he believed would be the world's first production jet fighter, the Heinkel 280, which would be powered by one or other of his jet engine projects – an all-Heinkel jewel for the Luftwaffe which would outperform every other aircraft in the skies around the world.

Despite Udet's apparent disinterest during his visit, Heinkel had persuaded him to licence all these developments by the end of 1939. But shortages of materials and manpower still dogged Heinkel as they dogged all the other German manufacturers. Heinkel was, however, prone to believe that his troubles were unique and stemmed much more from the animosity of Mauch and Schelp, and, when Mauch left the scene, Schelp alone. In his book, Udet becomes his far-sighted protector from Air Ministry opponents, while Schelp is asserted to have opposed his coup of 1941 – the purchase of a small aero-engine manufacturing company, Hirth Motoren, which gave him more manpower and machinery at a stroke. Hirth's experience was solely in piston engines, but the company had some turbo supercharger expertise. Heinkel paid six million marks for Hirth, which he regarded as excessive. Schelp's version of these negotiations is that he wanted Heinkel to acquire Hirth, that he believed Heinkel now had the capability to produce both airframes and the jet engines to power them, and that he was not opposed to any of these moves.

Again, the balance of truth seems to lie with Schelp, since Heinkel continued work with increasing momentum after his sponsor in Berlin, Udet, had shot himself. That he was to run into serious difficulties both with the engines and the airframe of the He 280 was none of Schelp's doing. It seems likelier that opposition to the Hirth deal came from Professor Willy Messerschmitt himself, who was not over-anxious to see competition from Heinkel in the form of his fighter project. This would not have gained the sympathy of Schelp, for whom competition was engrained in his philosophy, so long as it was kept within bounds which did not dissipate effort and waste resources. He stated that he was anxious to see Heinkel owning Hirth, and helped him acquire the company against Messerschmitt's wishes.

Difficulties there were, but nevertheless, barely a year and a half into the war, the Germans were almost ready to fly the world's first jet prototype fighter; and a second was soon to follow from Messerschmitt. All this was happening while in England, Whittle, the first man to patent a practical jet engine, was still awaiting take-off of the first British jet aircraft, the Gloster E28/39, a plane built to prove the principle of his engine, but not a prototype in the sense either of the Heinkel 280 or the Messerschmitt 262.

As Whittle drove away from Rugby after putting Pye on the train to London he could reflect on struggle and rejoice in success. He was carrying off an engineering stroke of genius; a mechanic's son would give the world a new way of travel. His name would belong on the short list which included Watt, Stephenson and Parsons. He could not foresee all the possibilities, but society would in some way be re-shaped by his invention. At thirty-two he was an outstanding engineer and airman. He had seen much and suffered somewhat on the journey; he knew the pain of being mocked and the agonies of nervous illness, he had seen jealousy warp the judgement of his fellow scientists and engineers. But he also had the balm of praise and trust from Henry Tizard and, shortly, senior RAF commander Arthur Tedder, two of the finest men in his field, who had courage and influence to match their convictions, and who walked in the right Whitehall corridors.

Whittle now knew the elements of leadership, how to extract from men and women that extra ounce of work before utter exhaustion set in; and he could inspire intense loyalty. But he was not yet up to the politics of Whitehall; he was poor at intrigue and naive in some of his encounters, even with his BT-II colleagues. Some lessons he had learned: as a young socialist he had experienced the failure of the capitalist system in one of its depressed cycles; he believed that it could not cope with a revolutionary idea. Although, he had managed to prise some finance from a merchant bank, the money was fitful in coming and always too little. He was sceptical of an engineering industry which, even at its most advanced, would not or could not try to meet his exacting needs. And he had also experienced the aridity of the official mind – as exemplified in the Air Ministry. He was very vulnerable, more so than any of his unknown jet pioneering competitors in Germany. All he possessed, apart from his mind, were his patents and a few shares in a small, rickety company which was already beginning to attract the ill-will of some of its future major competitors. The seeds of his success and failure were already being sown.

By mid-1939 it was inevitable that the first use of his jet engine would be military. The debate about whether it should power a fighter or a bomber reflected to some extent the confusion of aims within the RAF, caused by sudden pell-mell expansion. The spirit of Versailles had governed British visions of her aerial future: a nation which had lost three-quarters of a million men in the war to end wars was not going to run a strong air force once the slaughter was over. The futility of war was the lodestar of British government policy and general disarmament was the course to be steered. A decade after World War One a world disarmament conference met at Geneva, where aerial warfare was a major issue and the abandonment of bombing was an article of faith. Britain was the one nation with experience of the death, destruction and disruption possible by aerial bombardment by airship and aeroplane. German attacks on cities and towns in the UK between 1915 and 1918 had caused 1,413 deaths and 3,407 injured – nearly all of them civilian. The numbers were small (Britain lost 60,595 civilians in World War Two, and 146,777 were injured) but no other country had suffered in this way. The ferocious novelty of aerial attack had caused demoralization in some parts of the country and its indiscriminate nature seemed peculiarly horrible (in one of the worst raids forty-six children were killed in a Poplar school). Those who sought an end to aerial warfare were morally reinforced by the conviction (shared within the RAF) that there was no defence which could prevent the bombers getting through. Therefore, the bombers had to be outlawed.

The first shock to the disarmament conference was Germany's withdrawal, on the orders of Hitler, in 1933. When German rearmament became an undeniable fact, it was obvious that the RAF would have to be re-equipped and expanded. But what with? The 'invincibility' of the bomber argued for a strong bomber force with which to deter or strike at an enemy. In 1936 specifications were issued for the long-range heavy bombers of World War Two – the Stirling, Halifax and Manchester (later the famous Lancaster). But during the early 1930s a conviction was growing in the RAF that there *was* a defence against the bomber: this took shape as the eight-gun fighter, for which specifications were issued in 1934, and which materialized as the Hurricane and Spitfire. This sort of policy-making, in which manufacturers influenced the RAF and vice versa, did great credit to Britain, and the conversion to monoplane fighters would save the nation in 1940. The pursuit of speed as an end in itself in the Schneider Trophy races of the early 1930s also led to the development of conventional aero engines such as the Rolls-Royce

Merlin, which powered many of the fighters and bombers. Piston-engine development was in fact amazingly rapid and deserves a history to itself.

One last triumph set the seal on Britain's ultimate victory in the air. A scientific revolution took place when it was realized in 1934 by the Air Ministry's Directorate of Scientific Research that a war in the air would be lost unless science could be applied to the conquest of the bomber. (This was the same directorate, though with some differences in personnel, which was to be so grudging of Whittle in the later 1930s.) The conclusion came from a scientist of genius, A. P. Rowe, who convinced his director, H. E. Wimperis, who in turn persuaded the Air Minister, Lord Londonderry, to set up a committee to study air defence. Its chairman was Henry Tizard and the members included two Nobel prizewinners, Professor P. M. S. Blackett and Dr A. V. Hill. It was they who asked for a death ray and were given instead, by Robert Watson-Watt and A. F. Wilkins of the National Physical Laboratory, the basis of radar. The problem of detecting the oncoming bombers, their height, speed and numbers was on the way to solution. With Tizard (who was a brave and outstanding test pilot of World War One as well as a distinguished scientist, administrator and encourager of young people with ideas) and his committee, working with phenomenal exertion, a detection and attack system was ready for 1940. Often, as with Rowe and Wilkins, this work was done by people who have never received the proper credit for saving Britain.

In the same period the RAF's Director of Training, Arthur (later Air Chief Marshal Sir, and later still Lord) Tedder, foresaw the need for highly skilled people to use the technology which was being developed – irrespective of class, which was often a bugbear and created the RAF Volunteer Reservists, who were nowhere near as classless as he would have liked. Tedder moved on to become Director of Research and Development, and Whittle's champion. In his autobiography, significantly titled *With Prejudice*, Tedder wrote:

'Spot the Winner' was one of the preoccupations of my Directorate. The trouble was, the field was so big and the number of potential winners was so small. I found myself having to warn my staff that we could not afford to ignore any proposition. Many people would have dismissed as fanciful young Whittle's early claims. I can well remember Henry Tizard, on his way out with me to Lutterworth to see Whittle and his prototype of the first jet engine, trying to explain the difference between a jet engine and the old push-and-pull engine to which we were accustomed. I gathered that somehow the more difficult conditions got for the normal engine, the easier it was for the jet engine, and I remember remarking to Tizard that if anybody else had told me this story I would have regarded it as a confidence trick.

We went later to see the small machine shops which had been made available to Whittle on the first floor of British Thomson-Houston. One of the directors came round with us, and obviously was not particularly interested, if at all, in Whittle's idea, and kept on pressing us to come down to the floor and see a *real* turbine – enormous things they were. His reaction made me think of an experienced shipbuilder (in oak) dismissing as foolish an early iron ship, and saying 'Now there is a *real* ship'.

My recollection of the first engine or, rather, the test rig, was pure unadulterated Heath Robinson. In an enclosure in one corner of what looked like, and I believe was, a derelict motor garage, was an iron framework on which was mounted a combustion chamber with an undercarriage connected to what looked like nothing so much as a giant trout-fisher's spring balance – a typical Emett design. But more impressive was the glowing combustion chamber and the blazing blue jet flame roaring out into the open, added to which the fact that the thrust developed was considerably more than optimism, had suggested. Here was another gamble; a real war winner justifying the manufacture of an initial batch of engines and aircraft to match, straight off the drawing board.

That Tedder's appreciation of the possibilities of the jet was not matched by faster action may have been partly due to his posting in 1940 to be Air Officer Commanding-in-Chief, Middle East, even though by then the orders had been given. It is worth recalling the battle Tizard had to make the Air Ministry grasp the importance of the jet engine. At a meeting of the Aeronautical Research Committee's engine sub-committee in February 1937, Tizard remembered 'a very well known engineer saying that he would stake his whole reputation on his opinion that the scheme [the jet] would not work, and that it would be a waste of money to encourage it. I said at the time that we would guard against the loss of that gentleman's reputation by omitting his opinion from the minutes'. Tizard wrote to Lord Halsbury many years after his first meeting with Whittle: 'His suggestion was undoubtedly streets ahead of any other suggestion for the development of aircraft engines at the time. I knew it would cost a great deal of money; I knew that success was not certain; and yet I felt that it was of great national importance to spend the money.'

To some extent Whittle's concept was struggling against the same forces as those encountered by Schelp in Germany, though not by von Ohain, who was having a much clearer run under the protection of his speed-and-power-hungry patron. Just as the Luftwaffe was preparing itself for war, so was the RAF. It, too, envisaged a war in 1942, and there were enough problems in meeting even that deadline. In a single bound the RAF was changing from one aeronautical era to another, and in this kind of revolution it is all too easy to forget the day *after* tomorrow. Although the RAF was not quite so bedevilled by clashes of personality as the German Air Ministry and Luftwaffe, it had its own rows and political problems to surmount. The Chief of Air Staff, Marshal of the RAF Sir Edward Ellington, roughly the equivalent of Erhard Milch, was 'extremely weak in discussion and his utterances most confused' said one military diarist, Lt. Gen. Sir Henry Pownall, who added in his diary 'a cheerless cove . . . and the use of the words "good morning" are unfamiliar'.

Yet Ellington presided over enormous changes. Between 1934 and 1939 there were eight expansion schemes, some scrapped and superseded before a year was out. In the view of some historians, by the outbreak of war the various expansion schemes had left the RAF in disarray. Certainly the suppliers, Britain's aircraft industry, were in tumult and financial uncertainty, with sixteen sophisticated design teams at the head of thousands of workers existing hand to mouth in companies whose cash flows looked dismal because the paymaster, the Air Ministry, was anything but flush.

In a landscape so large it is not to be marvelled that Power Jets and Squadron Leader Whittle were little visible. That partly – but certainly not wholly – accounted for the fact that although Pye had blessed the work at last, nothing much tangible happened. Much more worrying was that when things did happen, the production decisions were amateur and the pathways chosen led in the wrong direction.

Power Jets received an Air Ministry contract for the first flight engine (for an experimental aeroplane) in July 1939, and British Thomson-Houston were contracted to make it. The financial situation eased slightly. BT-H increased its investment in the company by £2,000 and G. and J. Weir, the Scots engineering company, put in a further £2,000. Whittle seems to have fallen into the arms of BT-H because they were there, and knew of the project – nobody else was in sight – but it was to prove a major mistake. Whittle had already upset a faction within the company over the design of his blades, but, more seriously, he knew by 1939 that BT-H could not match the degree of precision engineering on which he was insisting. Nor did BT-H – as Tedder divined – consider the contract of major importance.

When war broke out in September 1939, the Air Ministry confirmed that Whittle could stay with the project and that work was to continue. However, the Air Ministry did precious little else to keep Whittle and his team together. Power Jets tried without success in January 1940 to borrow staff from BT-H, although they did loan him one brilliant engineer, Leslie Cheshire, who made important contributions to the jet. A small drawing office and workshop went up, but the workshop and its pathetically inadequate machine tools enabled Power Jets to make only modest modifications to engine parts. A request for better machine tools was turned down by the Air Ministry, which relented only in late 1940. Specialized test equipment was not authorized until late 1942.

The official historian notes: 'This shortage of ready money had a direct effect ... There is no doubt that the use of unsatisfactory components was the cause of many technical difficulties ... many parts which ought to have been scrapped had to be used again and again.' She concludes:

> The historical verdict may justly be that the expenses of the period (to 1939) were very low compared with the value of the research work done by Whittle ... The industrial background in which the Whittle unit was developed was quite unsuitable to push on the work with great speed, or to provide the resources which were needed, and it compares most unfavourably with the circumstances of von Ohain's development in Germany.

The outbreak of war, then, did not quicken the programme. Whittle's disagreements with BT-H and his suspicions about their ability to meet his needs had good factual bases. He was to write: 'Technical disagreements mostly had their origin in the very different background of the BT-H engineers and myself. I was an aeronautical engineer trained to think in terms of very low weight and great precision ... I saw these things through the eyes of a pilot as well as the eyes of an engineer.' Whittle knew that his engine needed rapid starting, quick response to control, 'and the ability to cope with a range of operating conditions as wide as take-off in the tropics to high-speed manoeuvring at very great heights where air temperatures would be 50° C below freezing point'.

BT-H engineers, on the other hand, were traditional designers and manufacturers of large generators for electric power stations, which stay in one spot and work in a known and narrow range of conditions. Their machines were constructed from

> massive castings and forgings weighing many tons and installed on heavy, rigid foundations. To save on manufacturing costs was far more important than to save on weight. Many of them had been twenty to thirty years and more in their profession and had little or no connection with modern aerodynamic theory ... Machine tools were correspondingly unsuited to the work. The factory was not temperature controlled and this is an important condition where great precision is required.
>
> It was a bit like expecting the makers of Big Ben to make a good job of a lady's wrist watch.

Despite his gifts as a communicator Whittle found it difficult to convert many of the traditionalists. He wanted the combustion chambers for his flight engines to be made of stainless steel $\frac{1}{64}$ in thick. It was a difficult job and BT-H claimed it was impossible. Whittle challenged one of their welders to do it and, with practice, he did. Stories like this spread and did not endear the impetuous pioneer to the experienced designer. It did not help that Whittle was quick-tempered and sometimes intolerant, partly because he felt that BT-H did not realize that while they could scrap a badly worked or worn component easily, a tiny company like Power Jets could not afford this luxury either in terms of time or money. On top of these problems, Power Jets in the persons of Frank Whittle and Lance Whyte often seemed to face the Air Ministry with arched backs and raised fur – and not without reason. Although the principle of the jet was now understood and accepted in Whitehall, the principle of Power Jets was not. Whittle wanted to manufacture his engines. But the Air Ministry believed that this would be intolerable to other manufacturers with whom they had to get along. How could they foster an RAF officer in a private company, thus themselves setting up a private manufacturer with an earth-shaking new idea in competition with the rest of the aero-engine industry?

Heavily involved in this debate were William Farren and W. L. Tweedie – the same Tweedie who had written to Whittle his formal brush-off letter in 1930. Whittle and Farren sat next to one another at lunch in February 1940 and what Farren said to Whittle so alarmed him that he subsequently sent a letter outlining the points that he understood Farren to have made:

1. An unselfish crowd of people put money into Power Jets. They had done a very good job of work but they would get no return on their money and would be lucky not to make a loss.

2. The Air Ministry would not allow Power Jets to manufacture. Some existing firms would do that.

3. The engine belonged to the Air Ministry and nobody else would make anything out of it except for manufacturing profit – that would of course exclude Power Jets.

4. The Air Ministry did not like Lance Whyte's suggestion (made in an effort to preserve at least some of Power Jets' position) that Power Jets should be *part* of an organization set up to manufacture.

5. Power Jets should raise more private money rather than depend on the Air Ministry – even though backers might well lose their money.

6. The Air Ministry would order only experimental engines from Power Jets.

To Whittle this was 'ripening the fruit for others to pluck. We have plenty of evidence that the wolves are gathering around the door, and I have a very depressing feeling that your sympathies lie with the wolves.' He sent a copy of this letter to Tedder, who told him not to worry too much about Farren. Then Farren phoned him to say that all he had tried to do was point out the kind of nasty things that *might* happen. He had been misunderstood: Power Jets had done a marvellous job and he and others felt it would be unjust if they did not reap the benefit.

Whittle's summary of Farren's views in fact turned out to be only too accurate a summary of what was to happen over the next few years, though the *dénouement* was not quite as ruthless as he had suggested. This atmosphere ensured that the early months of 1940 were spent wrangling over who was to produce Whittle's engines once they were ready for manufacture – a difficult stage in the life of any invention, since the inventor is only infrequently the best judge of how to mass-produce his idea, and often does not realize the great difference between building an exquisite prototype and designing an engine for the easiest and most economical production within a factory. Whittle was confirmed in his distrust of BT-H's capacities when he turned to the Rover Car Company, whose chief executives, two brothers named Wilks, were only too willing and eager to undertake manufacture – a bit too eager, as Whittle came to believe.

In approaching Rover, Whittle was following an almost chance suggestion by Tinling (of Power Jets) whose wife knew the wife of Maurice Wilks, Rover's chief engineer. It meant that he had circumvented the traditional aero-engine manufacturers, of whom he had even deeper distrust. However, he found that he could not reach a commercial agreement with Rover either. By this time the Air Ministry, who had at first looked coldly upon a car manufacturer joining the aviation business, began to see merit in the idea. The problem was, essentially, about who was to benefit from the founding of a new aero-engine industry. Whittle wanted to safeguard Power Jets' existence and its potential as a manufacturer. Rover wanted to make engines on terms favourable to them – in 1940 and after the war. Inevitably BT-H discovered that Whittle was talking to Rover as an alternative manufacturer and promptly refused to do any more work on their flight engine contract until the wrangle was sorted out in their favour.

The Air Ministry was now in a deep dilemma. They held that Whittle could not manufacture, of which there was no doubt because Power Jets had no equipment. Some argued internally that since the Crown had free use of Power Jets' patents, and of Squadron Leader Whittle, they held all the cards – 'including the joker', Tedder said one day, pointing to Whittle – and could do what they thought fit. Tedder took a calmer view and reassured Whittle that he would not be done down in any agreement that the Ministry might make. By April 1940 the Air Ministry decided (in a characteristically Whitehall gesture) that BT-H *and* Rover should share production of the engine. Power Jets was to be a research company only and would build no further development engines. The two manufacturing companies would be responsible for their own drawings and development work.

This decision seriously weakened Power Jets, and was to prove a disaster to them and – almost – to Britain. Lance Whyte intervened personally to try to defend the company's livelihood, only to find himself branded in Whitehall and by the manufacturers as 'difficult' – a name already indelibly stamped on Whittle's back. As if this were not enough, Whittle was finding it increasingly difficult to work with Whyte – a sentiment which probably had its roots in Whittle's temperament. Whyte was to leave the company in 1941, but after the war he was to write movingly of Whittle, and of this period of trial, stress and human failing:

From 1939 to 1941 the tension was never relaxed for a moment. We would leave board and committee meetings after exhausting battles with civil servants or with collaborating firms to return to engine tests at Lutterworth – often successful but once or twice ending in a shattering explosion – and frequently finish with night duty at the factory listening to the German bombers, as for example on the night of the first mass raid on Coventry, only twelve miles away. The days were an unbroken round of interviews, visits, discussions, arguments, all translated into a flow of decisions about increased staff, buildings and technical collaborations; and at the heart of it all Whittle's designs going steadily forward and the early models succeeding and failing and then again succeeding – and this against the fall of France, the rally under Churchill, the Battle of Britain, and the risk of invasion. Unbroken tension and excitement, with its result in nerves and illness.

At one critical stage Whittle himself could stand it no longer and as he lay in bed day after day the whole enterprise was shaken by the appalling doubt: had too much been gambled on one man and had that man taken on too much? Many were asking these questions. In the early summer of 1941 Power Jets was like a genius incarnated into a company, certainly brilliant and imaginative, but so unorthodox as to cause widespread alarm. Every month that passed after the summer of 1939 made it clearer that the gamble was worth while, but as the first flight tests grew nearer the doubts became graver: could an efficient engine really emerge from so unorthodox a background? Would not something go wrong at the last minute and justify the countless critics who distrusted or resented our rapid expansion at state expense?

Looking back at the rancour of the time, at the blatant self-interest and the jealousy and bitterness of human and professional relationships, it is hard to believe that early in 1940 Tedder and his staff, supported by Tizard, had included the jet engine in a short list of 'war winners' which they had drawn up. The implication was that each of the listed devices was to be developed as quickly as possible. This spirit was reinforced by the attitude of Tizard, who declared after one trial run that 'a prototype which does not break down in my presence is a production job'. He wrote to Whittle: 'Just a note to say how glad I was to have an opportunity of seeing your "child" in action. It really is a fascinating and impressive job and, having seen it, I shall certainly feel even more than before that it is up to me to do all I can to help it forward.'

It followed from the Air Ministry's conversion that they should now decide what aircraft was to be powered by the Whittle engine.

This was not an easy decision to take because the main patterns of the war had not yet emerged, and the arguments about what equipment would be needed were still being conducted with a crystal ball spirit. A high-speed, high-altitude aircraft was an obvious choice because those were the conditions for which the jet engine was designed. These characteristics argued at first for a bomber-reconnaissance aeroplane operating above 40,000 feet and at speeds way beyond the reach of any known German aircraft types. However, such an aeroplane would need a pressurized cabin to enable the crew to work in the rarified atmosphere, and that would mean a new and complicating factor to design into an aeroplane which was already a radical departure in aeronautical engineering.

Rather than take too many steps into the unknown all at once, the Air Ministry began to think in terms of a fighter with a pilot breathing oxygen in an unpressurized cockpit – a familiar enough concept in 1940. Two types were then considered: a heavy fighter of about 11,000 lb weight with a large amount of armament and a speed of around 400 mph, and a light fighter of 8,500 lb with smaller armament and a speed around 460 mph. The smaller fighter won the day because it would be able to catch any high-speed bomber likely to appear for some years. A contract had already been given to the Gloster Aeroplane Company to design and build a single-engined experimental aeroplane the E28/39 and on 12 May 1940 Gloster were ordered to 'proceed immediately with the design' of a twin-engined fighter which, four long years later, would enter service as the famous Gloster Meteor.

Whittle characteristically records that he had hoped that Power Jets would get the contract for the E28/39 and he had shown Pye some early drawings. However, Whittle was well satisfied with the choice of Gloster, a company which had built the RAF's last biplane fighter, the Gladiator, and which was now ready for, and capable of, more advanced work. The chief designer, George Carter, was an acknowledged leader in the industry and the company had in their chief test pilot, Flight Lieutenant P. E. G. (Gerry) Sayer, a man in whom Whittle had complete confidence and with whom he enjoyed a pleasant, easy relationship. There was to be little delay or fuss in designing the E28/39: it was providing an engine for it and for the Meteor that would be bedevilled by incompetence, distrust, personal animosity and bad faith.

In the early years of World War Two, Ernst Heinkel seemed to hold every card that would make him the man to lead the world into the jet age. Apart from Udet's admittedly ambivalent support, he had all the money he needed to finance his initiatives; and he seemed to have skimmed the cream of German scientists and engineers capable of designing and developing successful jet engines to fit into the world's first successful jet aeroplanes. Heinkel had a gift for picking people with advanced but workable ideas and providing them with the climate in which they could fulfil themselves, remembering always to whom the greater glory was due. In the Gunters, the identical twins Siegfried and Walter, he had bought a brilliant mathematician and a designer with an aesthete's eye for beautiful aircraft forms. He had recognized and bound by contract the gangling student from Göttingen, Hans von Ohain, who had repaid him with the world's first flyable jet engine. He had hired Max Adolf Mueller and some of his experienced, if temporarily disheartened, jet pioneers from Junkers. To cap it all, in 1939 he lured over Robert Lusser, development chief of Messerschmitt, who had done the preliminary studies for that company's jet fighter. (Heinkel was determined to beat Willy Messerschmitt into the skies with his own fighter: this rivalry and the lobbying in Berlin by these two formidable men was a powerful if incalculable factor in the story.) All this was apart from the rocket-propelled aircraft Heinkel was pioneering, together with alternatives to the pure jet, which included probably the world's first serious turbo-propeller venture, beating A. A. Griffith's work at Farnborough, at least on paper. Whatever went on among the bureaucrats in Berlin, Heinkel believed that he was going to show the world how. He had the ideas, and the resources to make them work.

His first step, once the Heinkel 178 had made the world's first jet flight, was to tell von Ohain to design the H E S6 engine with thrust increased from 1,100 to 1,300 lb. This was done with ease, because it required little more than modifications to von Ohain's existing centrifugal engine. However, the S6 and the 178 airframe gave disappointing results. The thrust was still low for the weight and size of the engine; the plane was directionally unstable at higher speeds, and the landing gear still refused to retract; above all there were problems with the long air intake and jet outlet pipe needed for an engine buried in the plane's fuselage. (All jet pioneers foresaw these same problems and almost all avoided them in roughly the same way: wing-mounted engines.)

Heinkel decided to scrap the historic 178 (which was taken to the Berlin Air Museum, where it was destroyed later in the war in an RAF bombing raid) and concentrate on a new single-seat fighter with two wing-mounted engines, to be called the Heinkel 280. Lusser was put in charge of its design and development. Heinkel now decided to develop two different engines for the 280 airframe. Mueller was to design an axial flow engine of the type on which he had worked at Junkers, while von Ohain was to reduce the diameter of his centrifugal flow engine by a major redesign. Von Ohain's engine was called the H E S8, or 001 in the Air Ministry series, and Mueller's the S30 or 006. The new centrifugal engine looked good on paper because its diameter was only half an inch greater than Junkers' new axial engine, the 004, on which Anselm Franze's team was working, and its weight was less than half that of the Franz concept. Its thrust was to be built up to around 1,300 lb. Mueller's engine, to be developed in parallel though more slowly, would have a thrust of about 1,700 lb and was to be ready in the summer of 1942, about a year behind von Ohain's design. A large new factory was to be built at Rostock to produce the engines.

According to Heinkel, Helmut Schelp was opposed to the idea of spreading the available engineering talent across two radically different engine types and even Heinkel concedes:

> In view of the shrinking number of specialists at my disposal he was doubtless right to some extent, but he was wrong insofar as at that stage of development in a new field it was not yet possible to adopt certain types and write off others. I was certainly right when I told these comparative newcomers to the ministry that they should not stop other developments by entrusting them to the various reluctant engine works which would be strained beyond their capacity . . . The capable scientists and designers now working together under me already knew the snags to be avoided, for our parallel developments embraced nearly the whole field.

They did, but Heinkel failed to see that he was overreaching himself, with consequences that would very nearly destroy his reputation completely in Berlin. However, throughout 1940 work went ahead on the engines and airframe, and there was no doubt that the Heinkel 280 would be a mighty leap forward. It was to be the world's first production jet to fly, the world's first jet fighter, the world's first aircraft to be fitted with an ejector seat for the pilot to bale out in an emergency, the world's first aircraft with a pressure cabin – though this was never achieved – and the world's first aircraft to fly with a fully retractable tricycle undercarriage. The new nosewheel was an important innovation because the aircraft could take off with its engine and tail parallel to the runway in a flying attitude. The Messerschmitt fighter at first was fitted with a tailwheel, which meant that the propulsion jet hit the runway at a downwards angle, something which was to cause trouble, as will be seen in a later chapter. Finally, of course, one or other of Heinkel's engines would be the world's first production jet engine.

The 280 had fine lines. A slender fuselage carried fuel and guns, twin fins and graceful wings with the engines attached in streamlined nacelles. It was an astonishingly advanced aircraft, designed knowingly for the jet age with all the innovations that entailed. The top speed would be 547 mph at 20,000 feet, faster by far than anything else at the time. At first, work was kept secret from the Air Ministry, but by March 1940, when Messerschmitt received a development contract for his fighter, Heinkel had talked and he also received a contract for the 280. By September 1940 one airframe was complete and two more prototypes were being built. The aircraft was now well ahead of its engines, so on 11 September, with dummy engine nacelles and the fuselage ballasted to the weight of engines and fuel, it was towed into the air by a Heinkel 111, cast off and tested in gliding flight. This gave the designers at least some idea of the plane's aerodynamic qualities and forty-one of these flights were made by March 1941. They seemed to show good pilot-handling and flight characteristics, despite the fact that Heinkel's team had stepped so far beyond the bounds of convention in their revolutionary design.

Although von Ohain's and Mueller's engines were now lagging behind seriously, it was possible by March 1941 to fit two of the 001 centrifugal engines to the wings and try a powered test flight, although they were developing only about 1,100 lb thrust against the desired 1,300 lb. All the same, the He 280 soared off the runway on its first jet-powered flight on 2 April – over a month ahead of the first British test flight of the E28/39 aircraft (best regarded as a superior counterpart of the He 178 rather than the He 280, which was the prototype of a fully fledged production fighter).

The 280's first flight went gingerly. The fuel tanks were only half filled and the Heinkel test pilot, Fritz Schaefer, turned over the River Warnow estuary, completed one circuit while keeping Marienehe in view, and then landed. By that time the fuel warning lights were glowing red. Schaefer did not retract the undercarriage, kept his height below 1,000 feet and probably did not exceed about 200 mph. The cowlings (covers) were left off the two engines because, during ground running tests, pools of unburnt fuel had collected in them, creating a fire hazard of the kind Whittle had encountered in the first runs of his engine.

Characteristically, Heinkel insisted on an immediate demonstration flight, which was held three days later, either at Marienehe or Rechlin, the secret German research station about seventy miles north of Berlin. Accounts of this demonstration differ, and documents about it no longer appear to exist. What is beyond dispute is that the spectators included Ernst Udet, Wolfram Eisenlohr, the sceptical head of the aero-engine section of the Air Ministry's technical department, Helmut Schelp, by now in charge of 'special' propulsion units under Eisenlohr, and Dr Lucht, chief of the engineering division. At this time it was highly probable that none of these men believed that the war would last long enough to require jet fighters.

According to Heinkel's account of the demonstration:

. . . the He 280 equipped with two He S8 jet units took off . . . on its first important flight for an exhibition display in competition with the fastest mass-produced Luftwaffe plane of its time, the Focke Wulf 190 [certainly an outstanding fighter]. By its extraordinary manoeuvrability and speed it completed four circles before the FW 190 had completed three. Warsitz was again the pilot.

At last it happened. Udet hurried over to me and said: 'I must thank you for what you have achieved here today. This is probably the proudest moment in the history of the Heinkel firm. If we had such machines on the Channel, so that the English could record their performance, they'd start scrapping the whole of their programme.' Eisenlohr, who was responsible for all power units, declared in Berlin the next day after his erstwhile reluctance: 'The kudos which must go to the Heinkel firm is enormous. This fact justifies their being allowed to go on working on engine development.'

The phrasing of this remark showed how much opposition the sale to me of the Hirth engine works had aroused behind the scenes. But the demonstration flight of the He 280 had been really decisive. Four days later I owned the four million mark Hirth engine factory, for which I had to pay six million marks, a fifty per cent rise. After the optimism of 1939 Udet must have come to the realization of how hopeless it was to keep up the strength of the Luftwaffe, even for a short time, without some quick and revolutionary development. I had no conception that Udet's breakdown and ultimate death would be bound up with this decisive step towards the change-over to jets.

How much of this is true? The German Air Ministry's top people certainly saw a demonstration in April, well before Udet's suicide on 17 November 1941, when he telephoned his girlfriend, Inge Bleyle, and said 'I can't stand it any more. I'm going to shoot myself. They're after me.' The girl then heard the shot which killed him. Udet's death was not directly related to jet – or any other – specific development. He became depressed after the outcome of the Battle of Britain and his problems mounted, partly because of the crazed atmosphere of Berlin politics, partly because of failures within his ministry to achieve performance and production targets for conventional aircraft. He was increasingly disregarded and derided and he believed that Milch and Goering were gunning for him. Most authorities agree that Udet made the remark about the British, quoted by Heinkel, some time in 1941 – Udet did not know of the British jet programme – although whether Eisenlohr ever said what Heinkel credits him with saying is open to doubt.

There probably was, however, some softening of attitude towards Heinkel when he was allowed to purchase Hirth. Opposition to this deal first came from Willy Messerschmitt, who lobbied the Air Ministry when he first heard about the deal earlier in the year. Messerschmitt's dislike of Heinkel was well attested. The personal and professional rivalry and jealousy between the two men was sharpened by competition for the desperately scarce commodity of trained manpower. Both were hard at work poaching scientists and engineers wherever they could be found – mostly from the universities – and both were skilled in bilking German labour laws. Heinkel's possession of Hirth, which had been advocated by Schelp since early 1941 (though Heinkel was never gracious enough to acknowledge this help), gave him an unfair advantage in Messerschmitt's view and he managed to block the sale by his machinations in Berlin for some months of 1941. Doubtless, Heinkel's apparently rapid progress with the He 280 persuaded the Air Ministry of the justice of his cause.

But it is not true that Udet and Eisenlohr experienced some

1 *above* Ernst Heinkel (*centre*) with Erich Warsitz (*left*) and Hans von Ohain (*right*).

2 *left* Max Hahn with the model jet engine made in his garage.

3 *top* The Heinkel He
178, the first aircraft
powered by a jet
engine.

4 *above* The Gloster
E28/39, the first
British jet aircraft.

5 *right* Frank
Whittle's first jet
engine.

6 *above* Frank Whittle and test pilot Gerry Sayer after the first jet flight on 15 May 1941.

7 *left* Whittle with his secretary Mary Phillips at Brownsover Hall, near Rugby, Power Jets' wartime planning office.

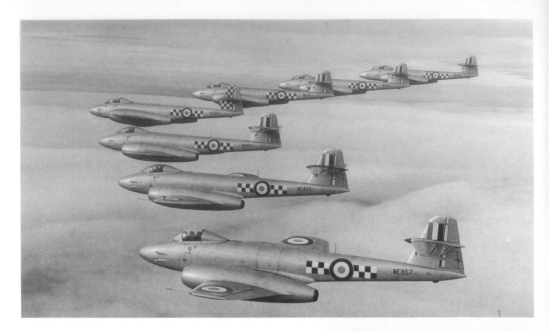

8 *above* Gloster Meteors, the
jet fighter planes fitted with
Whittle's engine and Rolls-
Royce development of it.

9 *below* Frank Whittle,
Harold Roxbee-Cox and Air
Chief Marshal Freeman,
August 1943.

10 *right* Lord Hives,
Chairman and Managing
Director of Rolls-Royce.

11 *left* Willy Messerschmitt with test pilot Fritz Wendel.

12 *below* The Messerschmitt Me 262; Wendel made the first pure jet-powered flight in it on 18 July 1942.

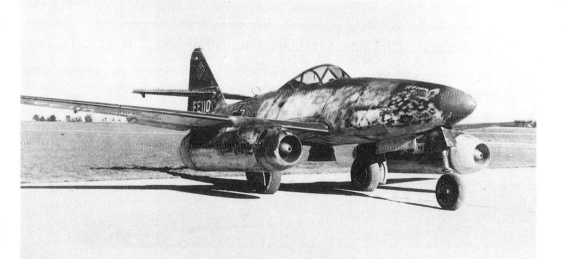

13 *above* The Bell
XP-59A Airacomet,
the first US jet
aircraft, first flown on
2 October 1942.

14 *left* Sanford Moss,
US pioneer of turbo-
superchargers and
head of General
Electric's turbine
research department.

15 *top* The Arado Ar 234, German operational bomber originally powered by Junkers Jumo 004 engines and first flown on 15 June 1943.

16 *above* The Heinkel He 162 Volksjäger – People's Fighter, designed and test-flown within ninety days and rolling off the production line by early 1945.

17 Frank Whittle and Hans von Ohain, meeting in the States in later life, when they became good friends.

18 Sir Frank meeting the Queen on being awarded the Order of Merit, July 1986.

miraculous conversion by the He 280 demonstration. The road to Marienehe or Rechlin was not the road to Damascus. The reliable historians of the Luftwaffe all agree that Udet and Milch, and their boss Goering, utterly failed to see throughout 1940 and 1941 that the aircraft they were providing for the air force were becoming out of date. They had learnt no lessons from the Battle of Britain, and the Battle of Russia still appeared a walkover. The view of the general staff in late 1941 was that the war effort did not need to be increased by production of more, or different, armaments, including aircraft. Standardization on known types kept production figures high, and that kept Hitler contented – or at least at bay. The chiefs were heavily insulated against the younger people – engineers and scientists, but especially the pilots, who knew by now that the machines in which they fought were on the verge of being outclassed. Jet engines, like other great innovations, were subversive of intellect and effort. They threatened the status quo and their development was to be held in check until the times permitted, preferably in peace, around 1943 or 1944.

The rest of Heinkel's story also seems exaggerated. A mock dog fight between a FW 190 and an He 280 did take place but, more probably, at a later date: it would have been a very risky initiative so soon after so cautious a first flight. And Warsitz was not the test pilot. The man who flew the 280 on its demonstration flight was Paul Bader, the Rechlin test pilot who had carried out most of the 280's gliding trials while it was awaiting its engines. Two English authors who interviewed Bader after the war, Richard Smith and Eddie Creek (*Jet Planes of the Third Reich*), tell a more convincing story: just before take-off Bader was handed by Robert Lusser, the architect of the 280, a small hammer. Lusser explained, with apologies, that there was as yet no means of jettisoning the cockpit canopy and should he have to leave in a hurry he might need the hammer to smash his way out. Bader put the hammer on his lap and took off. Test pilots of many nations will hear the ring of truth in this anecdote.

A far likelier version of the mock combat between the He 280 and the FW 190 is given by William Green (*Warplanes of the Third Reich*), who thinks that it took place in the spring of 1942 at Warnemünde. Heinkel believed that the 280 had proved itself and he could not understand why the Air Ministry was so apathetic towards his aeroplane. Green says that the Air Ministry was impressed enough by the demonstration to order thirteen pre-production aircraft. By this time, however, Heinkel's entire jet engine programme was in deep trouble and he was becoming seriously worried about his competitive stance, even though, in acquiring Hirth he had plant and skilled men – and he had overcome Willy Messerschmitt. Besides problems with the jet engines, the 280 airframe was also beset with difficulties. The plane suffered from tail flutter – it tended to oscillate under stress – a well-known characteristic of a new aircraft type which can usually be cured by development work. There had been two other mishaps: in January 1942 a 280 prototype crashed after icing up, the pilot escaped by ejector seat – believed to be the first man in the world to do so; and another prototype was damaged when a turbine blade in one of the engines broke loose.

Much worse for Heinkel, however, were the omens for the two engine types. Von Ohain's 001 was simply not giving enough power because its small diameter intake did not scoop in enough air for its all-important compressor. Mueller and his engineers, who had been transferred to the Hirth factory at Stuttgart, were in serious difficulties because their axial compressor was giving too much air for the turbine to cope with – a critical mismatch of the two. Engineering development is spattered with such paradoxes, but for Heinkel they were to prove fatal in the end. The Hirth works were not made for speedy construction of experimental engines and their esoteric components, so Mueller's engine did not run under its own (very limited) power in bench tests until the spring of 1942. By this time Anselm Franz's 004 was giving all that he had promised the Air Ministry – a thrust on ground test, for example, of nearly 2,000 lb, way ahead of anything Heinkel's teams could offer.

To Helmut Schelp, with his overview of the entire German jet programme, it seemed best for the Air Ministry and Luftwaffe to focus all efforts on the mass production of attack aircraft powered by the 004 and to turn Heinkel's efforts towards a second-generation engine beyond the 004, rather than persevere with designs which, at their best, would give no better performance than the 004. Schelp had already decided in his own mind what that engine should be: it would have an exceptionally complex diagonal centrifugal compressor matched to a further three axial stages. The diagonal mounting was another attempt to get the best of all worlds by using a centrifugal compressor with a reduced frontal area, thereby reducing air resistance (drag) on the aircraft.

When Schelp proposed this radical design to Heinkel, he characteristically jumped at the chance to meet a very stimulating challenge. An agreement was reached for the development of the new engine, designated 011, by 1943–4 (ludicrously optimistic). It was to have a thrust of 2,600 lb to start with and ultimately be capable of delivering

3,500 lb at sea level for a speed of 560 mph – a very formidable performance for such low altitude. Von Ohain was put in charge of the design: since Mueller's move to Stuttgart he had the Rostock facilities at his command. The layout of the 011 was completed by September 1942, and development of the centrifugal 01 was stopped. This engine never developed more than 1,300 lb and was all but obsolete at birth.

Schelp, the egregious young man in a rush, now made a critical mistake. Towards the end of 1942 he instructed Heinkel to drop all work on the Mueller engine, the S30 or 006, and concentrate his efforts on the 011. Mueller had quarrelled with Heinkel in May 1942 and had left the company. However, and this says much for the progress of Heinkel's limited number of engineers, the 006 was at last beginning to show great promise and by the end of 1942 it was giving around 1,900 lb of thrust – about the same as Franz's 004 – but for about half the weight – 857 lb against 1,650 lb. But Schelp flatly refused to believe that Heinkel's very small engine could give this performance on a service aircraft and, now that Udet was dead, he had enough power to see that his, not Heinkel's decision, was final.

This effectively doomed the He 280 fighter. With the loss of both the Heinkel engines intended for it, the prototype had to be fitted with heavier engines, especially the 004. This meant, among other things, shorter range and other performance penalties which gave the Air Ministry good reasons for preferring something else. After many anguished months Heinkel proposed a version of the He 280 fitted with two 004 engines and six 20 mm canon. By now, however, the Messerschmitt Me 262, modified for the 004, was giving better performance promise than the 280, which had been designed for lighter engines and armament. There was the usual confusion of intent within the Air Ministry, as well as the old dislike of Heinkel; at the same time Willy Messerschmitt's star was ascending – and giving great aid and comfort to the anti-Heinkel lobby – always powerful in itself. On 27 March 1943 Ernst Heinkel was ordered to abandon all He 280 development. Permission was given to complete nine prototypes, which were used only as test beds for various engine types – the 004 and also the 003, made by BMW. On the day of the death of the 280, Heinkel suffered another savage cut. He wrote of it later as 'one of the saddest experiences of my life and it was even more tragic as it ended with the complete failure of all my efforts at Zuffenhausen [his Hirth works at Stuttgart].'

Heinkel intended to centre all the jet engine work on Zuffenhausen. To avoid conflict between the two engine teams – Mueller's and von

Ohain's – Heinkel had appointed over them a manager named Dr Harold Wolff, with the rank of technical director, 'new developments'. Whatever his intent, what actually happened was that Wolff complained to Berlin about Heinkel's constant interference (a well-known phenomenon). Field Marshal Milch then sent the following message to Heinkel:

> In order to complete the project [the 011 engine] within the shortest possible time it is indispensable that there should be absolutely clear-cut directional control, and that this should be placed entirely in the hands of someone experienced in this field. In order to achieve this aim and to take the burden off your shoulders I have decided to entrust the whole of the Zuffenhausen factory to Dr Harold Wolff, with immediate effect. He is taking over this task and assuming full responsibility towards the Technical Department (of the Air Ministry). His management will continue until the delivery of the first 100 mass-produced 011s. When this goal has been reached I will inform you of my decisions. MILCH.

The first 100 engines were never built, let alone mass-produced. By the end of the war in 1945 a handful had been built for bench tests; not one flew under its own power. American intelligence engineers who saw plans and the remains of a few 011 engines when they overran the plant in 1945 were astonished by the audacity of the design, which was ahead of anything conceived at that time in the USA. But it was just that audacity, born of Schelp and nurtured by Heinkel, which ensured failure. In the end the two men simply ran out of time.

Yet Heinkel's failure was much more complex than that. How could it be that the man who looked supreme through 1939, 1940 and well into 1941 could become by 1943 the jet pioneer who took the hardest fall of all? The He 178 was a dead end; the He 280 was cancelled; the 001 and 006 engines were cancelled; and the 011, absorbing some of the best minds in German science and engineering, some of the most gifted jet pioneers in the world, had been taken out of Heinkel's hands and was staggering far behind its schedules. Heinkel's magnificent early strides (covering his parallel attempt to design rocket-propelled aircraft) ended in an aeroplane without an engine, a footnote in aviation history rather than the resounding chapter (or more) that it could have been; and this from the intellectual ferment which produced the world's first flyable jet.

That Heinkel was disliked and distrusted in Berlin, and that he showed a cavalier contempt for the powerful men he was upsetting, is well known and well attested. The roots of Milch's antagonism towards him lay in Heinkel's freebooting style, his wealth and independence, and his determination to use them via his friends to get his own way. The end of Udet was a powerful weakening of Heinkel's influence. Milch, though a man of great drive and determination, was a natural conservative for whom office and order were synonymous. Heinkel was an unruly innovator with too little respect for Berlin. As planemaker to the Luftwaffe his place was to sit down and get on with the task of producing thousands of He 111s for the short war, thus satisfying the chronometer-like beat of the production machine which Hitler wanted – save when he, too, went chasing after his special weapons. But Heinkel the innovator refused to behave as Berlin intended. Short or long war, he wanted to push ahead with planes that would make history – his history. Moreover, by 1943 distrust of Heinkel had real substance because, in Milch's view, he had completely failed to deliver the long-range heavy bomber, the Heinkel 177 or so-called Urals bomber, which could strike against distant targets in Britain and Russia with the effectiveness of the RAF and USAF bombers now beginning to cause such havoc in Germany. Although the He 177 was a piston-engined aircraft which should have been well within the German war machine's capability, it had gone badly awry, and this, right in the middle of the war, compounded all Heinkel's other supposed sins.

The He 177 was first ordered, amid much vacillation, for the Luftwaffe by Udet in 1938. The reason for the vacillation was the uncertainty over the Luftwaffe's needs. In 1938 war with Britain was still regarded by the German general staff, and those in the Nazi party who had the ear of Hitler, as very unlikely. The likely enemies at that time, were the Czechoslovaks and the Poles, and they could be dealt with by existing or forthcoming medium bombers. Udet suggested to Heinkel that Projekt 1041, the original He 177 project, should be regarded as an experimental aircraft. However, by mid-1939 war with Britain had become feasible and the British had embarked on their own heavy bomber programme. Heinkel was told to push ahead with the He 177 quickly.

The Heinkel team wanted a heavy bomber with two engines, rather than four, so that the wing surfaces on which they were to be mounted could be kept as clean and uncluttered as possible. The British had opted for four engines on the wings of the Sterling and Halifax types, but Heinkel argued for two engines developing 2,000 hp each. The aero-engine manufacturers, still at the stage of catching up with British engine development, could not, however, provide such engines and, rather than mount four engines of 1,000 hp each, Heinkel opted for two 1,000 hp engines to each wing, but each pair enclosed in one nacelle and coupled to drive one propeller. This did not work and after some spectacular mid-air engine fires Heinkel wanted to cancel the project and fit four separate engines. Udet's office refused this request because, by 1939, they had decided that the He 177 should also be a dive bomber and a four-engine dive bomber was ruled out because of the wing stresses and other problems which would arise. When Heinkel retorted that an aircraft of the He 177's size and weight could not, in any event, possibly be a dive bomber, Udet told him that it was essentially a twin-engined machine, that other twin-engined machines such as the (much lighter and smaller) Junkers Ju 88 could dive-bomb, so the He 177 had to be made to dive-bomb too. Heinkel was obliged to keep the coupled engines and strengthen the wings to withstand dive-bombing stresses. The result of this Alice-type piece of Udet's procurement policy was that some prototypes burst into flames or broke up in the air, killing many brave and able young men. By late 1942 only thirty-three He 177s had been accepted by the Luftwaffe, and only two were operational. The original production target called for 8,000 by 1943!

Udet was by now dead but Milch had his hands on a report from Rechlin showing that the strength of the He 177's wings was one-third below that estimated by Heinkel, who was now accused of neglecting the heavy bomber in order to concentrate production on the more profitable He 111, which by now had become the Luftwaffe's maid-of-all-work in its class – rather like the British Wellington. The hapless Heinkel, who had undoubtedly skimped work on the 177, had to listen to Milch declaring 'one can only weep'. Goering lamented:

> I do not have one single long-range bomber ... It is really the saddest chapter. I look at those four-engined bombers of the British and the Americans with truly enormous envy; they are far ahead of us here. I have never been so furious as when I saw this [coupled] 177 engine ... I believe I am right in saying that you cannot even take out all the sparking plugs without pulling the whole engine apart.

This was unctuous claptrap, but it must have been the more hard for Heinkel to bear as self-acknowledged innovator supreme, because he was being loaded with the blame for policies for which Goering and Milch, as well as Udet, were responsible. They had taken the crucial decisions lamely and with cavalier ignorance, four years previously. However, Heinkel was forced to admit that his technical office had not carried out sufficient fundamental work to make the modifications needed. Milch naturally now had to take production of the 177 out of Heinkel's hands. Instead of cancelling the project (which he ought to have done, but which would have left Germany without a heavy bomber at all and he, Milch, part of the collective guilt which would be revealed to Hitler's eyes), he gave the impossible job to Heinrich Hertel. Hertel had been Heinkel's (very able) technical director, who had been in overall charge of the He 178 venture. To him the He 177 project must have seemed a poisoned chalice. He had been technical director when the 177 project was agreed; he knew all the problems. He had left the company but now was forced to return to work on an aircraft in which he could not possibly place any faith. The He 177 had cost many lives – more, said the Luftwaffe sceptics, of their own comrades than the enemy. In 1944 the project was allowed to run quietly into the sands of defeat when the Luftwaffe generals had to acknowledge what their operational commanders had been telling them for some time: the aerial war was being lost for want of the best equipment.

Given the failure of the He 177 project and the damaging revelations to the High Command of Heinkel's own part in that failure, it became inevitable that Milch should also take jet development out of the hands of so thoroughly tiresome and unreliable a tycoon. The appointments of Wolff and Hertel came close together. Heinkel was discredited, and could be forgiven the feeling that his freedom, his life even, might be at risk. He was sent to the shades – until the final thunderclap of the war, when the Air Ministry again needed innovators and turned back to him in the hope of finding a saviour, too late.

Of course, Heinkel could be held to have failed in other respects. The principal reason for the failure to get flyable production jet engines from the 001 and 006 projects was the lack of qualified engineers and scientists available to him: he spread the brains too thin. He may well have had, in 1939, sufficient intellectual power among his staff to pursue two different research concepts, the centrifugal and the axial compressor jet engines, but he did not have the engineers and technical facilities needed to develop prototypes into convincing flight engines. A long chain of development separates an idea which may work on a bench in a shed from a product which can be produced in identical thousands to work in the skies, on earth, at sea or underwater – wherever the machine is designed to work. Anselm Franz knew this when he created the 004: Schelp may have thought it too conservative but Franz knew that this revolutionary concept had to be both revolutionary and conservative, so that it could be mass-produced to work at the limits then known from ground level to 40,000 feet. Few of the problems could be known exactly: they all had to be foreseen and designed in thermodynamic and material terms. Part of such an achievement must be inspiration, part experiment, part experience. Anselm Franz at Junkers had the ability to span the unknowns and he was cautious enough not to ask too much of his team – which was in any case always larger and better balanced than Heinkel's.

At Heinkel von Ohain was undoubtedly brilliant – Schelp told his American interrogators at the end of the war that he considered him to be among the best scientists in Germany – but he was inexperienced. Mueller had experience but he left Heinkel after a row just at the moment when the 006 was showing promise, just the moment when he was most needed to stay on and persevere, but perhaps it simply was not in Heinkel's nature to recognize and to keep the people who could have saved his reputation as well as his projects. Schelp, too, should have kept the 006 project in being rather than talking Heinkel out of it, but he was young and anxious to make big leaps.

German engineers who knew of Heinkel's work, who saw it in progress during the war, agree that it was well tuned to research projects but under-equipped and under-experienced for engine development and production. Around 150 engineers, designers and draughtsmen worked on the 011, in its time the most advanced design in the world. But Anselm Franz in the end managed to collect around him 500 such people to carry through the 004. Heinkel absurdly overstretched his resources in trying to develop two engines; even one would have taxed him. He should have had the wit and wisdom to see from his recent experience that in the 011 he was biting off more than his team could possibly chew. But that was not Heinkel's way; although capable of brilliance and the maker of some extremely handsome high-performance aeroplanes, he lacked the caution which warns against overweening ambitions, the prudence of the man determined to make something which would work, lacked von Ohain's guardian angel, perhaps. The gambler, the visionary, overcame the manufacturer too easily. Finally, it was one thing to be a noisy nuisance to the people in Berlin while there was a Udet to forgive and smooth the ruffled feathers. But once Udet was dead Heinkel's enemies were waiting for the mistakes which he readily obliged them by making: and then they cut him down.

Whittle's diary for 15 May 1941 reads: 'Evening – first flight of the E28.' Nothing more is said. The handwriting is that of his secretary, Mary Phillips. For Whittle it was the peak of thirteen years' struggle from 1928 when he first seriously proposed the idea – eleven years from the patents which make him beyond contest *the* jet pioneer, the man who designed an engine whose blazing jet alone would drive an aeroplane through the air.

The Gloster E28/39 (which ranks with Watt's steam engines, Stephenson's 'Rocket', Brunel's 'Britannia' and Parson's 'Turbinia') hangs today in the London Science Museum. Nearby is the W (for Whittle) 1, the first jet flight engine to be fitted to a British aircraft. Both commemorate the triumph of a timely idea – but something more: the human virtues of courage, steadfastness and endurance. Whittle is great not only because he was right, but because he never gave up. Samuel Smiles would have loved him, though Whittle's politics at the time were socialist and he would cheerfully have seen the nationalization of the whole of the British aero-engine industry.

The road to the slender, graceful E28 had been amazingly smooth, and shot with plenty of shafts of humour, to lighten the atrabilious rows that were going on between Whittle, his partners and BT-H, Rover and the Ministry of Aircraft Production, led by Churchill's henchman, the Canadian newspaper tycoon Lord Beaverbrook. The aircraft was to be purely for experiment and development. When he heard that its first flight was successful, Churchill immediately demanded 1,000 as soon as possible, not knowing that there would never be more than two and they would be kept as far away from combat as possible.

The job of an experimental aircraft is to tell engineers and scientists what to do (or not to do) next, and at this, the two E28/39s were outstanding. (E stands for Experimental, 28 is the Air Ministry specification number and 39 is the year it was issued). George Carter designed and Gloster made at their factory at Gloucester an outstanding little aeroplane without fuss or significant trouble. Whittle had designed the W1 engine and Power Jets subcontracted the construction work to BT-H. From spares for the W1 flight engine, a test bench engine, the W1X, was also built and run at Lutterworth. This was not officially approved but it was extremely useful because experience in testing it suggested modifications to the W1 which were incorporated before it flew.

The W1X was used for taxiing trials on Gloster's grass airfield at Hucclecote, just outside the city. It was installed by Bob Feilden, now Dr Feilden (FRS and much else besides), who was to become one of the most distinguished engineering designers of his day, but who was then twenty-four and had done less than a year's work for Power Jets. Feilden was a Cambridge graduate with a first class honours degree – just as Whittle was – who had taken a job with the Unilever soap company and worked on research at the model factory at Port Sunlight, on the Wirral, where the philanthropic Lord Leverhulme had built a model village for his workers. Feilden wanted to get into war work and he filled in a standard Ministry of Labour form on which he stated he had done work for Brown Boveri on boilers. This was spotted by a retired director of the National Physical Laboratory, Carl Hall, who was combing the country for highly qualified engineers with talent. Feilden was told to report to Power Jets for an interview with Lance Whyte at the intensely secret Lutterworth works. No reason was given, just an official Ministry of Labour green card.

When Feilden presented himself, he recalled many years later:

Lance Whyte said, 'D'you know what we do here?' I thought it was probably something to do with carburettor jets, but I took a stab and said, 'Is it anything to do with aircraft gas turbines?' Whyte immediately blenched, got out a form and made me sign the Official Secrets Act there and then. What he did not know at the time was that while I was at Cambridge I had done an industrial 'sandwich' course in industry at BT-H in 1936 and I'd heard a whisper about Whittle's work while I was there.

Anyway, Power Jets signed me up for £3 per week and I went to live with three other young bachelors – there was no time to be anything else – and we were very well looked after by a retired nurse who was our landlady and who put up with all our irregular hours marvellously. I was there with one of my old Cambridge contemporaries, Geoffrey Bone.

PJ was a pretty ramshackle affair. The building was filthy and the jet engine – everyone referred to it most secretively as 'the unit' – was mounted on a rubber-tyred trolley with the big spring balance to measure the thrust. In October we were all given one week's holiday while they tried to clean out all the foundry sand in the place. If we got fifteen minutes' running per test with the unit we thought we were lucky – eventually we got up to an hour and that was considered incredible.

By early 1941 Feilden had shown that he was prepared to grapple with real problems when they arose – he was a 'hands on' man who preferred practical work to theory. He worked on combustion, which called for greater intensities than had ever been achieved before.

When we decided to instal the W1X for taxiing, Whittle came to Bone and me, and a third engineer called van Milligan. He had some straws and he held them behind his back in a corner of the workshop. I was lucky enough to pick the one to instal the taxiing engine, while Geoffrey Bone got the one to instal the flight engine.

We took our engine very secretly on a truck from Lutterworth to Gloucester at the height of the war. I remember that for the first time I had sleepless nights over my work, waking up in a cold sweat wondering if we had put the split pin in the centre of the turbine shaft. Of course we had – but this indicates the pressure we all felt to do the best possible job.

One evening in April, fairly late, we had finished everything and the aircraft was taken on to the grass airfield and the engine was run up with the test pilot, Gerry Sayer, at the controls. It started very nicely and we got up to 13,500 revs per minute, at which we hoped the aircraft would roll quite nicely and we could do a little taxiing around the airfield and see that all was well.

It barely moved at all on the wet grass in early April. We went away disconsolate. However, the following day we ran the engine up to a rather higher speed and the aircraft luckily moved. Finally we got up to 16,500 rpm and the aircraft did a short hop off the ground as well as the taxi. That was one of the most marvellous moments of my life. I was standing beside the number two test pilot, Michael Daunt. He just said, 'Thank God it flew straight.' I said 'Why ever shouldn't it? – Newton's Laws and all that.' But he said, 'No, we have all been scared stiff by this jet engine because we've seen compressed air jets in the workshop squabbing about all over the place and thoroughly unstable. We thought this aircraft was going to do the same thing.'

Whittle also watched the hop:

Gerry Sayer looked disappointed on the first run-up. We were not worried because we knew how rapidly the thrust increased at the upper end of the engine speed range. The next morning I made a few taxiing runs in which I reached a maximum speed of about 60 mph. The complete absence of vibration, the big reductions in noise compared with conventional aircraft, the excellent view from the cockpit and the simplicity of the controls added up to an impressive combination.

After lunch we increased the engine speed limit. Sayer taxied off to the downwind edge of the airfield. This made me suspect that he intended to do more than merely trundle over the grass, though we had warned him that the engine was thoroughly unairworthy. It had never been intended for flight in the first place and it had had a number of misadventures on the test bench. Sayer turned into wind, released the brakes and rapidly gained speed. We saw his elevators go up in an effort to get the tail down. He was a little too successful in this because the tail blister struck the ground and the aircraft pitched forward on its nosewheel. A second or two later it left the ground and after being airborne for about 200 yards landed . . . Sayer's only criticism was that the aeroplane was a bit reluctant to get its tail down during take-off but he seemed confident that he would have no difficulty in making a controlled flight.

Early in May, the E28 was partly dismantled and driven under wraps by road to RAF Cranwell. The W1 had been thoroughly ground-tested and a maximum flight speed of 16,500 rpm was set, giving a thrust of 860 lb. Cranwell was chosen because of its isolation in Lincolnshire, its concrete runways and clear approaches. It was also the place where cadet Whittle had written the thesis which eventually brought him to this moment. Geoffrey Bone, installing the flight engine, recalls that he shared a room at Cranwell with a Flight Lieutenant Brown of the Fleet Air Arm, who was extremely curious about the hangar in which the E28 was having its engine installed. It was out of bounds and cordoned off for many hundreds of yards, and Brown took to flying his Grumman Martlet fighter straight at the hangar doors to see how close a look he could get before pulling his aircraft up and over the building. He never cracked the secret.

The Power Jets' team had to keep their mouths resolutely shut, in the officers' mess as well as everywhere else, and the stories that spread about the plane gave them endless amusement. After the first flight one officer announced, 'It's easy old boy – just sucks itself along like a giant Hoover.' Another officer – and this rumour was naturally the strongest – said that the E28 had a Merlin engine in its bowels which drove a small four-blade propeller buried in the fuselage. A pilot officer who saw the plane in the air could not think afterwards what was strange about it. Suddenly he realized and blurted out to his drinking party, 'My God, chaps, I must be going round the bend – it hadn't got a propeller!' The pubs in Newark resounded to stories of the plane that climbed vertically, belching flames and black smoke. The E28 did neither but it was an eloquent tribute to the new sound in the sky and the surge of power which even its tiny engine gave. Most endearing, though, was the comment by labourer Jack Smedley, quoted previously: '. . . we were used to seeing aeroplanes with propellers. It just turned into wind and runned along the ground just like a partridge . . .'

On 15 May Whittle was in his office at Lutterworth. The weather looked unfit for test flying but the day later brightened up and he drove back to Cranwell to find patches of blue sky and a higher cloud base in the early evening. Sayer rolled the aircraft at 7.40 pm and the E28 lifted off 600 yards down the runway, climbing into cloud and going into a long circuit before a confident and perfect landing. He flew for seventeen minutes and as he taxied the E28 to the small group of spectators, he gave the thumbs-up sign. The flight had been near-perfect except for Sayer having to use a hand pump to lower and lock the nosewheel. His first flight report, on a standard form, included the item, airscrew type and number, against which he wrote: 'No airscrew fitted with this method of propulsion.' The Air Ministry and Ministry of Aircraft Production had both declined to send a film crew to record the occasion.

Accounts of the flight suggest it was almost anticlimactic. There was some tension, but nobody admitted it. Whittle professed to anxiety about the pilot and airframe, and no doubt Carter worried about the engine. What built up in the days to come was a tidal wave of conviction that engine and airframe were greater than anyone had realized. Performance was better than predicted and the E28 went through trials faster than anyone had dared to hope. By 21 May a demonstration flight was given to Sir Archibald Sinclair, Air Minister, his senior officials and representatives from BT-H and Rover, together with other plane and engine-makers, among them Sir Geoffrey de Havilland and T. O. M. Sopwith of Hawker Siddeley. The E28 swept over their heads at 350 mph, went through some glorious climbing turns and left the spectators spellbound, except for Sir John Buchanan, a civil servant from the Ministry of Aircraft Production who said that it was too good to be true: 'There is bound to be trouble ahead.'

So there was. But for the moment there was time to wonder at the power, speed and beauty Whittle and Carter had created. By the end of May the first set of trials was complete. The engine ran for ten hours without need to take its covers off – an extraordinary achievement – and the plane made seventeen trouble-free flights. Total running time for the engine, including ground tests, was thirty-nine hours and fifty-seven minutes. When stripped, it was in perfect condition. The W1 weighed 623 lb for its 860 lb thrust (which approximates to something near 1,000 hp) and it constituted an immediate challenge to the most advanced piston engines. It promised high standards of reliability, simplicity and less time between overhauls, and it used cheaper grade fuel. Nobody could foresee how far it could be developed, but it was obvious that a new chapter in engines was being opened and the possibilities were incalculable. In wartime Britain no one could know that the W1 was superior to any German challenger available at that moment, although the enemy would pull ahead later. The W1 also served notice to the entire piston-engine community. It was a notice that quickly reached the eyes of the manufacturers, who were beginning to think of their stake in the future – for the conviction was growing that there would be a future, a peace in which Germany had been defeated and Britain had the whole sky to herself, with no limits.

This could not turn out to Whittle's advantage. Almost inevitably, every step which he took from now on would in some way weaken his position. Power Jets were denied the means of making engines and had to ally themselves totally with a good manufacturer. They failed to do so. Because of the war, the secrets of jet engine design and development would have to be shared freely with other British manufacturers. Very soon they would have to be shared with the USA – an enormously risky step from Power Jets' point of view. Every milestone on the road to exploitation would prove a headstone for the company. As the manufacturers grew in knowledge and experience once they had the secrets of the jet and worked on engines of their own, so Whittle and Power Jets' independence lessened. Whittle had his patents, but they were not invulnerable – even apart from the Crown's rights as free user. A clever manufacturer could challenge, weaken and negate them by his own design and development work, which he could in turn patent himself.

Whittle's job was to be patriotic and share his knowledge with others in Britain's struggle. The others could take the knowledge for nothing, with the certainty that they would profit after the war.

Nearly fifty years on, the recollections of the original Power Jets' team nearly all include stories of some aero-engine maker saying that Whittle must of course disgorge – and quickly. As one said: 'I clearly remember hearing in a manufacturer's lavatory one director saying to another after lunch, "Whittle's difficult. We must cut him down to size and then cut him out."' To this day, Whittle's disciples, a tenacious band, believe that he was never rewarded sufficiently, whatever his prickly shortcomings. 'They gave him a knighthood and quite a lot of money,' Lord Kings Norton commented. 'But I'm not sure that it was enough. I feel he should have had more, and if I thought I could get him more I would – say, an OM. There was a lot of dirty work.' (A few weeks after this comment, in January 1986, the Queen appointed Whittle to the Order of Merit, the special distinction for eminent men and women which is limited to twenty-four and included at that time figures such as Henry Moore, Dorothy Hodgkin, Lords Zuckerman and Penney, the Earl of Stockton and Sir Peter Medawar.)

Lord Kings Norton stepped on to the jet engine stage early in 1940 as Dr Harold Roxbee Cox (later Sir, and later still, awarded a peerage, he took the title of Lord Kings Norton). He was a gifted engineer who had done original work to overcome the problem of flutter in aircraft structures. A small, sometimes self-important, bustling man, he had come to the civil service from RAE Farnborough. Before that he had helped design the R101, Britain's ill-fated state-built airship; his life had been saved by the fact that there was no room for him on the flight to India which ended in the airship's fatal crash in northern France in 1930. He regards himself to this day as 'Whittle's entrepreneur'. Certainly he was his champion throughout the war and says of those days that 'Britain very nearly threw the whole thing away'. He became embroiled in the conflict when he was appointed Deputy Director of Research and Development at the Ministry of Aircraft Production and given special responsibility for the entire jet engine field. Like others on the scene, he does not overlook the fact that Whittle often behaved like a prima donna, and that Rover, with some able engineers, were not always wrong. It was to him that both sides expressed their grievances – when they were not going behind everyone's back to express them to more senior people.

Within the civil service, as the engineering success of Power Jets progressed, the anomalies of the situation became more and more pressing. How could the state finance a serving RAF officer and his private company in an apparently privileged position, yet avoid the aero-engine manufacturers' charges that Whitehall was using public money to subsidise a competitor – an upstart who had simply had a good idea and was now being bolstered up by the taxpayer without the taxpayers' knowledge? In 1942 one senior civil servant wrote to the Director of Scientific Research at the Ministry of Aircraft Production:

As I pointed out over a year ago, Power Jets, long since subsidised 100 per cent by the department, is for practical purposes as much an MAP establishment as the RAE, and yet retains the advantages of control by its own Board of Directors ... I have not the slightest doubt that at some future date, if not during, certainly after, the war some sort of enquiry will be instituted into this firm's operations and we permanent officials will be called to give evidence, probably under conditions when the emergencies of the time when actions were or were not taken, will either have been forgotten or appear different in perspective.

Again in 1942, Major George Bulman (retired service ranks were still prized and used), a senior civil servant in charge of engine development and production, wrote:

I deprecate at this stage any encouragement to Power Jets to plan any extension of the facilities already given to them at public expense, which are very generous [sic] in proportion to their practical experience and the standing of their organization ... Power Jets is subsidised 100 per cent by the state ... and I have felt for a long time some uneasiness as regards the responsibilities being incurred ... this is an appropriate time for a discussion of the whole situation ...

As far back as April 1940 a minute from Tedder about problems with BT-H and Rover runs: '... This raises the second difficulty, which is how to keep Power Jets alive. We do not want to exclude Power Jets – or give them a *most undesirable* control. It is essential that the organization which is ultimately going to produce should have control.' [author's italics]

That was something nobody appeared willing or ready finally to settle. The issues rolled back and forth during the years between 1940 and 1944. The ways in which they were handled were frequently incompetent and often barely savoury. The detailed negotiations took months and years, filling quantities of files in the Public Record Office and involving dense technical arguments in the fight to develop a British jet engine. The struggles of the time (which was desperate: in 1940 the government considered evacuating Power Jets to Canada) make disagreeable reading today. In the air thousands of young men were dying; on the ground, a handful of rich manufacturers fought about the rights and profits which might come from the jet after the war. The engine manufacturers hungered for their share of a new product which none had had the wit to invent, yet by which all were determined to gain somehow; and if that meant cutting Whittle's throat, so be it. The engine itself languished for long periods during this struggle. Doubtless the manufacturers could argue that they were defending the legitimate peacetime interests of themselves and their shareholders, but that is not how it looks half a century on.

With hindsight, Whittle would have done better to have gone straight to Rolls-Royce with his invention, which was the eventual solution. They were the best engine-makers in Britain – and believed themselves to be the best in the world. He did not do so because the company was filled with war work – the brilliant Merlin engine, for example – and because Rolls was a manufacturer of the type he thought safer to avoid in his own interests. Also, he hankered in his heart to become a manufacturer himself. Whittle's engine was, after all, his child, and what engineer would lightly pass up the chance of seeing the cowling of a great and revolutionary engine stamped WHITTLE, as RR is stamped on so many cowlings flying on jet engines around the world today?

In 1940, however, Whittle, the Air Ministry and later the Ministry of Aircraft Production expected BT-H and Rover to be their manufacturers. BT-H were to drop out after a while, a traditional company which suffered from terrestrial vision. Rover were a terrestrial company too, but in the Wilks brothers they had at the top two excellent engineers who wanted to become airborne. Such were the origins of the battle which soon began to rumble. Rover would have to develop the engine as well as make it. This was a difficult job for which, as car manufacturers, they were not fitted, so the Air Ministry and MAP agreed that development should be jointly undertaken by Power Jets and Rover. Power Jets were to deal with the science: the aerodynamic and thermodynamic work; Rover were to be responsible for structural and mechanical work for a production engine. Whittle was to advise and comment on all design changes they might wish or need to make. Collaboration with Power Jets and its chief engineer was essential, and so were conventional good relations. But Rover believed that they could follow any promising line without necessarily referring to Power Jets – or even, at times, the Ministry. Two years, 1941–2, were virtually frittered away while all sides argued about their interpretations of these responsibilities.

Early in 1940 a policy document drawn up by the Air Ministry had spelt out the relationships, though in misty terms. Rover and BT-H were to be given an order for development of prototype engines and were to start preparations for the production of 125 units: each was to carry out development testing. Power Jets were to be employed by the Air Ministry to act as consultants to the prospective manufacturers and were to give full design information to them while continuing to do research. 'The closest collaboration between Power Jets as advisers and consultants, and BT-H and Rover is essential to the success of the scheme.'

To speed up production Whittle was asked to pass drawings over to Rover, but Power Jets demurred over this until more terms, especially regarding the patent position, had been agreed, and the company submitted a counter proposal for technical collaboration with the other two companies. This stated that Power Jets would be responsible for all design, research and experimental work, and the manufacturers were to inform Power Jets of any experimental results, improvements, manufacturing processes etc., immediately such matters arose. Power Jets also sought an undertaking that the contractors should devote the whole of their work to Whittle engines and none to any other gas turbine save with the consent of the Air Ministry, with Power Jets having the right to state their views on any such consent. Power Jets took the line that if technical cooperation were to be complete, they should be informed of improvements so that duplication would be avoided, while at the same time Whittle's company should be protected against any 'misuse of the circumstances'.

When Tedder telephoned Lance Whyte about this proposal on 18 April 1940, he had the conversation recorded. Part of it went:

Mr Whyte, when I saw you here I thought I made it clear that as regards our relationship with you, although we had free rights over Whittle's designs and inventions and could enforce them, at the same time we recognize fully that we are under a moral obligation – a moral obligation, I repeat – to Power Jets and I assured you in the presence of Mr Pickles, representing the Directorate of Contracts, that we would see that our obligation was adhered to. What more could you want?

These words, ceaselessly quoted by one side or the other, crackle with increasing acrimony through the correspondence and records of meetings for the next three years. Rover saw Whittle's powers as too limiting on them and they flatly refused to enter into any agreement which might bind them after the war. Power Jets, on the other hand, had to give Rover their patent secrets in their engineering drawings and naturally saw Rover's refusal to be bound as commercial robbery with an all too clear intent. The government officials in the middle all too often prevaricated: they inclined towards Power Jets when Rover was the complainant or towards Rover when Whittle and Power Jets were complaining. This was not the exercise of impartiality so much as weakness. Their internal minutes frequently betray a sense of irritation with Power Jets' and Whittle's ambiguous independence, and an acquiesence in Rover's right to go its own way. This was particularly true among officials in charge of engine development. The research and development men were more in sympathy with Power Jets' outlook. Nor were men of the stature of Tedder, admittedly in the press of war with all its terrifying responsibilities, at all definitive. They often seemed to prevaricate when Whittle asked them to make clear choices. To him this looked like pandering to traditional manufacturers – in this case companies which were not even in the aero-engine business. Doubtless Whittle's independence and his anomalous position as a serving officer able to guide the fortunes of a private company proved irksome. Proposals were frequently made to cut Power Jets out of the whole process (some as early as 1940) while returning Whittle to active service. But time and again Whittle was seen – generally by the most senior officials – to be indispensable, and nobody felt able to disband Power Jets, or to nationalize it.

As relations grew more and more strained through 1940, the issue of post-war rights became even more apparent, even though the national plight was desperate. S. B. Wilks wrote to the Air Ministry contracts department (undated but apparently midsummer): 'If you are going to ask me to accept any restrictions as the result of my taking on this work which would put me in a worse position commercially than I should be if I had nothing to do with it, then I obviously cannot accept the work, and as we are a controlled factory you must use your powers and instruct us to do the job, and leave the matter to be cleared up afterwards.'

The Air Ministry did not want to go that far but they did want to find for Power Jets the sort of pigeon-hole they could understand. At one point they suggested that the company should be taken over by BT-H and a chief engineer of experience and initiative installed, either alongside Whittle or, if necessary, without him. Rover incessantly pointed out that if they accepted restrictive contracts they would find themselves hampered after the war, whereas a company which had not signed a contract had only to buy an engine, strip it and make and sell others like it, since Power Jets' patents would by then have expired.

The source of much discontent was a meeting Sir Henry Tizard called at the BT-H works on 2 January 1941, which was attended by representatives of Rover, BT-H, Power Jets and Vauxhall, another motor manufacturer. The official minute says the reason for this meeting was 'to determine the necessary steps to be taken in order to ensure that the production of an engine giving a thrust at sea level of not less than 1,600 lb should commence in this country as soon as possible at a rate which should increase, say, to 2,000 engines a year in not more than eighteen months'. It was decided that Rover should be given the contract for the production engines but Whittle says that no decision was taken on which engine was to be produced (there were designs for two). Later that month it was agreed that the engine should be based on Power Jets' designs, which could be modified only to ease production, and with Power Jets' approval. Vauxhall dropped out of the running at this point and so, apparently, did BT-H a little later. Whittle was very clear about which design was to be manufactured. In February he received assurances about Rover's status from the Ministry's director of engine development and production, Major Bulman (one of the men who were so worried about Power Jets' anomalous position). Mr Wilks of Rover was to be the authority for all sub-contracts and allocations of materials, and Bulman concluded: 'I take the opportunity of again confirming to you my verbal assurance that we are all combining and concentrating on the objective of bringing your child into effective RAF manhood at the earliest possible moment.'

Whittle maintains that Wilks put a much wider construction on his brief and he worried that Power Jets appeared to be at the mercy of Rover for their supplies. In any case, the seeds of trouble had been sown much earlier. Roxbee Cox and his colleagues were already having to deal with the problem of Rover using Power Jets' drawings with the company's name deleted from them. To Rover this was an incidental: the names of Power Jets' draughtsmen were still there. Rover's endorsement read: 'This drawing is the property of the

Rover company and is loaned on condition that it is not reproduced, copied or otherwise made use of in any form except directly for the exclusive benefit of the Rover company.' Asked for an opinion on this dispute, the Treasury solicitor wrote: 'The action of the Rover company in substituting their own name for that of Power Jets strikes me as questionable but I do not know of any grounds on which the department could challenge it.' The judgement, too, seems questionable. To Whittle and Power Jets it seemed to fit in with the conspiracy theory.

In this atmosphere the job of people like Roxbee Cox became one of assuaging feelings as much as getting on with the jet. And the jet *did* get on, as far as Power Jets were able to push ahead. In July 1940 a momentous leap had solved the problems of combustion of the air-fuel mixture which provided the propelling jet. Materials which could withstand the great temperatures produced by burning the mixture hotter and hotter were not the only problems to be solved. Good results on the test rigs could not be repeated in the combustors installed in experimental engines. Was this because pressure conditions were different – in test rigs the air supply was only slightly above atmospheric?

Combustion tests were tried out at Dartford using a very large compressor intended for the construction of the tunnel under the Thames (held up because of the war). Power Jets' men had to travel from Lutterworth to Dartford with combustors, which were attached to the compressor in great secrecy on the building site. The rig showed that pressure was not the problem and the difficulties seemed intractable until Isaac Lubbock of Shell, hearing something of the trouble, suggested that they try a combustor with which his engineers were experimenting. The fuel in it was injected in a fine mist of droplets through a controllable atomizing burner. The combustor was brought to Lutterworth by car overnight and, because of the much finer control possible, it worked. Within a week Power Jets advised the Ministry that this was the basis of future combustors for the jet engine. It was a small-sounding development but one which marked the defeat of one of the most difficult obstacles in the way of a successful engine.

The W2 engine was designed and Rover set to work on it, only to find that Power Jets were not satisfied with it and were redesigning it as the W2B, scheduled as the engine for the Gloster Meteor fighter and designed to give 1,600 lb thrust. Rover accepted Power Jets' drawings with the proviso that they could make minor alterations. This resulted in further arguments, into which Tedder and Tizard were drawn, about who was responsible for which elements in the design. But conflicts were blurred rather than resolved.

Nor did feelings within the Ministry of Aircraft Production towards Power Jets mellow. On 10 May 1941 an unnamed official minuted an opinion that his Ministry should increase its shareholding in Power Jets

> to secure present control and to assure ourselves of an adequate share of the fruits (if any) of any later commercial exploitation. The company has shown itself hostile to such an increase and is negotiating with a third party for additional finance. I understand we have taken steps to see that no outside finance is provided ... We shall also be in the happy position of controlling the entire board ... We shall probably encounter strenuous opposition to our attempt to increase our shareholding. In that case our 'big stick' is the threat to withhold funds and withdraw Wing Commander Whittle.

The attitude that Whittle was Royal Air Force property and could be returned to active service at any time is at least understandable but the assumption that he could be replaced by any competent chief engineer is extraordinary. As the pros and cons were weighed in Whitehall, the key factor of Whittle's genius was ignored. Throughout 1941 the civil servants kept on wrangling about Power Jets. A suggestion was made that Whittle should be transferred to Farnborough or to Rover and instructed to work with their teams while the assets of Power Jets were seized. None of these proposals materialized. For Rover, the Wilks brothers complained throughout the year that they had not had a contract for the job; the Ministry retorted that it was because of the complex legal problems which their complaints, among many, had caused. Rover were to build the engine in two factories at Clitheroe and Barnoldswick, converted mills high in the Lancashire uplands, but by the end of 1941 remarkably little had been achieved and men, women and raw materials waited while the warring factions went their ways. The W2 engine was completed, but it was the failure Whittle had predicted – and one for which he took personal responsibility.

A fundamental problem of this engine was 'surging', which plagued all the jet pioneers and plagues their successors to this day in certain circumstances. In an engine surge, the flow of air through the engine falls, accidentally, below a minimum critical level needed to turn the engine. Violent pulsations throb in the compressors and turbines, and the airflow pauses for a second, completely reverses its flow and surges out of the front in a violent cough, an explosive sound, before naturally stabilizing. This is frightening to see and hear, and in ground-based turbines it can blow out the walls of test plant. In the air it can be caused by an aircraft side-slipping, shearing off the volume of air reaching the intakes. In 1941 surging was a potentially dangerous new phenomenon which Power Jets had to solve – in the case of the W2 it was caused by design faults. All the same, optimism abounded after the first flight and the Ministry hopefully set production targets of 1,200 engines and 500 aircraft to be ready by the spring of 1943, a touching faith since they were literally ordering them off the drawing board, with little or no time for the massive ground and air testing programme of prototypes and development engines, let alone the final production model. Whittle himself thought the target was unlikely to be reached. Design changes were bound to be needed as experience accumulated and these would surely entail production delays – as the knight from the Ministry had warned.

The flight of the E28/39 came and went without the Ministry switching allegiance from Rover, as Whittle had come to hope they would. There were also troubles at Power Jets. Whittle was undoubtedly difficult to work with in this period. Lance Whyte, who had been a faithful pioneer, resigned and Tinling became chairman. In practice these men had to be subservient to Whittle's genius: without him there was no company; it was dominated by him and its structure was probably inimical to the huge problems of mass production. Power Jets' staff were undoubtedly gifted design and experimental engineers, just as Heinkel's team were at Marienehe, but they were not experienced in the team work and the long haul of the type which Anselm Franz was engaged in at Junkers. 'We were probably all prima donnas,' as Feilden remarked many years later. Production would require different minds, different temperaments.

Despite the early promise of the jet, there was also dithering at the highest level during this period. At one stage even Sir Henry Tizard began to feel that jet flight was for the post-war world, but he changed his mind and told Whittle he was delighted with the progress on combustion problems. When he learnt of the successful first flight, he stretched out a piece of paper on his desk in his wartime offices in Thames House, on the London Embankment, and began to rough out the future of the jet engine, to the delight of his assistants. However, he was still cautious. In mid-May he wrote to Professor Lindemann, Churchill's scientific adviser:

The aircraft with the experimental engine has done some very satisfactory flights . . . At the same time we have a long way to go yet . . . We have not yet had anything like a type test, even of an experimental engine approximating in size and power to the project engine for which the aircraft has been designed. So we must not be too optimistic. I am sure the outstanding problems can be solved – the great thing is to solve them in time . . .

Lindemann apparently shared this view (although the two men personally hated one another) and passed the advice on to Churchill, who had no stomach for this sort of temporizing. On 13 July one of his famous war minutes landed on the desk of the Minister of Aircraft Production, Lord Brabazon, headed 'Action this day:

Will you convene this week a meeting of the necessary authorities, including the S of S [Secretary of State] and C A S [Chief of Air Staff] and Lord Cherwell [as Lindemann had just become] and report to me whether in the circumstances we ought not to proceed forthwith in the production of the Whittle aircraft without waiting for a pilot model of Mark 11. If this latter course is adopted we shall be delayed till January or February, and very high-level German bombers may well appear over the British Isles in the interval. I am assured that the production of say 1,000 W H I T T L E S would not cut in upon existing types of aircraft to any serious extent.

Five days later Tizard, Cherwell and Brabazon were among those who met at the Ministry. The whole question was thrashed out exhaustively and it was decided that Gloster should speed up their plans. Nobody appeared to ask about progress with the engine and there was no whisper of the Ministry's inability to produce even a draft contract for Rover to discuss. Brabazon, who had taken Lord Beaverbrook's place as Air Minister, was drawn almost comically into the arena. A friend of Churchill, he was lazy, rich, brave, impeccably upper-class, a safe Tory, pioneer pilot and lover of fast cars. In his autobiography, he wrote:

One of my proudest associations was with Air Commodore Sir Frank Whittle, inventor of the world's first [sic] successful jet. Inventive geniuses are difficult people and must be treated as prima donnas and encouraged in every way, but a minister can never do anything right. I believed so much in his invention that I wanted to help in every way I could and have nothing to reproach myself about in this matter, but to show how you can get into trouble Whittle refers in his book to my over-enthusiasm and to the fact that my daily enquiries after progress were causing him to feel like a hunted man. I must plead guilty to writing him a note telling him that my short visit [to Lutterworth] gave me more interest and enjoyment than any which had fallen to my lot since joining the Ministry; and I certainly telephoned frequently until Air Marshall Linnell [Director of Scientific Research] passed me a hint saying that everything possible was being done and that Whittle shouldn't really be bothered by constant enquiries.

Brabazon's note to Whittle read: 'So sorry things are not behaving themselves. I am afraid there are going to be a lot of headaches coming your way. Don't be discouraged. Just plug along, it will all arrange itself. Any way I can help, just ask, everything is at your disposal. You've got a good crowd round you. I have nothing but confidence in the future.' He went on to claim that 'I fully understood Whittle's needs in the matter of a full-scale test plant and did all I could to help in the development of this remarkable invention'.

Many people have claimed long afterwards that they did all they could to help but, if so, their names do not start out of the official documents of the time. Whatever Brabazon thought he was doing, his intervention took place at a point when there was a very good chance of losing the Power Jets/Rover project because of personal, technical and managerial failures on a grand scale. The time had come to place the design, development and production of an operational jet above all personal or company considerations, calling on the skills and determination of everyone – public servants, industrialists, engineers, scientists – and the genius of Whittle. There is no evidence that Whittle would not have responded to this call, but there is much material to suggest that nobody had the vision and conviction required to take the ruthless decisions that were now needed because of earlier prevarication and incompetence.

The paralysis of will dates from early 1941, when the Ministry of Aircraft Production appeared to believe that the matter had been settled when it divided responsibilities between Power Jets and Rover. It completely miscalculated the way in which the partners would look to the future, and the terms of reference were ambiguous. Direct responsibilities were insufficiently identified and not pinned firmly on one body, or person, or another. Within the Ministry, jet engine development was entrusted to a branch accustomed to dealing with orthodox manufacturers of piston engines – the traditionalists. This is a classic mistake in innovation, where the premium is on evaluating new thinking, not on invoking old experience. Also, there was deliberate deviation from an old-established civil service principle that the firm which designed a piece of equipment should also be responsible for its development and production. Power Jets could not do this before 1942 because it was forbidden to do so. Whitehall had set its face against the one canon in its rules that might have been some use: expansion of the company's facilities for just these purposes was constantly denied or begrudged.

Collapse might still have been avoided if there had been a good relationship between Whittle's company and Rover. Instead there was jealousy, suspicion and downright enmity, which did not stem only from personal rivalries. Rover were to show that they were unequal to the task. Their own technical staff, divided between car engineers and newcomers drafted in to work on the jet engine, were split and unhappy, and by 1942 only a handful of engines had been made for test. The records make it difficult to judge how many; Rover's own records left the civil servants unable to ascertain quite what was being done with the hundreds of thousands of pounds which, by now, were being poured annually into their factories. Late in 1941 Power Jets were, at last, allowed to make their own experimental engines and a factory at Whetstone, near Lutterworth, was sanctioned. Building had begun when, at this crucial moment, on 10 December, Whittle, worn out, suffered a nervous collapse and had to rest for a complete month – he was not fully fit for a much longer period. The rumour in Whitehall, faithfully relayed, was 'Whittle? He's gone round the bend, old boy.' In fact, Whittle was meeting his personal crisis, at the same time as Rover were advancing their claims for an increased share of the project, by a stealth which was later to embarrass them and be their undoing. During 1941 they had completed just two engines, one delivered to Power Jets in October, the other for Rover in December; by April 1942 they had completed eight W2Bs and were going ahead with another five. But Power Jets had now shifted their sights to a better engine and work had begun on a complete redesign, known as the W2/500.

By 1942 it was clear that Rover felt themselves free, because of all the troubles with the W2 series, to go ahead with a complete redesign of their own, the B26. They did not disclose this major departure to Whittle: the designs were slipped into the end of a routine production meeting between the Ministry, Power Jets and Rover on 11 February, with Rover engineers arguing that the changes made production easier. Principally, the changes hinged on giving air a straight flow through the entire engine, instead of convoluting the flow through the combustion chambers, a necessity forced upon Whittle by the economies in materials demanded of him in 1938. He already had plans for a 'straight through' engine but had not produced them because of the urgency of getting on with a production version. Rover were undoubtedly right to go for a 'straight through' design but there was a query over whether they had informed the Ministry that they were making a major redesign. At first the Ministry said not. Rover certainly had not informed Whittle or any other member of Power Jets and were thus in fundamental breach of an understanding – no contract had yet been signed – that any major changes should be sanctioned by the Ministry after discussion with Power Jets. Two months after the disclosure, however, it was discovered within the Ministry that one of their officials, Major Ross, of the engine development section, *had* sanctioned Rover's redesign. Senior Ministry officials like Linnell were profoundly embarrassed to learn that they had not known what their own officials were sanctioning or why they were sanctioning it, and Whittle was asked to accept Linnell's assurance that Ross had acted in good faith.

Rover had, however, taken a step too far in putting forward the B26. The redesign was not only beyond their remit but they did not have the necessary basic skills or knowledge in aerodynamics and thermodynamics, and by now were not listening to the people who had these skills. Ross's sanction demonstrated to the Whittle camp the sympathetic climate towards Rover and how little they could expect under the existing regime. What he and Power Jets had hinted at was now proved: Rover wanted to go their own way and the piston-engine warriors of Whitehall were prepared to let them. Whittle produced a devastating critique of Rover's behaviour, which he sent to Air Marshal Linnell, stating that Rover had neither the will nor the ability to make the engine and that if things were allowed to drag on, the engine would be officially declared impractical or too far ahead of its time and the project would be lost. He received powerful support from Hayne Constant at Farnborough, who pointed out in a letter to the Ministry that, when compared with the latest version of the W2B, the B26 offered few advantages: the problems of surging and blade failure were more important than those which Rover were trying to tackle. Constant concluded:

... the general layout of the B26 offers some attractive features, but none of the improvements suggested are essential to the development of the engine. We suggest that with the production programme delayed by blade failures, time should not be spent at present on non-essential modifications, and we recommend that the Rover Co be instructed not to proceed with the manufacture until a Whittle-type engine has been proved to be reliable.

The depth of Whittle's bitterness can be felt in a personal letter he sent to Linnell in April 1942, when the internal row was at its height:

It has been the custom of certain individuals to treat me as a gifted amateur, inventor, etc and to talk of 'taking my child and sending it away to school', to say I have no production experience, etc, and, I believe, to represent me as a somewhat difficult and temperamental individual. On the one hand a good deal of lip service has been paid to my achievements, but on the other hand it has been implied that I am only fit to have 'bright ideas' with the results that, as it seems to me, I have been regarded as being either too biased to make a good judgement or to give good advice on matters of policy.

I am in a far stronger position now to say these things than I was a year ago, because the advice, etc, that I gave then, in so far as it is on the record, can be weighed against events as they have turned out.

Embarrassed civil servants now turned their attention to the actual state of affairs on the shop floors at Clitheroe and Barnoldswick. It was clear that, for an investment of £1.5 million and 1,600 skilled workers, the nation was getting almost nothing in return. Workers were making components but there was little assembly and overall very little work was being done because of the lack of agreement as to what work should be done. Twelve engines were required for test immediately in April, but the Wilks brothers admitted that because of blade and casing problems they could give no future date for their probable delivery. So much for the projected flow of 2,000 engines per year from 1943. Later in 1942, when the situation was desperate, a civil servant named Hamilton-Eddy wrote to another named Cairns in the Ministry:

Expenditure to 31 March 1942 amounted to £778,000 and since then to 30 November we have advanced a further £886,000 making a total of £1,664,000 to date . . . I am concerned at the lack of any operating statement and of any real information as to what Rover have done with the money. I know they are doing experimental work, but I have heard somewhere that this experimental work was limited to £30,000. [Rover have] received at least two orders from Contracts, one of which, if I remember rightly, was for about 600 engines, the other being much smaller. So far as I am aware, we have received to date some 16 engines, but I have only the vaguest idea what is really happening . . . and I do not seem to be able to get a lot of information.

What is really concerning me is this: how long must this branch go on authorizing cash requisitions at a rate of £100,000 a month with no knowledge at all as to the purpose to which the company are applying the wages and the materials they are buying . . . ?

On 11 December the Minister wrote to his Chief Executive, Sir Wilfred Freeman: '. . . in my talk with Hives [head of Rolls-Royce] yesterday he gave a very depressing account of the state of affairs in the Rover W2B factory. I didn't realize before the scale of this work . . . Have you any recent report on it at all? We really must get this whole matter cleared up so that the job can be got on with quietly . . .' Three days later he again wrote to Freeman: '. . . I think a report should be made upon this to see if we can't get better use out of 1,600 bodies and £1½ million of capital. Perhaps Roxbee Cox would report urgently.'

It had taken two years for Rover, with all its equipment and manpower, to make around twenty engines; no final figure was ever arrived at. It was a scandal of considerable proportions, which had to be hushed up. In December Sir Wilfred Freeman, a gifted and far-seeing administrator who was appalled by what had now been discovered, sent for Whittle to tell him that he had considered closing down the entire job. Whittle's account tells how Freeman paced his room back and forth, speaking forcefully and abruptly, making rapid gestures with his arms; every jet engine up to then, Freeman exclaimed, was a flop or likely to be one. The inventor, in poor health and feeling particularly overstrained on this day, protested feebly while Freeman continued his harangue, blaming Whittle personally for the failure of the W2B. Whittle managed to demur at this, but he was then subjected to a tirade. 'Here was the state of affairs I had long foreseen,' said Whittle many years later. 'Though I had been deprived of any effective control of the development of the W2B long before, I was being blamed for the results of a policy which had failed.'

As tempers cooled, Freeman told Whittle that, apart from closure, he had considered putting the companies under the central direction of Rolls-Royce, excluding the Rover management and making Power Jets subservient to them. He felt that the board of Power Jets had ceased to have any useful function and was considering having

Williams and Tinling recalled to the RAF compulsorily, together with Johnson. The management of the Clitheroe and Barnoldswick plants would be transferred to Rolls-Royce although the Wilks brothers did not yet know this. Whittle finally protested that he was unwell, tired and sick with the whole project, and when Freeman asked whether what he had said made Whittle feel any worse, Whittle replied that he had been unable to take it in. Freeman closed the interview by saying that Whittle's brain would be required for some time yet.

Whittle was soothed afterwards by a silent spectator of the interview, Air Marshal Linnell, who advised him that some of what had been said was for effect. Rolls-Royce were to go ahead with the W2/500 engine at the Lancashire factories and, as Whittle learnt later, Power Jets was to keep some sort of autonomy. The Ministry had at last opted for the only feasible solution, and Freeman now insisted that his own house be put in order. Responsibility for jet engine development was taken out of the hands of the traditionalists and vested in a new deputy directorate solely responsible for research and development of gas turbines. At its head would be Dr Harold Roxbee Cox, who remained Whittle's staunch defender, as he had been since early 1940.

Roxbee Cox had begun in 1941 to lay the foundations of a general jet engine industry and he suggested to Ernest (later Lord) Hives, head of Rolls-Royce, that a central clearing house of information and experience on jet engine design, development and production should be set up. This became the Gas Turbine Collaboration Committee, which met for the first time under Roxbee Cox's chairmanship in November 1941. In his opening remarks he told the committee that they were 'the midwives of a new era'. By early 1942 eleven companies were working on jet projects, among them de Havilland, Bristol, Armstrong Siddeley, Rover and Rolls-Royce. Whittle and Power Jets were loyal members, although it was not in their self-interest to be so. Whittle wrote: 'Frankly we did not receive the proposal with any enthusiasm at first because it seemed likely to complicate matters rather than otherwise, and add yet further to the burden on us . . . but we later became enthusiastic supporters and I am firmly convinced that Britain owes much of its technical superiority in this field to GTCC . . .' In his eighties, Roxbee Cox, now Lord Kings Norton, commented:

I was responsible for GTCC although Hives sometimes gets the credit. I thought of it because it was essential to spread the task, especially with the state of affairs at Rover. It was a kind of technical diaspora of knowledge throughout the industry and the meeting worked beautifully. We took it in turns to meet quarterly at each manufacturer's headquarters and it was invaluable to progress. Whatever happened elsewhere there was an excellent, unselfish spirit and people did act disinterestedly, putting their work and experiences in the pool. It was part of the war time spirit of co-operation to get on with the job.

GTCC may have been a bright deed in a dark world; at least it ensured that whatever happened to Power Jets and Rover there would be an independent British jet effort. But the central conduct of affairs had been chaotic. Two years, 1941 and 1942, were allowed to elapse before Whitehall could bring itself to intervene ruthlessly. Meanwhile, Rover tinkered with the connivance of officials at the Ministry of Aircraft Production, and in the middle of the greatest war in history, with Britain in an exceptionally desperate position, 1,600 men and women and £1.5 million worth of equipment were allowed to languish in north Lancashire.

It is still argued today that the delay did no real harm, that the RAF did not need high-flying jet fighters because it was no longer fighting that kind of war and that it was possible to develop much more reliable and airworthy engines *because* of the longer research and development times available. The apologists would even ask us to accept that Whittle's health problems were a blessing which ultimately turned to the national advantage. The apologists, however, must answer questions too. If the Gloster Meteor had been able to enter service in 1942 instead of 1944, what impact would it have had on the war? What light does it throw on the judgement of very senior civil servants that Whittle's return to active service should ever have been considered? What value was served by starving Power Jets of essential resources?

The truth is that the main British jet project was mismanaged before the war and during its first three years by the Air Ministry and the Ministry of Aircraft Production, whose failures were never the subject of the enquiry which ought to have been held into them. Inefficiency starts out of almost every page of the records available. The internal strictures about the anomalies of Power Jets are there for all to see, but there is no parallel comment on the performance of officials. Their attitudes as they minute away their days are of a piece with their toleration of their own and Rover's failure to carry out their duties to the nation. About Rover there is barely a word of complaint, about Power Jets little but complaint. At the end of the day – and in the nick of time – the project was saved by those outside the mainstream of traditional engine development: Roxbee Cox from Farnborough, Hives from Rolls-Royce, Whittle from within his own company. What chance would *he* have had to further his ideas from within the RAF or the civil service? For him it was essential to be a crusader with his own staff. Power Jets answered a national need which could not have been met through official channels because of the institutionalized nature of the men and organizations involved. They were – and are – not there to innovate.

The militarily titled men at the Ministry watched as the weeks and months whiled away, and their own executives were taken completely by surprise when failure clamoured so loudly that at last it had to be faced. The official historian's verdict is more judicious; of Rover she says:

> They took little or no trouble to establish good working relations with Power Jets and did not make nearly enough use of the very valuable work being done and of the very great knowledge and experience of Air Commodore Whittle, the designer. Much of the blame . . . must therefore rest with Rover. On the other hand the attitude of Power Jets was one of suspicion and resentment – both excessive if understandable . . . When, during 1941, it became clear that Rover were not asking Air Commodore Whittle's advice or informing Power Jets before making design changes, the latter began to put the worst construction on Rover's motives.

Rover had been sacked, but they then virtually asked for an official denial and one last cynical rite was observed. On 21 January 1943 Roxbee Cox wrote to Air Marshal Linnell:

> I met Mr S. B. Wilks at Clitheroe on 20 January. He said that in some quarters (he mentioned Glosters) there is a misunderstanding of Rover's position, the prevalent notion being that Rover had been sacked for incompetence and replaced by Rolls-Royce; Rover personnel were therefore received somewhat coolly. . . . Mr Wilks asked . . . that an official letter should be sent to his company stating whether or not we attach any blame to them. Mr Wilks pointed out that his company had clearly stated for a long time past that the W2B is no good, but I doubt his wisdom in urging this point in his defence . . . Mr Hives, in search of a formula, suggested that the change was associated with a 'concentration of industry' . . . I gathered he [Wilks] would prefer a clear statement

that the change over is in no way due to any fault or failing on the part of the Rover company, but this I think we must deny him. . . .

On 24 January Air Marshal Linnell wrote to Wilks:

Now that we are concentrating our efforts by a closer co-ordination of the work at Barnoldswick and Clitheroe with that of Rolls-Royce and Power Jets, it is an appropriate time to refer to the work which the Rover company has done for us under the more difficult conditions when they were more on their own.

We here are appreciative of the work which your people, both in workshop and office, have done in the shadow organization of Waterloo Mill and Bankfield Shed [the two Lancashire sites]. They set out at our direction on a programme of production which had to be cut back for reasons over which they had no control, and it is highly creditable that despite the inevitable disappointments they continued to work with enthusiasm and make a solid contribution to the advancement of this special work.

It may well be that some of them felt from time to time that the number of engines which they produced was incommensurate with their increasing effort. They were, however, and are, working over new and difficult ground, and their contribution to the national effort is not one whit less than that of men and women who have the good fortune to see their work contributing to a satisfying flow of production.

It was surely the kindest way out.

On 25 July 1944 a Mosquito photographic reconnaisance plane from the Royal Air Force base at Benson, Oxfordshire, was flying at 29,000 feet near Munich, Bavaria, taking oblique pictures of the city, when the observer in the two-man crew, Pilot Officer A. S. Lobban, spotted a twin-engined fighter closing fast about 400 yards astern. The pilot, Flight Lieutenant A. E. Wall, was surprised. Solo Merlin-engined Mosquitos on high altitude reconnaisance missions were generally reckoned to fly too high and too fast for any German intercepter fighter to challenge them. That was why the Mosquito was unarmed, a daring design assumption made by Sir Geoffrey de Havilland when he proposed the plane, and backed by Sir Wilfred Freeman, whose staff at the Ministry of Aircraft Production called the aircraft Freeman's Folly, until its performance in service showed with whom the folly actually lay.

Flt Lt. Wall slammed his throttle levers fully forward and lost 1,000 feet in a shallow dive in which he reached 412 mph, an escape speed at least equal to that of any German fighter of the time. Still his attacker came on and shot past the Mosquito, turning to attack again. Wall and Lobban now recognized the German as a Messerschmitt Me 262 jet fighter, of whose impending action in service Allied intelligence had been warning for some months. Wall pulled the Mosquito into a tight evasive turn to starboard. The Me 262 was now 2,000 yards astern and closing again. At 800 yards the German pilot opened fire but missed as Wall wrenched the Mosquito to port. In the dog fight that developed, the tighter turns of the Mosquito caused the 262's pilot to miss his quarry each time. On his fifth attack the German dived from 700 yards and climbed into the attack from below. Again Wall successfully avoided his cannon fire and dived into some cumulus cloud for cover. When he came out three or four minutes later his antagonist had gone and he continued his flight to an Adriatic airfield in safety.

Thus runs the British combat report of the first recorded encounter between an Allied aircraft and a German jet, although German pilots had been claiming victories among American bombers over Germany since April, four months earlier. Just two days after the Mosquito incident, British Meteor 1 fighters of 616 Squadron, based at Manston, Kent, powered by two Whittle W2B/23C jet engines, were given operational clearance to attack German V1 pilotless bombers flying over south-east England. The jet age had officially arrived.

On the German side the new aviation era opened with what should have been a shattering symbiosis. Two world firsts – the first operational jet fighter, the Me 262, and the first production jet engine, the Junkers Jumo 004 – came together in what might well have been a breathtaking *coup de théâtre*. That it was not, was not the fault of German industry, which gave its country a significant lead with an aircraft which could have won back for Germany control of the West European skies, with all that might have meant in prolonging the agony of World War Two. But the 262 came too late for that, even though it had been a weapon in the shaping for six tumultuous years from 1938. The visionary genius behind aeroplane and engine ultimately failed to influence the greatest war in history because of the powers of inertia in human affairs and in technology.

As mentioned earlier, Hans Antz of the German Air Ministry had asked Messerschmitt to prepare designs for a radical jet fighter for the Luftwaffe. By late autumn 1938 a design contract had been issued, specifying the use of two BMW jet engines which, it was then thought, would give 1,320 lb thrust and be available by December 1939. The 262 was always seen as an intercepter fighter and at a stroke it was to add 200 mph to the speed of front-line fighters and give formidable performance at height, where piston and propeller performance fell off rapidly. It would be a sleek all-metal monoplane, its two jet engines mounted in the roots of the wings, which would probably be swept back to delay the effects of compressibility – the tendency for air to build up as a bow wave as the speed of sound, the so-called sound barrier, was approached.

Early work was carried out by Robert Lusser at Messerschmitt and when Lusser went to Heinkel design responsibility passed to Waldemar Voigt. The Messerschmitt company produced a mock-up for inspection in January 1940 and in March a contract was issued for three prototypes for flight testing – just at the time Heinkel received his prototype contract for the He 280. A link of enmity and suspicion bound Heinkel and Messerschmitt; and Messerschmitt was even more disliked by Erhard Milch, the field marshal who was now Goering's deputy and secretary of state at the Air Ministry. Milch's feud with Messerschmitt extended back ten years and has some bearing on Messerschmitt's progress and the attitude in Berlin towards this jet pioneer and his company.

Wilhelm Messerschmitt was born in Frankfurt on 26 June 1898. His parents were wealthy and he had a sound engineering training at Munich Technical University. His youth ensured that he missed the First World War, but he was precocious and in 1923 when still in his mid-twenties he set up, with family backing, an aircraft company called Flugzeugbau Messerschmitt based at Bamberg, Bavaria. He designed and built several successful gliders and sailplanes, including the S15, S16 Bubi and S16a Betty sailplanes with engines – devised to defeat the Allied ban on Germany building aircraft, let alone having an air force. However, Messerschmitt's formidable creative genius and love of aircraft and flying soared above mere international treaties and by 1925 he had designed a two-seat tandem-powered monoplane, the M17 Ello. Growing in experience and ambition, the tall, dark and sparingly spoken designer now conceived and built the M18 light transport for pilot and three passengers, an advanced plane for its day because it had an all-metal structure. The visionary Messerschmitt had a clear understanding of where aircraft construction was leading and he was using metal for his structures long before wood and fabric designers were abandoning their materials.

Messerschmitt was firmly on the road that would lead him to the creation of two historic aeroplanes, the Bf 109 piston-engined fighter and the Me 262 jet, but he first had to overcome the determination of Erhard Milch never to award him a contract. Milch indeed virtually told him that he was of no value to the German aircraft industry and advised him to join the brain drain and pursue his career in another country. This sensational misjudgement dated from 1928, by which time Messerschmitt had merged his company with Bayerische Flugzeugwerke – B FW for short – which had among its founders Ernst Udet. B FW, which had suffered various vicissitudes and had large fundings from the Bavarian state government, was also building transport aircraft but it lacked a gifted engineer to head its design team. The amalgamation meant that Messerschmitt provided the designs, retaining design rights, patents and independence, while B FW would produce Messerschmitt's planes. The two companies thus kept separate entities but worked as one from offices and plant at Augsburg.

Messerschmitt's successful four-seat transport, the all-metal M18, was followed by the M19 two-seat sports monoplane and then the M20, an ambitious ten-seat transport. The young German airline,

Lufthansa, of which the managing director was Erhard Milch, placed a contract for ten M20s but in 1929 cancelled the order when the prototype was destroyed in an accident. Another prototype was quickly built but Messerschmitt's company could not afford to repay the airline's deposit and was forced into bankruptcy, showing a loss of 600,000 marks. Messerschmitt, left with several half-built aircraft, held that the cancellation of the order was panicky and unnecessary and a bitter row broke out between him and Milch. Although Lufthansa reinstated its order when the second M20 was built and flown successfully, it came too late for the dispute to be cooled and indeed BFW's action, through the receiver, in forcing Lufthansa to take delivery of the unwanted M20s, together with the M28 high-speed postal monoplane, probably added to the venom which the two men felt for one another.

BFW was back on its feet by May 1933, with Willy Messerschmitt as joint managing director. By now Milch was Secretary of State for Aviation under Reichsmarshal Goering and the Nazis were in power. Successful designs continued to flow but Milch tried to frustrate Messerschmitt by restricting BFW to manufacturing under licence the designs of other companies, among them Dornier and Heinkel. This in fact strengthened Messerschmitt's financial hand because this business was profitable and by 1935 BFW was expanding to build five different aircraft types. Faced with a ban on his creative genius within Germany, Messerschmitt had sought design commissions from other countries and Rumania had ordered a six-passenger transport, the M36. Another cabin monoplane, the M37, was begun.

Milch's anger was roused to greater heat when he learnt of these developments and he prompted one of his Air Ministry officials, Oberstleutnant Wilhelm Wimmer, to rebuke BFW for accepting foreign orders. Messerschmitt, with the backing of his colleagues, retorted that the Air Ministry's failure to award them any design contracts at all – at the instigation of the Air Minister – forced them to look abroad. Messerschmitt's name might be poison, but the Air Ministry was now spurred to give BFW a commission: a competition aircraft to take part in the 1934 Challenge de Tourisme Internationale. In the previous challenge, in 1932, the Poles had taken leading places and the Germans were determined to set about righting that slight and proving that they dominated European aviation. Willy Messerschmitt promptly rose to the occasion by designing and building the Bf 108, an advanced two-seater with some excellent design innovations – metal structure again, flush-riveted skin, retractable undercarriage, enclosed cabin and what would now be called a high-technology wing with movable slots and flaps. Flight trials of the Bf 108 quickly showed that it was a very promising aircraft.

Meanwhile Messerschmitt was offered the chair of aeronautical design at Danzig Technical University. Danzig was a European free state and acceptance would mean that Messerschmitt would join the small but steady flow of people leaving Germany because of their distrust and fear of the Nazi regime. Seeing a means of gauging his value to the Air Ministry, he artlessly enquired of Berlin whether, in the light of the offer, there was much significance attached to his work for Germany and what his influence on German aviation might be in the future. At Milch's behest, Oberstleutnant Wimmer advised Messerschmitt to go to Danzig because his work was of no importance to Germany and was not expected to be in future, but friends of Messerschmitt, believing that things had gone far enough, persuaded him to stay in Germany despite his wounded *amour propre*. Among them was an engineer named Fritz Loeb, who shortly afterwards got Wimmer's job at the Air Ministry. Milch, angered by Messerschmitt's decision to stay in Germany, seized another chance to humiliate him when one of the six Bf 108s in the Challenge team crashed. Theo Osterkamp, the team manager, was put up to argue that the 108 was unsafe, and two other team pilots felt free to insult Messerschmitt openly. However, Loeb again intervened, pointing out that the official test pilots at Rechlin had approved the aircraft, and he flew from Augsburg to Berlin to tell Milch personally that Osterkamp should be fired and, by implication, that he should stop being so foolish as to try to get rid of the nation's greatest aircraft designer. Milch refused to fire the team manager but the criticism of the 108 became muted. The plane proved to be the fastest entered in the Challenge and, though Poland again beat Germany overall, it was held to have performed well.

Messerschmitt went on to design the Spitfire's great Battle of Britain antagonist, the Bf 109, one of the world's great aircraft and a Luftwaffe mainstay throughout the war. When Udet inspected it at Augsburg, the wartime ace noted its closed cockpit, monoplane design and a retractable undercarriage, and boomed: 'This will never be a fighter!' But the barnstorming days of front-line dogfights were over and Udet realized that in the 109 he had a deadly killing machine. By 1938–39 Messerschmitt's standing and abilities were internationally acknowledged. He was secure against the displeasure of the mighty Milch – though only temporarily, for the enmity would break out again during the war – and he now had design supervision of Projekt 1065 – the Messerschmitt 262.

Waldemar Voigt, who worked for Messerschmitt, gave a lecture in 1974 to the American Aviation Historical Society which contained an account of the way Messerschmitt worked. Voigt recalled how Messerschmitt encouraged his advanced designers to work in teams, while he himself directed overall and created the climate in which innovation could thrive. He tended to work only on projects that interested him intellectually – the days of hack-work were now over. Each project leader was responsible in the last analysis for the work of his team, but a good deal of latitude was encouraged in in-dividuals. Messerschmitt was humorous, but sparing in his praise; Voigt recalled that after the 262's successful first jet-propelled flight Messerschmitt said to him: 'You know, Herr Voigt, you might become a good detail designer.'

At his Augsburg plant at the outbreak of war there were about 175 engineers, a third of whom were in advanced design while the other two-thirds were concerned with structural design of hardware. The advanced design teams were an elite for whom money was not a consideration: if a job needed to be done, it was assumed to be essential and the money would be found and spent. The team would look at the state of the art in any particular field to see where it could be advanced, would sell the new concept to the Air Ministry and then do the aerodynamics and overall design. Once a mock-up of a design was accepted and a contract placed for development, the advanced team's job was largely done and the hardware engineers set to work to build the prototype. Voigt was paid bonuses by Messerschmitt and it was within his personal power to raise the pay of the engineers working for him. The amounts were coupled to success in the volume production of a design, so these men had an interest in designing for successful and rapid manufacturing, which was not marred by the constant dissonance of the British side between the separate staffs of Power Jets and Rover.

Although each of Voigt's engineers was a specialist, each was expected to see his specialism in the overall context of the team and the concept on which they were working. Messerschmitt knew and worked closely with all the specialists; he scrutinized their drawings, making changes as he thought necessary – which in practice meant frequently. This fairly loose system of management worked well on a project like the 262, where precedent was non-existent and the premium was on creative thinking within the bounds of what was thought possible with the engine they were given to power their aircraft: any designer is completely dependent on his power plant. Messerschmitt, Voigt and their colleagues were given some idea of engine weight and power, and knew that the 262 had to have an endurance – maximum time in the air – of one hour for a top speed of around 530 mph. They settled early on for twin engines with straight wings and a tail wheel undercarriage. This was a very conventional layout: Heinkel's team were already thinking in more advanced terms for the He 280, though their thinking was of course a company secret. The Messerschmitt design evolved slowly into a swept-wing tricycle undercarriage design. Because the wing was too thin to accommodate the landing wheels they had to retract into the fuselage, which determined the plane's triangular shape in cross-section and gave it a shark-like appearance, though it was unofficially named *Schwalbe* – Swallow. Changes in the size and weight of the engines, outside Messerschmitt's jurisdiction, had their influence on the design: growth in the diameter of the engine intakes meant that they had to be moved from the slender wing roots and housed in nacelles under the wings. (The American post-war preference for engine pods under the wings of their large civil and military aircraft stems partly from this early decision.) The basic design, arrived at by May 1940, was only sparingly wind-tunnel tested, since there were no large high-speed tunnels available.

By the summer of 1940 Projekt 1065 began to encounter the two main difficulties that were to dog its life. They did not occur within Messerschmitt, but were to do with engine development and the indifference towards advanced designs within the Air Ministry and the top echelons of the Luftwaffe. When BMW had acquired the Bramo company in a merger in 1939, Bramo's design for an axial compressor jet, decided on through the persuasive powers of Schelp and Mauch, was adapted to use the turbine already being developed by BMW. This was the 003 project, designed to give a thrust of 1,320 lb at 560 mph, which had hollow turbine blades in order to cool them and withstand the very high combustion temperature of the engine – 1,652°F. The axial compressor, chosen because of its small diameter, was designed by Dr W. Encke, of the Aerodynamic Research Establishment at Göttingen. However, engineers soon found that the temperatures of the gases leaving the combustor were too high for the turbine blades and in late 1939 the combustion temperature was lowered to 1,382°F. But this in turn meant that when the engine was first run in early 1940 it gave a thrust of only 570 lb. The difficulties show the critical interrelation of the key components of a jet engine and the penalties paid for mismatches of the parts – compressor, combustor and turbine.

To obtain the thrust required at a lower temperature meant a redesign of the compressor to take a much larger mass flow of air into the engine. A lower combustor temperature in turn spoiled the efficiency of the turbine because it altered the velocity of the gases flowing through its blades. That in turn altered the performance of the compressor up front, to which the turbine was linked on the single shaft running through the engine. Serious faults were also found in the combustion chamber. In short, a major re-design of the engines was called for by 1940 and was eventually to take almost two years. Forewarned of trouble, the Messerschmitt team decided to complete the Projekt 1065 prototype with two rocket motors instead, but because these could not be completed in time for flying, this idea had to be discarded.

In the end, the Me 262's first flight was to be useful, but not noble. V1, the prototype, was fitted with a twelve-cylinder piston engine and propeller in the nose in order to do some rudimentary airframe testing. With test pilot Fritz Wendel at the controls, V1 first flew on 18 April 1941 from the Messerschmitt airfield at Augsburg. The engine gave low acceleration and the high-speed wing offered only just enough lift for Wendel to clear the boundary hedge at the end of the runway. V1's level flight speed was only 260 mph, but Wendel reported very good flying characteristics. In shallow dives at full throttle things were not so good: beyond 335 mph Wendel encountered severe buffeting and the elevators misbehaved. However, minor modifications sorted these problems out and Wendel and his fellow test pilot, Karby Bauer, flew the plane throughout the following summer without mishap. In November the first BMW 003 jet engines reached Augsburg from Berlin. They were expected to give 1,015 lb thrust – well below their specified power – and were fitted to V1, but Messerschmitt decided, luckily, to keep the piston engine and propeller in use for the first flight, on 25 March 1942.

On the day, using all three engines, Wendel barely managed to clear the boundary hedge because the weight of the additional engines was only just overcome by their meagre thrust. As Wendel edged 160 feet in a shallow climb, the port jet engine flamed out – its ignition jet failed, as a pilot light goes out – and seconds later the starboard jet did the same. V1 could barely stay in the air but with superb airmanship Wendel completed a circuit and put the plane safely down on the runway. Anguished BMW engineers removed the engines at once. Broken compressor blades had caused the failure, but what had caused them to fail was a mystery: neither engine exceeded the speeds at which they had been run in ground tests. The engineers went back to Berlin to face an inescapable fact: the thrust rating was so poor that the engine would have to undergo another complete redesign to admit a still greater mass flow of air to the engine. The compressor blade failures were almost incidental.

However, Anselm Franz was now confident of the Jumo 004 and two of these engines were fitted to the third prototype, V3, and made ready for flight on the morning of 18 July 1942. The 004 was larger than the 003 and heavier; it required a larger nacelle to house it, which meant an increase in the fin and rudder area for the airframe. The aircraft was taken to Leipheim, where there was a 1,200-yard runway, the same length as Augsburg, but with a smoother tarmac surface. With an all-up weight of 11,000 lb and engines rated at 1,850 lb thrust, the (by now) rather heavy aeroplane was ready for its first jet flight. But during taxi trials on the morning of the flight Wendel discovered that by the time he had covered 875 yards of the runway he could not raise the tailwheel off the ground for a conventional take-off (the 262 only later gained a tricycle undercarriage with a nose wheel). V3's elevators were masked by the wing so that they were not giving the lift essential to get the plane's tail up into a take-off attitude. At a runway-side conference, one of the test team suggested that Wendel should try a touch of brake at 112 mph – the speed he was supposed to unstick and become airborne – the idea being to use the brakes to jerk the aeroplane's nose forward and down, lifting the tailwheel off the runway so that V3 could become airborne.

It worked. At 8.40 in the morning Wendel lifted off for a twelve-minute flight on jet engines alone. Anselm Franz, a nervous spectator of the runway conference and of the take-off itself, recounted many years later:

Before the flight it took us two days fooling around regulating the engines. The weather was terrible, the thrust from the engines was unequal and we had our two best mechanics as well as the senior engineers making very delicate adjustments by hand. We had to do it all by hand – it was automatic only much later on. I can remember standing on one side of the cockpit talking to Wendel and Dr Schmidt, my chief of engine test, on the other. Then we went and stood with the rest of the group.

The plane rolled away very slowly at first and from the perspective where we were standing it spent an age getting smaller and smaller down the runway and I said to someone, 'My God, what's happening? He's getting to the end of the airfield and he's too slow.' But that was only our view because when he was at the end, suddenly he took it up and, boy, with a speed like you never saw before it went up like a rocket, vertically upwards and disappeared into the cloud.

At this moment it was clear to me that the jet age had begun.

Wendel himself was filled with enthusiasm – for a test pilot: 'Immediately I touched the brakes the tail lifted and the elevators started to bite. My engines ran like clockwork and it was a sheer pleasure to fly the aeroplane – seldom have I been so enthusiastic about a first flight with a new type.'

Just after noon on the same day Wendel took off again in V3 and began to explore its handling in the air. He noticed that, when banking, the airflow detached from the centre section of the wing, a problem quickly solved by aerodynamic modifications. The speed performance of the aircraft on subsequent tests was excellent, except for some tailplane instability beyond 430 mph, which, too, was quickly cured.

Once V3 had completed another six flights, the Messerschmitt team decided to bring in a test pilot from the official test centre at Rechlin, a cautious manoeuvre on the road to bringing Goering and Milch to watch a full-blown demonstration. A pilot named Beauvais arrived at Leipheim from Rechlin on 17 August and after Fritz Wendel had carefully explained to him the 'kick start' needed for take-off, which he now regarded as routine, he turned the plane over to Beauvais, positioning himself beside the runway at the 875 yard mark to make sure there would be no mistake. Unfortunately, there was. Beauvais did not get the aircraft up to its unstick speed, and he could not touch the brakes until 985 yards, when the tail rose, only to flop down again. He tried once more, but failed again. On his third attempt Beauvais lifted off, but his wheels cut through the corn in the field beyond the boundary, a wing tip hit a manure heap, and V3 performed an ignominious ground loop – a circle on its wheels on the ground. Beauvais was only slightly injured but the psychological effect on the test team was sharp.

The piston-engined V1 continued flying in the hands of Wendel and Bauer, however, and the third prototype, V2, also fitted with 004s, was test flown from Lechfeld airfield on 1 October. The Messerschmitt team now requested more prototypes and Milch authorized two, with fifteen pre-production aircraft – the intermediates between prototypes and front-line aircraft. These were to be powered by Ansel Franz's 004B, the brilliant redesign which was to give roughly the same power as the 004A but with its weight cut by almost 200 lb. By early 1943 V3 had been repaired and flew from Lechfeld with another test pilot, Wolfgang Spate, at the controls. On his second flight Spate almost lost his life when both jets flamed out at almost 10,000 feet. At 5,000 feet he attempted to relight and it was not until 1,500 feet that one engine came to life, the other seconds later. The flame-out was caused by the airflow hitting the compressor blades at a sharp angle in a side-slip, which created a strong braking effect on them, cutting the engine. Spate's place was now taken by another test pilot, Ostertag, also one of Wendel's assistants. On his first flight his plane, V3, went into an irrecoverable dive from only 1,500 feet and he was killed. The cause of the crash could not be found, and several more unexplained fatal accidents happened in similar circumstances. Suspicions began to centre on the cone in the rear of the engine exhaust. Every jet engine has this cone, which moves to allow for changes in pressure, temperature and height. Although later done automatically, in the early 004s the pilot had to make these fairly sensitive adjustments manually and it became certain that in these crashes the cone was detaching itself from its mounting and completely blocking the jet nozzle. This caused the engine to flame out instantly and the aircraft dived into the ground because it was impossible to relight.

Although the 262 had not yet reached the stage where it could be ordered for Luftwaffe service, both the Messerschmitt and Franz teams thought that interest should be judiciously courted in the right circles. The hierarchy still took the view that the jet's day lay far ahead in the future, and production lines for existing types should not be disrupted by well-meaning enthusiasts; their time would come in the late 1940s and 1950s when, it was assumed, the war had been won and it was time to consider new types of aircraft and engines. By early 1943, however, experienced Luftwaffe pilots recognized, as officials at the Air Ministry did not, that some of their aircraft were already outclassed and others were on the road to obsolescence, which was apparent on the eastern as well as on the western front. In April, when V4, the fourth prototype, was ready for testing, test pilot Spate sought out Adolf Galland and gave him a glowing account of the Me 262's potential. Galland, a General of Fighters, was exactly the right person to influence. He was a popular hero, a young fighter ace who had come through the Battle of Britain with distinction and was one of a group of outstanding combat pilots promoted to high rank in the Luftwaffe command.

On 22 April he visited Lechfeld and flew V4 himself. Anselm Franz recalls the first Galland flight vividly:

He came along with his high boots and riding crop and ordered everybody away, although he had never been in the aircraft before. I was up there on the wing when he started the engines. I started to explain to him what he could do, what he could not do, but he didn't have any time. He just said, 'OK, OK, I understand, get off please. I want to go.' When he came down, he ran over and gave me a kind of embrace and said this was the greatest sailplane he ever flew – it was so quiet, without vibration compared with piston engines.

This, and a subsequent flight by Galland a month later, were landmarks in the 262's road to active service. After his second flight with the 262, Galland personally reported to Goering:

This model is a tremendous stroke of fortune for us. It puts us way out in front, provided the enemy continues to use piston engines. As far as I can tell, the fuselage seems to be entirely satisfactory, and the engines are everything that has been claimed for them, except for their performance during take off and landing. This aircraft opens up entirely new possibilities as far as tactics are concerned.

Galland never doubted after his flights that the day of the jet had come and it should be put in the hands of his fighter pilots as quickly as possible. He thought the aircraft needed greater endurance (flying time), which would mean larger fuel tanks and additional weight, and he and his comrades in ensuing discussions with the flight test team also pointed out that 'kick take-offs' were all very well, but it was time to fit a tricycle undercarriage. Willy Messerschmitt burst into one discussion to say: 'Should we not put the 262 into production as it is? Does it not embody sufficient advances to justify the start of production? We could do all the modifications as we went along.'

Messerschmitt badly needed the 262 fillip. During 1942 one of his piston-engine designs, the twin-engined Me 210, a replacement for the Me 110, had proved a complete failure. Production was halted after ninety aircraft had left the assembly line, with the inevitable impact on the production-obsessed regime, and the Luftwaffe suffered the shattering loss of a planned 600 aircraft. Those that had been delivered were killing pilots weekly and Messerschmitt's company lost 30 million Reichsmarks in cancelled orders. Not only was the company in financial trouble but Erhard Milch used the moment to resume his feud with Willy Messerschmitt, personally dismissing him from the chairmanship and managing directorship of his own company and appointing the chairman of the shareholders' committee, Theo Croneiss, in his stead. Although Croneiss was an old acquaintance, and although Milch allowed Messerschmitt to continue his design leadership, Messerschmitt was seriously injured by this blow and the Me 262, with all its possibilities, offered balm and a future worth working for.

Galland suggested that conventional fighter production should be restricted to the still-formidable Focke Wulf 190 and that the whole of the Messerschmitt Bf 109 capacity should be switched to the Me 262. This powerful advocacy led the usually conservative procurement and supply committee of the Air Ministry to decide on 2 June 1943 that the Me 262 should be put into production because of its superior speed and many other qualities. This would make possible the fundamental change which Luftwaffe thinkers were beginning to grasp: the Luftwaffe would have to be turned into a great defensive force to save the Third Reich from the RAF and the USAF, which were beginning to cause critical damage to the cities. (The terrible destruction of Hamburg in July/August 1943 caused deep fear in Goering and Goebbels.) Lesser officers knew by now that the war was probably lost, not only because of what was happening in the west, but because the Russians, too, were building aircraft which were beginning to match their own on the eastern front – and building them in incredible numbers. The east was no longer a Luftwaffe shooting gallery.

None of this, however, was clear to Hitler – or so Milch claimed. When, in September, he announced a fighter production target of 4,000 aircraft a month, and Galland demanded that at least twenty-five per cent of these should be 262s, Milch said he could not be expected to stop all other projects just because of the jet fighter: 'The Führer feels the risk is too great. I personally would go ahead and produce it as we planned. However, as a soldier I have no choice but to obey orders. If the Führer orders caution we must be cautious.' One did not quarrel with orders in Germany.

Messerschmitt and Galland appealed personally to Goering, who said he would intercede personally with Hitler – a process which had been known to reduce the obese Reichsmarshall to blubber but which on this occasion led to the formation of a special committee to guide development of the jet fighter. Membership included Anselm Franz as well as Messerschmitt. Goering descended on Augsburg with Milch and Galland, ostensibly to consult the Messerschmitt company on production feasibility – these were the days when jigging and tooling up of the factories became the paramount problems – but he asked for an answer to Hitler's question whether the 262 could carry bombs. Messerschmitt replied that it had always been envisaged that the aircraft could carry a couple of 500 lb bombs or one 1,000 pounder. Goering said that this was all the Führer wanted to know but he personally would like to know when the bomber variant would be ready. Messerschmitt, unable to dissemble any longer, admitted that the racks had yet to be designed and, when further questioned by Goering, claimed that the job could be done in a fortnight. The Reichsmarshall concluded correctly that Messerschmitt had given no thought to the 262's possible role as a light bomber. He was also disturbed to hear that at that moment only one prototype was available for testing.

Messerschmitt assumed that the bomber discussion could safely be forgotten as incidental – indeed, a red herring – whereas it was to become one of the more famous internal rows within the Nazi hierarchy, a diversion which would lead to the charge that Hitler fatally delayed the pitting of the war-winning 262 fighter against the Allies because he insisted on trying to convert it into a bomber. This argument has little validity but it has been used by air historians and strategists as yet another example of Hitler's disastrous misjudgements in the conduct of the war. Albert Speer, Hitler's armaments minister, claims in his self-serving memoirs that he personally (and by inference, courageously) argued with the Führer against his decision. Whether he did or not, his assertion that the hardening of Hitler's mental arteries made the 262 'the most valuable of our secret weapons . . . worthless' is quite untrue.

The real problem was that neither fighter nor jet engine was ready for production. The early aircraft could only be flown by the most skilful test pilots; young service pilots of experience would have had difficulty converting to it and pilots new to squadron service from flying school would have killed themselves in it. In any case, no factory facilities were likely to be available for some time. By June 1943, prototype V5 was flown with a nosewheel. The piston engine was taken out of V1 and it was flown on jet engines, only to have one of them burn out in flight – the aircraft was badly damaged in a forced landing. A pre-production 262 aircraft, V6, became available in November 1943 and it was fitted with the new 004B engine, the lighter engine which gave 1,980 lb of thrust. On 26 November, V4 and V6 were at Insterburg for a demonstration flight before Hitler and Goering and although V4 flamed out on take-off, V6 was very effectively flown. Hitler is asserted to have said afterwards that the aircraft must become a blitz-bomber but on 5 December

Hitler's aide was writing to Goering only that the Führer placed

> tremendous importance on the production of jet-propelled aircraft
> for employment as fighter-bombers. It is imperative that the
> Luftwaffe has a number of jet fighter-bombers ready for front
> commitment by spring 1944. Any difficulties occasioned by labour
> or raw material shortages will be resolved by the exploitation of
> Luftwaffe resources until such time as existing shortages can be
> made up [sic]. The Führer feels that a delay in our jet fighter
> programme would be tantamount to irresponsible negligence. The
> Führer had directed that bimonthly written reports be made to
> him concerning the progress of the Me 262 and the Ar 234 [a jet
> reconnaissance bomber].

This hardly amounts to holding up the 262 to make of it something
which it is not, but suggests rather that Hitler was looking for
something with which to strike hard and fast at Allied beach-heads
in a western front invasion.

Speer gave the Me 262 top priority, but at Messerschmitt and
Junkers a great deal of development work on airframe and engine
remained to be done. The airframe was at first built at a plant at
Kottern, for which Speer promised 1,800 skilled workers, who were
weeks late arriving. Another bellicose Nazi in the armaments ministry
under Speer, Otto Saur, now became self-appointed trouble-shooter
to the whole project. His shouted telephone orders were remembered
with keen dislike forty years later by Anselm Franz, not least
because his harassed team were already working eighty-hour weeks.
Saur's self-introduction to Franz was characteristic.

> I was in my office, when there came a call and my secretary said,
> 'There's somebody who wants to speak to you, he doesn't give his
> name but he insists.' The voice shouted, 'This is Engineer Saur'
> and I had no idea who it was. He said, 'Don't you understand?
> Saur? and then I realized who it was. It was the big shot, in charge
> of engine and aircraft production. It was three, four o'clock in the
> afternoon and he just said, 'Get in a car and come to room so-
> and-so at the Air Ministry.' I said 'What's the problem?' and he
> said I'd hear when I got there. That was the way they operated – it
> could be anybody. I walked into the room and there was only a
> desk, a little lieutenant sitting there. He got up right away and
> took me to Saur.

This meeting was the prelude to a journey on Goering's armoured
train from Berlin to Regensburg to the demonstration of the 262.

Franz recalled that the journey was a nightmare because of a massed raid by the USAF on Weiner Neustadt, south of Vienna; the train made its own contribution to the flak barrage, while Goering and senior officers attempted to direct the air defences as they travelled south – a journey of a type becoming familiar to a country under night and day bombardment. Franz recalled that Goering's attitude was unfriendly but that on later visits to Dessau he was friendly and even encouraging. He found that Hitler, whom he expected to be raucous, was a soft-spoken man who asked intelligent and penetrating questions.

Saur regarded the 262 project as a personal crusade once he realized its importance. With Gauleiter Sauckel of Thuringia, he laid plans to convert underground mine workings into safe plants for the production of airframes, plans which were later supplanted by more ingenious and easier methods of dispersing manufacture. Both engine and airframe engineers were now exerting their utmost efforts to clear the fighter for mass production and by the beginning of 1944 the 004's performance on test was extremely promising. Most of the bugs were out of the engine, although there were difficulties in getting and shaping the materials needed for the hot-burning parts of the jet. When the engine was 'frozen' for production – design and development were held to have been completed – some of the work was removed to the notorious underground forced labour factory at Nordhausen.

Early in 1944 all the pre-production aircraft had been delivered and were being tested. Production aircraft began to emerge from the factories, but many could not be flown because engine production was not matching airframes. On Franz's own estimates: 'Production in early 1944 was very, very slow over several months, but by the middle of the year it started to go up and in many ways it then went on faster than anyone could expect.' During those early months Franz and many others were treated by Saur to bullying and threatening behaviour, accompanied by the setting of impossible target production figures. Often he achieved nothing more than mere resentment.

More trouble broke out at the top when Hitler, in conference with Saur, Goering and Milch, learnt that Me 262s were being delivered without bomb racks. 'Not a single one of my orders has been obeyed,' he raged. Milch suggested gently that the plane had, after all, been designed as a fighter, which infuriated Hitler still further. Nobody dared to point out that the aircraft so far delivered were barely ready for combat – any more than were their pilots, who were often given only the barest familiarization before being sent into the attack.

In early 1944 Messerschmitt had sanctioned exploration of a bomber version which might carry a load of up to 2,000 lb of bombs. Racks were fitted under the fuselage. More hair-raising, a 1,000 or 2,000 lb bomb was fitted with wooden wings and towed behind the aircraft. This flying bomb sat on a trolley which was jettisoned on take-off and the pilot would then, so the theory went, fly the plane and bomb to the target, where he would go into a shallow dive, aim and release the bomb, and climb away at top speed. This contraption was not popular, even with test pilots. One, Gerde Linder, was forced to bail out when an uncontrollable oscillation was set up between aircraft and bomb, and on another occasion he was forced to land aircraft and bomb together because the latter could not be detached in flight. The towed bomb concept was abandoned, but Hitler's wishes had still to be satisfied.

On 29 May 1944, at yet another conference, Goering, speaking to an audience which included Messerschmitt and Galland, suggested that the term 'fighter-bomber' should in future be dropped in favour of 'super-speed bomber'. He explained that it was not that the Führer wanted to exclude the fighter role, just that current production should be of the super-speed bomber. It was the Führer's wish that the bomb capacity, racks, bombsight and tactics should be sorted out, and then the role as fighter could be considered. Goering implored his audience to do nothing to upset Hitler: 'The commands of the Führer must remain inviolable,' he exclaimed, slapping down the hapless Messerschmitt when a slip of the tongue made him refer to the aircraft as 'the fighter'.

This bizarre turn of events resulted in the famous Führer-Order of 8 June 1944 – two days after the Allied landings in Normandy. The order was the upshot of a conference with Saur, in which he permitted *testing* of the 262 as a fighter, but under no circumstances was bomber production to be delayed: '. . . not until results of these tests have been concluded will fighter production be permitted to start. Once this point has been reached there is no reason why production capacity cannot be divided between the two models.' This Führer-Order has given birth to the legend that only Hitler's obduracy prevented the Me 262 going into fighter service early enough to deal some very heavy blows against an unprepared enemy, especially British and American bombers, and is used as an argument that the war would have gone differently if only Hitler had not intervened. Speer in *Inside the Third Reich*, writes:

At the end of June 1944 Goering and I once more tried to make

Hitler see these points [that the 262 should be turned on American bombers]. Air Force pilots were spoiling to use them against the American fleets. But here was one of those moments when Hitler's preferences were insuperable . . . The more we tried to dissuade him the more stubbornly he held to it. To mollify us somewhat, he spoke of some day, in the future, when he would let the aircraft be used, at least partially, as a fighter.

Speer contends that the general staff were counting on the fighter to bring about a decisive turning point in the air war and that Hitler's mad determination cost them valuable time:

In the autumn of 1944 he finally and characteristically brushed aside the whole controversy by flatly forbidding any further discussion on the subject. When I telephoned General Kreipe, the new chief of staff of the air force, to inform him of what I wanted to write to Hitler in my mid-September report on the question of jet planes, he strongly advised me not even to allude to the matter. At the very mention of the Me 262, Hitler was likely to fly off the handle, he said. And I would only be making trouble for him, since Hitler would assume that the air force chief of staff had put me up to it.

Speer loftily says that he withdrew from the fray after telling Hitler that it was a grave error to make fighter planes serve as bombers. Be that as it may, from mid-1944 both fighter and fighter-bomber versions of the Me 262 began to roll off the production lines. It was certainly an aircraft which caused strange notions to enter the heads of those near the seat of power, particularly of those lacking the technical knowledge to enable them to judge what was actually happening. Engineer Saur led this band, telling a meeting on 22 June:

We deserve to be soundly reproached. During September and October last year we made certain promises which were not based on fact, but on pure wishful thinking. We simply assumed we would have a goodly number of machines available for rigorous testing by January or February: we assumed we would produce at least thirty or forty during March, sixty per month by May and soon thereafter seventy-five to eighty per month. It is now June and we do not have one single machine in operational service. We have only ourselves to blame – we were incapable of finding the resources, incapable of concentrating our efforts, and incapable of approaching the problem with the energy and determination warranted by its vital importance. The development and production of the Me 262 has been attended by a number of mysterious machinations – this sort of thing must come to an end immediately! I will not be lied to and deceived any longer!

Saur's ramblings were based on little more than his own delusions. But he was not alone. In August Kreipe was to obtain minor concessions from Hitler: every twentieth 262 could be a fighter, he was told, and in September, when Kreipe handed in his resignation, Hitler conceded that the 262 could be produced as a fighter provided that each one could carry at least one 500 lb bomb in an emergency.

In fact there were no mysterious conspiracies behind the delays in introducing the Me 262 into service. What delays there were had much more to do with the situation inside Germany generally, where production delays of all kinds were mounting as the war machine was being increasingly smashed by bombing. On Anselm Franz's own statement, the supply of 004 production engines did not get into its stride until the spring of 1944 and, even then, production of fighter airframes was outstripping engines. The truth is that the world's first production jet fighter was doomed from the start, along with the Third Reich. What might be a much more potent criticism of the German jet fighter programme is the cancellation of the Heinkel 280 and its promising engine, for they could have been in mass production by 1944. This was, almost certainly, a major error. But the Germans were not alone in error. In England, jet production had stood still, though all was not yet lost: a meeting had been arranged in the Swan and Royal pub in the Lancashire town of Clitheroe.

Clitheroe is one of those neat limestone towns in north Lancashire that look from the air like a scattering of grey pebbles between the green and gritstone hills of the Pennines. Its main street climbs to a ruined Norman castle (the smallest keep in England – Clitheroe's sole claim to architectural distinction) and on it stands the Swan and Royal, which, in 1942, was a snug firelit old pub where you could still get a decent five bob dinner – five shillings (twenty-five pence) being the maximum charge allowed in food-rationed Britain.

Into the Swan's restaurant one November evening trooped three men, the first, the party's evident leader, a medium-tall man, in his mid-fifties, built like a bull and loaded with suppressed energy. This was Ernest Hives, Rolls-Royce's works manager. The second, more diffident member of the party, grey-suited and middle-aged, was Rover's joint chief engineer, S. B. Wilks, who was suffering the twin scourges of Whitehall and Whittle. The third man was a six-foot-plus gangling thirty-five-year old with a receding chin and poorly fitting clothes: Dr Stanley Hooker – later Sir Stanley – who, by the time he was thirty-two, had added a third more power to the great Rolls-Royce Merlin piston engine, revivifying the Spitfire, converting the American Mustang from a mediocrity to a great long-range fighter and making of the Mosquito and Lancaster two of the war's invincible aeroplanes. After Whittle, Hooker would become Britain's most important jet pioneer, the man who rescued the jet engine from Rover's ruin, made a production engine out of it, and – above all – thought bigger in terms of thrust than any other jet engineer in Britain excepting Whittle.

Many years later Stanley Hooker recalled that the conversation over coffee had run on the lines:

Hives: Why are you playing around with this jet engine? It's not your line of business, you grub around on the ground and I hear from Hooker here that things are going from bad to worse with Whittle.

Wilks: We can't get on with him at all. I want to be shot of the whole business.

Hives: I'll tell you what I'll do. You give us the jet job and I'll give you our tank engine factory in Nottingham.

'In no time at all,' Sir Stanley related, 'the deal was done.' The Nottingham factory which Hives swapped for the jet plant was producing a tank engine called Meteor (in fact an unsupercharged Merlin) and Rover would run the factory for many years after the takeover. In his autobiography (*Not Much of an Engineer*) Sir Stanley writes: 'There was no talk of money, and no talk of getting government agreement. I suspect that Hives had already done that, but I never knew or cared. When two such big men get together, decisions of this magnitude can be made on the spot.'

This awe was misplaced. The change was being engineered in Whitehall and Hives had almost certainly been prompted by Freeman to make the unofficial approach. The Air Ministry had spent some months coming round to a decision it should have taken three years previously – to put the jet engine in the hands of those who could manage it and make it successfully and as far back as the previous April, Freeman and Linnell had discussed a handover which would put Power Jets and Whittle at Hives' disposal. To Hives the decision was to be the key to Rolls-Royce's future, the step which ensured that the company would have world pre-eminence after the war. Although he was at this time works manager, he would be elected to the board the following year, to become managing director in 1946 and chairman in 1950, when he also became Lord Hives, first baron. He would be at or near the top for twenty years.

Hives was the fourth of the great Rolls-Royce dynasts, following Charles Stewart Rolls, and Henry Royce and Claude Johnson, who, after Rolls was killed in 1910, went on to build an engineering legend which was admired and envied world-wide. Hives first joined the company from a Reading garage, then went to Napier before returning to Rolls in 1908 as a road test driver; he was one of the first men to reach 100 mph on a racing track. He had no formal engineering education, having left school at fifteen, but in 1915, when Royce designed his first aero engine, the Eagle, Hives directed its development. This engine powered the Vimy bomber of Alcock and Brown on the first direct transatlantic flight, and it was followed by a long line of successful engines, all developed under Hives' direction, culminating in the Merlin. He was an intuitive leader ('and an honest rogue' said Frank Whittle. 'He always let you know beforehand when he was going to do you down.'). He loved responsibility, success, power, snooker and the voice of Miss Ethel Merman. He built up such contacts and influence in Whitehall and the RAF that Rolls operated with an autonomy envied and often resented by all other manufacturers. He never sought advice, never resented criticism, and was one of the few engineers ever to influence government policy.

When he 'decided to go all out for the jet' (his words) he made the most important decision in the company's history – but he was led to it by Stanley Hooker, who had joined Rolls in 1938 on an intriguing arrangement which left him to find his own level in the company. He quickly did, and it was very near the top. He was a prima donna and while working on one engine was always thinking about the next, not always with complete success. After a grammar school education, he had taken a course in mathematics at Imperial College where he became interested in hydrodynamics (the flow of fluids) and was able to take von Karman's works on vortexes further than the great scientist-engineer had done. This led him on to an interest in aerodynamics and work on the compressibility of air, which would almost inevitably lead him to Whittle and the jet. First, however, he had gone to do research at Oxford, where he became interested in supersonics, and he joined Rolls after coming to Hives' notice as a promising young man whose analytical talents might benefit the company's approach to engineering problems. Left to float in the first few weeks, and to absorb the Rolls atmosphere, Hooker stumbled on the fact that Merlin superchargers, though the best in the world, were still less efficient than they could be: his improvements to them added 70 mph to the speed of the Spitfire, 10,000 feet to its fighting altitude, and supercharged his own career in the process. Then he heard of Whittle.

Hayne Constant made the introduction early in 1940 when he took Hooker down to Lutterworth to show him the test rig – a pigsty compared with the facilities of Rolls in Derby. Hooker watched an engine test run: 'I felt conscious that I was in the presence of great power – whether it was useful power I had no idea.' Indeed, the promise of the jet escaped Hooker for some months. The dawning came as he fell gradually under Whittle's spell and as he began to equate pounds of thrust with the horsepower measurement with which he was more familiar. Later in 1940 Hooker learnt that the engine was giving some 800 lb thrust and in August he passed this figure to Hives, who said that it would not blow the skin off a rice pudding. Hooker was able to show him that the thrust of a Merlin piston engine flying in a Spitfire at 300 mph was about 840 lb, and here was a crude experimental engine which was giving nearly that much power already. Hives immediately made plans to go to Lutterworth the following Sunday. As Whittle showed him round, Hives asked where the other engines were and, when Whittle explained the poverty of his resources, he invited him to send drawings to Derby so that they could make some parts for him; money was not mentioned. This collaboration was confined to making turbine blades, gear casings and some other components, all of which was very welcome to Whittle; it also served, of course, to keep Hives and Hooker broadly aware of the developments Whittle was making.

Early in 1941 Whittle heard from Tizard that Rolls were going ahead with a jet project of their own. This alarmed him at first, but it turned out to be the work of A. A. Griffith, who had left Farnborough to join Rolls at the beginning of the war. His complicated engine, called the CR1, was based on the axial principle. Each of its blade wheels was free-running, with no rotating shaft connecting them; the inner blading was a turbine stage, the outer a compressor stage. Alternate wheels were contra-rotating. Air entered at the rear of the engine, travelling forward through the compressor stages to a combustor at the front of the engine. After burning, the hot gas then expanded backwards through the turbine stages. Griffith had at last acknowledged that a pure jet could drive an aeroplane and he had dropped the propeller once and for all, but in his first full engine project he plumped for a particularly complex design. Unsurprisingly, the CR1 quickly ran into severe difficulties and none of the calculated efficiencies was ever reached

Griffith was undoubtedly a brilliant theoretician with attractive personal characteristics to those whose company he accepted, but, to quote Hooker's opinion: 'He was bigoted in favour of the axial compressor and had reported unfavourably on Whittle's engine . . . He was a curious loner, whose thinking was years ahead of his time. His fertile brain would produce some radical new idea for an engine which he would push hard; but once others took up the idea he would lose interest and pass on to his next invention. He had no concept of the team effort which is required to produce a real engine.'

The experience with Griffith's engine made Hives sceptical of jet propulsion in general, and it took Whittle and Hooker to convince him of the inherent simplicity of the idea and that the problems which presented themselves during development could be solved by commonsense approaches. Hives' appetite for the jet market was also sharpened by the knowledge that some of his competitors were already rolling with their own projects. As his personal assistant of the time, Alec Harvey-Bailey, wrote in a memoir (*Hives, the Quiet Tiger*):

> Padding round the gas turbine set-up, like the quiet tiger he was, Hives saw that Metro-Vick were designing engines, as was Frank Halford for de Havilland. The Americans were also heavily involved. Hives saw that as sub-contractor to Power Jets, Rolls-Royce would miss a great opportunity. After discussions with the Ministry of Aircraft Production he approached Wilks of Rover on the question of Rolls-Royce taking over the management of the factories at Barnoldswick and Clitheroe. According to a note written by Hives on 28 December 1942 Wilks accepted the proposal that Rolls-Royce should take over the gas turbine business and, although it was not spelt out, Rover would accept the tank engine project in exchange.

In his note Hives wrote:

> We want to make it clear that the mere fact of changing the management from Rover to Rolls-Royce will not in itself produce results. Rolls-Royce can only undertake this project on condition that they are allowed to operate it in a similar way to that in which they run their own business . . . In other words we must have complete control, subject to the technical policy laid down by M A P . . . The first responsibility we shall assume is the technical responsibility, and in addition, to decide on what types and numbers of turbines should be manufactured.

Thus Rolls-Royce entered the gas turbine field, at no cost to themselves other than the wages of a handful of men whom they appointed to run the two plants. All the capital equipment had been paid for by the government; wages were similarly paid for wartime work. Considering the prize offered, there can be few manufacturers in history who have taken up a key new technology at such little risk and expense in order to assure their future. The contractual details remained to be argued with the Ministry, but Hives had pulled off a great coup, calling all the shots and dictating his own terms to everyone, including Whitehall and Power Jets. Men, women, machine tools and jigs, materials and drawings were all sitting there awaiting orders. His timing had been impeccable: the early engines were not far from acceptability, much of the sweat of the job was over and all the contenders were exhausted. It was for such reasons that Hives came to head Rolls-Royce. Jets for tanks was one of the industrial bargains of the century.

The end for Wilks and Rover came with a meeting with the Minister for Aircraft Production, who minuted on 18 December:

I saw Mr Wilks this afternoon and arranged with him:
1. Rover will hand over the two factories to Rolls-Royce
2. He will see Mr Hives and arrange the details of handing over to their mutual convenience
3. If they have any differences they can come to me and I will settle them. Permanent Secretary please see to this
4. He will now communicate formally with Rolls and Rover
5. As there is no formal agreement with Rover I said we would leave it to him and Rolls as in 2 above to settle a fair and convenient method of handing over
6. Neither he nor I made any suggestions as to MAP accepting any liability or being bound to any particular terms of notice

RSC

The initials were those of Richard Stafford Cripps, the brilliant left-wing statesman, scientist and lawyer, who had been appointed minister by Churchill only a month previously, and had had intensive briefings by Freeman on the chaos which was supposed to be Britain's jet engine programme.

In December Hives appointed Hooker chief engineer of the jet project and personally toured the two Lancashire mills. His works manager's eye saw what Rover had failed to see: the Waterloo mill was wholly inadequate. He immediately closed it and made Barnoldswick into an experimental and development centre. The tempo of work changed completely. The 1,600 workers and their extensive equipment were focussed immediately on the task of getting the W2B engine right and ready for RAF service.

There was, however, still the matter of the Rolls–Power Jets relationship. The Ministry concluded that they should not, at least for the moment, seize the assets and merge Whittle's company with Rolls-Royce; nor did they force a merger of the two. Instead in a change of heart in Whitehall for unknown reasons, Power Jets was to keep its autonomy and carry out design, research and development work in its (by now) well-equipped plant at Whetstone. Hives visited Power Jets with a delegation from Rolls-Royce and met the board. He told them bluntly that his company intended to be the centre for the whole of jet propulsion engine work in Britain (something which would come about only some twenty years later). Any Ministry

proposal that might place Rolls in a position subservient to Power
Jets would, he stressed, be quite unacceptable because until Rolls-
Royce came on the scene the venture was all but dead and Rolls
were the sole instrument of their survival. (The Power Jets' team
demurred but Hives ignored them.) Rolls were going to conduct their
jet engine programme in the way they thought best for the country
and for Rolls-Royce.

To reinforce the message, Hooker personally told Whittle:

> Frank, you must realize that now that Rolls-Royce have taken
> over and intend to put their full weight behind your engine,
> control must necessarily pass to us. With the facilities at our
> disposal it is no use your trying to compete. On the contrary you
> must join with us and give us the benefits of your talents and
> experience . . . I will keep you fully informed and I hope you will
> look to me as your man, only too anxious to have direction and
> advice from you.

It must have been obvious to Whittle that control of the project
was out of the question and that influence with Rolls-Royce was at
best tenuous. In fact both sides were so relieved with their respective
positions (Power Jets still had an independent existence) that the will
to work together overrode all other considerations. It is clear from
interviews and the written record that collaboration was effective,
perhaps the more so in this case for being carried out with unwritten
rules.

In early 1943 Whittle went, for the first time, to Barnoldswick,
where much had been heard, not always to his credit, of this enigmatic
genius. He addressed the whole plant, and the magic of his personality
and enthusiasm, though a little dimmed through tiredness and ill
health, was enough to fire the workers – who had already realized that
with the advent of Rolls Royce they would be put to work usefully.
After all the conflict everyone wanted to work smoothly. Whittle
records that 'technical consultation between us was unaffected and
the atmosphere was so cordial that it gave rise to firm and lasting
friendships between the engineers of the two companies'. In confirma-
tion, Hooker wrote in his autobiography: 'I have often heard it said –
indeed it was the current view in many influential circles – that Frank
Whittle was an awkward and difficult man to deal with. This I
absolutely deny. In the more than forty years that I have known him,
we have never had a disagreement. Although Rolls-Royce was
destined to take his engine away from him I personally have never
had from him anything but encouragement and generous help.'

When Rolls took over at Barnoldswick, the management and senior engineers, all Rover appointees, were given the option of returning or remaining. Some of the best, sensing a quickening pulse, decided to stay, among them Adrian Lombard, a natural engineer without any formal training who would become chief engineer and technical director of the whole of Rolls-Royce before his tragically early death from heart disease in 1967. The team that was left were young, mostly in their mid-thirties, like Hooker and Whittle, and they rapidly organized a unified workforce, with an effective test programme for all the existing engines on the four available test beds. None of the completed engines had run for more than a few hours under Rover's aegis, but protracted engine-running was essential to the Rolls programme.

The tests were conducted on a very simple basis. An engine was run until a fault or breakage occurred, when the mishap was analysed, the fault righted or the part replaced with a strengthened part. Then the engine was run again until the next failure, which received the same treatment. This 'run and bust' philosophy was applied within the stringent 100-hour test criterion laid down by the Ministry: an engine must have run 100 trouble-free hours before it was accepted for use. Total running time under Rover management had never been more than 100 hours a month but in January 1943, as Rolls took over, it jumped to 396 hours and mounted almost every month thereafter. By June 1943 it was possible to instal engines in the Gloster Meteor prototype fighter which had been standing embarrassingly engine-less at Gloster for a whole year while the wrangles over engines were played out between Whitehall, Rover and Power Jets. Much flight test data came from an engine fitted into the tail of a converted Wellington bomber and another E28/39 prototype was added to the flight programme.

Rolls concentrated first of all on their version of the W2B, in order to get that right, while Whittle focussed on its successors, the W2/500 and the W2/700. By May 1943 the W2B – still basically a Whittle engine – passed its 100-hour test at its rating of 1,600 lb thrust; the next goal was 2,000 lb thrust. In October this engine was christened Welland, establishing a Rolls-Royce practice of naming jet engines after British rivers, echoing the idea of flow.

The Meteor's top speed of little more than 400 mph brought protests from the piston engine designers and manufacturers that the performance gain was so small that MAP and the Air Ministry might just as well not have invested the effort. A typical complainant was Roy (later Sir Roy) Fedden, the chief engineer of the Bristol

Aeroplane Company and a fine designer. He wrote a letter of protest to Sir Wilfred Freeman, who passed it on to Hives for his comment; he in turn asked Hooker for his views. Between them they were able to point out to Freeman that with the improvements under way a piston engine would need to exceed 4,000 hp to compete with improved Wellands and a later engine, the Derwent, which would give 2,000 lb thrust (this again was a W2B-based engine, but with a twenty-five per cent gain on the Welland). A 4,000 hp engine would need thirty-six cylinders and would have been a vast, heavy and cumbersome mass for airframe designers to cope with. Fedden, persuaded, quickly changed his views.

Successive improvements were made to the engine and airframe of the Meteor, which became a first class front-line fighter almost immediately after the end of the war in 1945. In November of that year a Meteor set a world speed record of 606 mph. Versions of the Meteor set various other records and the performance gain within two years in relaxed peacetime conditions convinced any lingering doubters that the jet engine would eventually supplant the piston engine for any but light aircraft.

In any event, another jet engine of much more formidable power was coming into service from another source altogether: de Havilland, a company noted for its genius, independence and pioneering spirit from its beginnings in the First World War. Under the direction of Sir Geoffrey de Havilland the company was instrumental in providing the engines for the Gloster Meteor's first flight on 5 March 1943 – three months ahead of the intended Rover/Rolls-Royce engines and an eloquent comment on Rover's performance over the previous three years. De Havilland's engine was designed, developed and the first production runs begun in little more than eighteen months, and the de Havilland Vampire fighter in which it flew was designed and built in sixteen months. De Havilland had of course produced one of the aerial war winners – the Mosquito, a beautiful innovative wooden fighter bomber which for much of the war was the fastest aircraft flying, as well as the most versatile. It was the brain-child of Sir Geoffrey himself.

The combination of the H1 Goblin jet engine and the Vampire airframe would have achieved similar stature had it been available in time for war service, for it was a brilliant conception. It was the product of three minds: Sir Geoffrey de Havilland, the company's founder and chief, Frank Halford, an unqualified but outstanding engine designer, and George Bishop, the airframe designer who went on to create the Comet, the world's first passenger jet liner. Of the three, de Havilland was the intellectual as well as de facto chief. He was a man of deep sensibility, self-effacing, unaffected and selfless, who led by discussion rather than diktat, without any loss of natural authority. By training he was a mechanical engineer, but he was unqualified in any branch of aeronautical engineering since the discipline simply did not exist when he had been inspired by the Wright brothers in the 1900s to build his own aeroplane and engine. He may be said to have been one of the inventors of airframe and aero engine design. This gentle, good man was devoted in his spare time to natural history and when he selected a Hampshire field for the first flight of his first aeroplane he put markers over two larks' nests so that he would not run over them on taxi or take-off. The larks were spared but a few hundred feet into the flight his aeroplane literally came apart at the seams and he crashed ignominiously, though he escaped unharmed. Two of his three sons were, however, killed in flying accidents – one testing the fastest jet plane of its day – and these tragedies broke his wife's health and hastened her death: the family paid the supreme price for pioneering.

De Havilland formed his own company in 1920 and set his heart on civil aviation; he designed military aircraft only when the country's needs dictated it. He profoundly distrusted official wisdom throughout his life, a scepticism that dated from reading a War Office memorandum of 1909 which stated: 'We have decided to cease making experiments with aeroplanes as it has proved too costly, namely £2,500.' He remained an innovator all his life, believing that great designers are born with an innate facility for form; a deep understanding of mechanical engineering is needed, together with experience, but the gift was probably already there. He held that good designers first created a mental picture of the aeroplane, visualizing shape and relationships. Once the picture had been built up in the head, it could be transferred to the drawing board. After that, the designer had to make sure that each part was strong enough, and as easy as possible to make, repair and maintain. It was also important to resist taking on more work than could be done well. The result of these maxims in his case was a line of some of the most beautiful aeroplanes ever made.

In Frank Halford he found an engine designer without training or formal qualifications who had a natural gift which resulted in some fine piston and jet engines. Bulman, the Ministry's director of engine research and development, said of him: 'He was the essentially creative artist, anxious to get-on-with-the-next and a little too apt to leave to his devoted staff the drudgery and sweat of carrying his last-but-one design into production. He had immense magnetic and dynamic charm, but his mind was ever busy with his engines.'

De Havilland, Halford and Bishop, the airframe designer, flew from their factory at Hatfield one day in May 1941 to watch some of the earliest flight trials of the E28/39. They realized immediately that a new era in aviation was opening and decided that they would answer Air Ministry specification E6/41 for a single seat jet fighter. (The Meteor was built to a 1940 specification and the Air Ministry in its latest specification was calling for a more advanced single engine aircraft.) Halford determined on a much higher thrust engine and, with the benefit of collaboration directly with Power Jets and later multilaterally through the Gas Turbine Collaboration Committee, he set to work to design an engine of 3,000 lb thrust, the most powerful in the world for a short time. This was the H1 or Goblin, and it was broadly similar to the Whittle engines, using a centrifugal compressor driven by a single stage turbine.

De Havilland's team were no mere copyists, however, and their designs offered some interesting solutions to the problems which the jet age was beginning to pose for designers. They wanted a 'straight through' design in which air was not required to perform any reverse-flows within the engine. One of the reasons that Whittle had designed bends in his airflow was that he wanted to keep the shaft between turbine and compressor as short as possible to avoid whirling. (A shaft whirls or vibrates like a violin string when the number of revolutions per minute at which it is turning equals the natural frequency of the part.) Whittle's short shaft dealt with this problem but it meant that there was not enough room to interpose the combustion or chambers, between compressor and turbine. They had to be unted out of the straight line and the air had to be conducted round bends in the piping to reach them. Halford designed a longer shaft so that he could place his combustors along the straight line of the engine; and he solved the problem of whirling by using a larger diameter shaft which was thicker and more rigid. (When Rover engineers saw this design they realized its superiority, and it was their attempt to do the same thing with their B26 that culminated in the row with Whittle and their dismissal.)

The Vampire's tail was attached to the end of twin booms instead of a conventional fuselage, because the designers could afford only minimal power loss from the jet pipe, which therefore had to be as short as possible. Instead of a fuselage they had thus built jet engine and pipe into the stubby cockpit-engine nacelle to which the wings were attached. The nacelle structure borrowed an important feature from the piston engine Mosquito: it was made with a plywood-balsa-plywood sandwich, beautifully light and very strong. The Vampire was the first service fighter with a top speed exceeding 500 mph. The prototype's first flight was in September 1943, not far behind the Meteor, although the Vampire had been designed and built in so much shorter a time.

Now that an industrial programme for the design and construction of jet engines was beginning to emerge through the smoke of inter-necine warfare, how stood the jet engine and the organizations which should have been spearheading progress – Power Jets, the RAE and Rolls-Royce? Although the decision to order the W2 engine off the drawing board without due development time had ended in disaster, and the Meteor programme had been set back two years, there had been some crucial progress in engine design. Surging was becoming a controllable phenomenon, but repeated blade failures, caused mainly by high temperature running and chafing against heat-distorted casings, were still a major problem. The alloy used in blades since early 1939 was Rex 78, produced by Firth Vickers, and though good, it was not good enough. During 1941, however, a new alloy called Nimonic 80, produced by Mond Nickel, became available. Tests by the National Physical Laboratory were very promising and the adoption of this material for turbine blades, the design of which was being constantly refined, went some way to alleviating the problem. Impeller failure, frequently caused by vibra-tion, was another major snag, and the impeller was now regarded as the weakest part of the engine. Strengthening the blades went some way to solving the difficulty, but the most ingenious solution was to raise the speed at which the natural frequency of vibration occurred to a point higher than the operating speed of the unit. Shortage of skills in handling advanced materials was another bugbear from which the projects suffered – as British industry suffers to this day – and the acquisition of skills was a slow and often painful process in the press of a wartime economy.

Power Jets were at this time showing great resourcefulness in designing machine tools to handle new shaping and forming proces-ses, of which the beneficiaries (through the GTCC) were the entire jet engine community. Power Jets were much better equipped to deal with problems of this kind because of their new factory at Whetstone, four miles south of Leicester. This purpose-built plant, conceded by the Ministry after pressure from believers like Tizard and (to be fair) Brabazon, would enable Power Jets to build up to twelve complete development engines per year. It provided 80,000 square feet of factory space, palatial after Lutterworth, and by the spring of 1942 test beds were being installed. There was, however, still no guarantee of a long-term future for the company, which could not therefore offer its senior designers and engineers good, secure contracts. Whittle felt that this led to low morale, as did the sense that, whatever they did, Rolls Royce and the rest of the GTCC members would be the beneficiaries, not Power Jets. Productivity at Whetstone was not as high as at Lutterworth, which Whittle blamed on low standards among the newly recruited workers, and a small group of communist agitators, although the management of the company also seems to have been somewhat amateurish. It was the view of abler engineers that, while people like Williams and Tinling were adequate for the running of a comparatively small research and development company, Whetstone found them out of their depths. Thus, despite the increase in staff and facilities, and the capability of building engines, Power Jets in 1943 was not a happy place and there was a good deal of unrest. Whittle's magnetism and drive were missing because he was suffering from continuous nervous overstrain caused by years of overwork and conflict.

The tempo of work at the Royal Aircraft Establishment had meanwhile increased rapidly after the successful early flights of the E28/39 in May 1941. Later that year Hayne Constant was made head of engine development and he set up a turbine division under Dr William Hawthorne, who returned to the RAE following a year's secondment to Power Jets. Here, too, an assortment of huts was giving way to purpose-built engine test houses, a workshop, laboratory and an office block. This small centre was set up at Pyestock, a village on the opposite side of the airfield from the main research centre, and was very quickly to become world-famous for its research and test work. The virtue of the RAE's set-up was that work could be conducted away from the daily clattering rush to get engines built and tested. The staff could experiment carefully on components that were giving consistent trouble. Turbines and compressors could be more carefully matched to give the best performance possible; combustion experiments could be given a scientific basis; exhaust gases examined spectrographically; fatigue failure of blades probed with the best scientific equipment of the day. None of this could be done on the factory floor, but all of it was of great importance in building up a body of knowledge for the development of the aircraft gas turbine. All the companies taking part in the programme benefited from the results: a national programme was taking shape.

The R A E were also collaborating with Metropolitan Vickers on their own ambitious F2 axial flow jet engine. The first engine was completed towards the end of 1941 and testing started in December. Its early significance was that by October 1943 two F2s could be fitted as flight engines to a Gloster Meteor, which flew for the first time on 13 November, the first British flight of an axial flow engine. The development of the F2 was a relatively smooth affair: it gave around 2,000 lb thrust and was a good example of successful collaboration between a research establishment and an industrial company.

From the spring of 1943 onwards the R A E also became the base for flight tests of the two E28 experimental aeroplanes. Several records were set up in these times, not all of them intentional. In July 1943 the second aeroplane developed loss of aileron control while being flown at more than 30,000 feet by Squadron Leader W. D. Davie. As the aircraft tumbled uncontrollably through the sky, Davie baled out and broke all height records for a parachute jump. One of the Farnborough test pilots, Wing Commander Charles McClure, recalled many years later the record he established as the first man to re-light a jet engine in the sky.

I put the E28 in a stall turn over Farnborough on my third flight of the day. I put on full rudder and the aircraft tilted slightly on its back as it came round. I was diving slightly over the vertical from about 7,000 feet. Then the whole aircraft shuddered violently. The fin [the vertical part of the tail] had stalled, and the rudder was locked solidly to one side. I used great force on the control column but the rudder then locked in the opposite direction. The aircraft again shuddered violently. I managed to straighten the rudder and the aircraft became stable in a vertical dive at about 300 mph. As I pulled back on the stick each wing stalled in turn and I thought we were going to spin. I pulled out of the dive to discover that the engine flame had gone out. A few days beforehand a spark plug had been rigged in the combustor against just this emergency. It was attached to a switch in the cockpit – a crude arrangement but better than nothing. I flicked the switch but the engine did not re-light, probably because the high speed was compressing the gas away from the sides of the tubes and the spark. I left the switch on and, as we were rather low, prepared for an emergency dead stick [no engine] landing at Farnborough. As the speed fell off I saw the jet pipe temperature gauge start to rise – the engine had re-lighted. I landed normally, if a little shaken. Nobody on the ground realized that there had been anything wrong.

McClure added that it was not until the 1960s that he really felt safe in an aeroplane.

Rolls-Royce had officially taken over the Barnoldswick and Clitheroe factories on 1 April 1943, although Hooker and his team had moved in during January and already begun a remarkable transformation of the scene. They found a disheartened workforce which was mistrustful of management after the Rover débâcle, but the pace of work imposed by Rolls-Royce, and the evident sense of purpose, soon raised morale. Most of the workers were local people but a large contingent of young women, who proved highly skilled in their use of machine tools, lived in a hostel which was soon christened Virgin Villas. The W2 engines were still giving only 1,250 to 1,400 lb thrust against a design expectation of 1,600 lb, so Hooker's team decided not to wait for improvements but to press ahead with long-running trials which would at least establish the engines' mechanical integrity and reliability. Hooker and the metallurgists decided to settle for Nimonic 80 – eighty per cent nickel – for blade material, which turned out to be so reliable that it was used for the next ten years in a variety of engines. Efforts were concentrated on increasing the thrust of the Welland, which was modified to take twenty-five per cent greater airflow and named the Derwent 1. It gave 2,000 lb thrust and by the end of 1944 it was powering a much improved Meteor, the mark 111. Some 500 Derwents were made by the end of the war – a considerable though belated achievement. At last, the British jet engine industry was working well.

The conquest of America was now to come.

Invention and innovation are supposed to be the twin engines of American power. Allied to the laser vision and vaulting flight of the symbolic national eagle, and fuelled by the restless spirit of the individual and the ruthless winds of competition, they have made the USA the greatest power on earth. Or so the legend says.

On 10 June 1940, a few weeks after contracts had been awarded for the Heinkel 280 and Messerschmitt 262, a committee of the United States National Academy of Sciences reported: 'In its present state, and even considering the improvements possible . . . the gas turbine engine can hardly be considered a feasible application to airplanes mainly because of the difficulty in complying with the stringent weight requirements imposed by aeronautics.' Thus, twenty years on, American engineers repeated the errors of their English colleagues.

America's passport to the jet age had to be handed to them by two Englishmen, Air Vice Marshal Linnell and Dr Harold Roxbee Cox, thirteen months later, in a sunlit Whitehall office. On 22 July 1941 they met two American government representatives, Mr Schultz and Colonel A. J. Lyon, and described to them in detail the work of Whittle and Power Jets. Three days later they took the Americans to meet Whittle and his colleagues at their primitive plant. Later still, they took the two to see the Gloster factory and the E28 prototypes. Drawings and data were given to the Americans under the free trade in secrets which had been established by the British on the assumption that one day America would be in the war as an ally, that she must be prepared for the day and that she must be made the arsenal of democracy through the lease-lend principle, an imaginative act of self-interest often described as the most unselfish act in history.

The deal in this particular secret was remarkably advantageous to the Americans. Without paying any significant sum and without any real discussion of the patent situation, America was given a new technology with which to transform aviation. She entered the jet age – which in five short years she would dominate – via the small back rooms in Britain where, however uncertainly, the revolution was being forged. The Whitehall meeting put on a formal basis other hints, official and unofficial, which had begun with leaks from a British mission to America led by Sir Henry Tizard in 1940. The Americans were astonished to find that Britain was so far down a road which their Academy of Sciences had told them was blocked and it is indeed a matter of wonder that the Americans failed to invent the jet. If necessity is the mother of invention, then the USA, with its imaginative developments in civil aviation, forced along by the need for rapid business travel over its vast land mass, certainly needed the thrust of the jet to fly fast and high. Indeed, for many years the US stood on the brink of its discovery through the work of lone and disregarded inventors but, tantalizingly, the country of the individual spirit drew back from the final step for which a handful of pioneers were striving with almost as much vision as Whittle and von Ohain.

In August 1939, on the eve of World War Two, when von Ohain's engine first flew and the German Air Ministry was at last sorting out its act with German manufacturers, and when even the British Air Ministry had agreed to buy up Whittle's work and make a jet engine that would fly, American aviation was gorged with innovation. The US airlines and their manufacturers had developed and equipped the world's largest and most advanced commercial airline system. It was so well engined by manufacturers such as Wright, Pratt and Whitney, and Allison that there seemed to be no great impetus to go higher and faster – in some ways a testament to the great steps already taken with the piston and the propeller. The twelve-seat Ford Tri-motor, a noisy, spartan but reliable work horse of the 1920s, had a cruising speed of 95 mph, but within a few years the greatest workhorse of them all – and the first commercial aeroplane to make a profit without any subsidy   the Douglas DC3 Dakota, cruised at almost 200 mph.

As far back as the 1920s the metal monoplane was seen as the way to the future and the end of the fabric-covered biplane was evident in the work of Lockheed, Douglas and Boeing, whose engineers were harnessed successfully to solving the problems of the all-metal era. With the powerful radial piston engines of Wright and Pratt, US airlines were supreme. True, those engines were knobbly, flat-fronted, of large diameter, and therefore responsible for very large amounts of drag, but the National Advisory Committee for Aeronautics devised a streamlined engine cowling which cut drag by up to twenty per cent and enhanced air cooling, solving these complex problems through brilliant theoretical and practical work.

The propeller, rejected by Whittle and von Ohain, was enjoying a new and vital lease of life which kept its development parallel with the new generations of aero engine. The problem with the propeller was that the angle of the spinning blade which was right for take-off and climb was not the best for cruising flight, and the angle for high speed was not the best for flying round low looking for partly obscured airfields. All this was solved by varying the pitch or angle of the blade in flight – in the early days by the pilot himself, but later automatically. Other engine improvements would have been as nothing without this development, which revolutionized commercial flying because of its dramatic effect on fuel economy and performance at different heights.

Along with greater engine power and propeller efficiency went a large number of accompanying improvements – the retractable undercarriage, flaps for braking and increasing lift at take-off and landing, and de-icers to clear the wings and propellers of a major hazard of the American climate. In the two decades between the wars American designers transformed the face of commercial aviation without having to worry about newfangled power plants; indeed, their cup was overflowing with innovations which produced lines of beautiful and successful aeroplanes which comfortably led the rest of the world.

Boeing first revolutionized air transport with the 247, which was the world's first cantilever wing, all-metal, twin-engined monoplane. It could carry a full load (including ten passengers) coast-to-coast in the USA in twenty hours. When it first flew in 1933 sixty were ordered by United Airlines. Boeing, together with Pratt and Whitney, who supplied the engines, Hamilton Standard (propellers) and United, realized that if all the 247s were delivered to United before any other airline was allowed to buy, they had a clamp on modern air transport for two to three years. Two competing airlines, Continental and Western, determined to break this attempt at a stranglehold and asked the brilliant young designer Donald Douglas to produce a plane at least the equal of the 247. Douglas accepted the challenge and the result was the DC1, which carried four more passengers for the same operating costs. There followed the DC2 and then, in 1936, the DC3, affectionately known as the Gooney Bird, of which hundreds are still flying in different parts of an otherwise unimaginably changed world of the 1980s. In the 1930s Boeing also produced the world's first four-engined airliner, the Stratocruiser, which was developed into a transatlantic carrier for the war and after.

Geography favoured the development of American airlines and provided the spur for engine and airframe manufacturers. All civil flying could take place within one country – there were no national boundaries to overfly – and all flights were overland, where it was not too difficult to provide navigational beacons and a pattern of emergency airfields. The American business population was regaining its confidence and affluence after the great slump and could afford the price. Although the railroad system was excellent, the ninety hours by rail from Los Angeles to Newark, New Jersey, looked antique when compared with the fifteen to twenty hours offered by the airlines from 1934. In Europe, the Germans had the most advanced airline system, but the excellent railroads over shorter distances did not encourage air passenger traffic to anything like the same extent. In Britain, with a much smaller land mass and an intricate rail network, this was even more true, although the British and the Dutch, for reasons of empire, did some remarkable pioneering to the Far East and Australia. British governments did little, however, to foster commercial flight – far less than their American and German counterparts – and Imperial's equipment, of vast biplanes with ocean liner standards of comfort, reflected an elitist view of air travel which ruled throughout the years up to the war.

The American government, by sharp contrast, was a major shaper and former of the US airlines. Government air mail subsidies originating in the 1920s brought many operators into existence – 400 by 1925, though a lot faded out of existence very rapidly. In 1930 Postmaster General Walter Brown, with a ruthless eye on the future, invited only big business conglomerates to tender for coast-to-coast routes, ensuring that the future would lie with large and financially strong operators using large and more economical aircraft. Brown was able to extend or consolidate routes where, in his judgement, the public interest would be promoted. He used such executive power to redraw the American airline map, excluding small operators from lucrative mail contracts; selected major carriers could share the principal routes between them. From such structure-rigging, giants such as TWA and United became king.

Brown's policies were continued to some extent by the Roosevelt administration but manufacturers were forced to sever their financial ties with the airlines and, although the big four kept their transcontinental routes, airlines such as Braniff and Delta were able to emerge. The network of mail routes, heavily subsidized, covering many thousands of miles, not only strengthened the new airlines, it gave them the clout to demand technologically more and more advanced and reliable aircraft, forcing the pace of change along. Manufacturers could also use the experience gained on military contracts such as the famous B17 bomber to help develop civil airliners such as the Stratocruiser. Government subsidy, the business climate and the innate thrustfulness of American industry and commerce are reflected in the figures for passenger miles travelled. In 1929 all the airliners of the world flew 96 million passenger miles; by 1939 they flew 1,395 million miles, a thirteen-fold increase in ten years. In 1929 the US accounted for 38 million passenger miles (European airlines 49 million) but by 1939 American airlines flew 754 million passenger miles against Europe's 434 million.

Immersed in such convulsive changes and beset by airlines demanding reliability and safety at the same time as speed and economy, it may not be surprising that the American aircraft industry was not particularly receptive to revolutionary ideas like the jet. They had their laps full of innovation already. The engine manufacturers, glutted with demands for ever more sophisticated versions of the same thing, had neither the spur nor the vision to make the quantum leap into the jet age. And the turbine manufacturers in the USA, though formidable, were firmly terrestrial in their ambitions – they had no thoughts about turbines for aircraft flight.

There was one exception. Dr Sanford A. Moss, born in 1872, had become obsessed as a sixteen-year-old mechanic with the idea that if fuel could be burnt in compressed air there would be major increases in energy output. He took his ideas to the University of California and by 1900 he had gained a BSc and MSc. For his doctoral thesis at Cornell University he began a theoretical examination of the gas turbine and in 1903 he successfully produced enough energy to drive a turbine by burning gas in a pressurized chamber – claimed to be a world's first. Moss's experiments at Cornell were carried out in a laboratory under Dr William Durand, one of the university's most prominent members of faculty, who complained that 'whatever Moss is doing it is not likely to be worth the noise, smoke and smell – indeed it is likely to be worth nothing at all.' Since he had to live with the output of Moss's experiments, Durand's complaint was not wholly unreasonable, but his prediction was wrong – as Durand was to recall many years later.

Moss's thesis on gas turbines drew some interest from engineers at General Electric (GE), the great power company which was deeply involved in the still-new technology of producing steam turbines for electricity generation. GE had been formed by a marriage in 1892 between the two major forces in the electrification of the USA, the Edison General Electric Company and the Thomson-Houston Company, whose British subsidiary was to nurture Whittle in his early days with Power Jets. GE's success owed a lot to the legendary intellectual curiosity of Thomas Edison, but other great engineers around him also encouraged a climate of research-guided achievement and innovation which made the company formidable. In Europe, Charles Parsons in Britain and de Laval in Sweden had each advanced steam turbine technology in the 1880s with practical turbines and Friedrich Stolze in Germany had demonstrated a gas turbine in 1872.

When Moss joined GE in the early 1900s his enthusiasm for the gas turbine idea was damped by the stock responses: lack of high temperature materials and low compressor and turbine efficiencies; the energy output did not justify the fuel consumed. Moss was assigned to GE's steam turbine department at Lynn, Massachusetts, the works which had been the headquarters of the Thomson–Houston company before the merger. He was lucky to be attached to a gifted group led by Elihu Thomson, a great pioneer of the electrical and turbine industries, and the advance of turbine technology became his life. Moss quickly became a leader in his field and through him and his team GE had built up by 1917 a useful business building centrifugal compressors for blast furnaces and a number of other applications requiring large amounts of low pressure compressed air.

By 1917 Moss had established a turbine research department at Lynn and in April, when the US entered World War One, the department was put on military work. In the autumn Moss again met his Cornell Professor, Durand, who had become head of the new National Advisory Committee for Aeronautics (NACA). Durand was by now sufficiently mollified to accept the value of Moss's work and he asked him – and GE – to develop and test an aero-engine booster. This work was to bring Moss to within a microdistance of inventing the jet engine and must be one of the great near-misses in the history of invention.

The concept of a booster had already been proposed by a Swiss engineer, Alfred Buechi, to his employers, Brown Boveri. His idea was to use the exhaust gases of a piston engine, always wasted into the air, to drive a turbine which, linked to a compressor, would drive compressed air back to the engine, boosting its power. By 1916 the idea was taken over by a Frenchman, Auguste Rateau, who was responsible for the world's first turbo-superchargers, or boosters, which were fitted to French warplanes to give them a height advantage over the Western Front before the end of the war.

Rateau's work was turned over to NACA with the condition that he and his company should be allowed to develop an engine booster for the army air force. NACA awarded development work both to Rateau and to GE, represented by Moss. The Rateau and Moss superchargers had one crucial difference: the Rateau design called for the turbine to be enclosed without cooling provisions – usual practice for steam turbines, which however operated at very much lower temperatures, while Moss, recalling his work at Cornell and Lynn, held that the turbine should be provided with cooling air.

The first real tests of the two projects showed Moss's virtues as a true visionary. The army called for a demonstration at full speed for an engine run of fifteen minutes – but at sea level. Moss objected because the true test of the supercharger was its ability to run at height and he proposed to do the test on the highest accessible mountain top. Thus Pikes Peak (14,109 feet) near Colorado Springs became a technology landmark as well as a scenic adornment. The engine, its test mount, fuel tanks, instruments, workshop, spares and the whole test crew had to be put together and taken two and a half miles into the sky. Nonetheless, Congress appropriated the funds and a Liberty piston engine of 350 hp at sea level was calibrated and hauled up to the heights. Run without a supercharger, it developed only 230 hp in June 1918 up on the peak. Tests with it, and with Rateau's challenger, went on until October, as the weather began to worsen. The GE supercharged engine eventually gave 356 hp – 6 hp better than sea level – and Moss won his contract. Just one month later the army cancelled the project, along with all other military contracts, because of the Armistice agreement.

GE thus won and lost its first contract for an aircraft supercharger within eighteen months. However, engineers at the US Army Air Corps Power Plant Laboratory – now Wright Patterson Air Force base, Dayton, and one of the major research bases of jet propulsion – decided in 1919 that the GE turbo-supercharger was to be one of its most important future projects, so Moss's team at Lynn were assured that their work was not wasted. Dayton, home of the bicycle shop where the Wright brothers gave birth to their flying machines, was thus the scene in the early 1920s of Army Air Corps-GE experiments with an improved supercharger with a 400 hp Liberty engine. Major Rudolph Schneider piloted a La Père biplane powered by this engine and its supercharger to 33,133 feet on 27 February 1920. At 60°F below zero – in an open cockpit – Schneider lost consciousness and his plane dived to 4,000 feet before he revived to make a safe landing. This world altitude record proved the efficiency of the turbo-supercharger and in the following year Lieutenant J. A. Macready climbed a La Père to 40,800 feet to clinch the point.

In 1921 the supercharger again scored in a major debate about the future of air power. Colonel Billy Mitchell put forward views about the superiority of the aeroplane as a war weapon, arguing that bombers were more effective than surface ships and guns against naval targets. The War Department, riled, gave him two captured German battleships, moored 100 miles off Virginia, to prove his point, requiring his Martin bombers not only to cover this distance from land and return, but to bomb from a height no lower than 15,000 feet. These were nearly impossible conditions for aircraft and engines of the time. Mitchell responded by installing G E turbo-superchargers to give the planes their range and altitude, and he successfully sank the ships, teaching the American warriors a lesson that they would have forgotten again by the time of Pearl Harbor.

A safely isolationist America of the 1920s did not pursue Mitchell's point in peacetime. In the 1930s, though, the Army Air Corps kept G E turbine research ticking over, especially in high temperature work, and by the middle of the decade high altitude turbo-superchargers were again becoming significantly interesting to manufacturers. G E were now being urged to reduce the weight of their designs and on 5 July 1937 a Northrop Gamma monoplane fitted with the new Moss turbo-supercharger was flown at 37,000 feet between Kansas City and Dayton — the first 'over the weather' flight between distant cities. The Army Air Corps decided to instal the turbo-supercharger on its prototype Boeing 299, forerunner of the B17 Flying Fortress, to enable a 1,000 hp engine to maintain full power at 25,000 feet.

These developments were to lead to the relatively high altitude long-range bombers and fighters which were to take part in the great aerial battles over Europe in the 1940s. Aerial warfare was revolutionized by engineers such as Moss getting as much as possible out of the existing technology. The turbo-superchargers were in mass production by G E in the 1940s, Moss and his gifted team had overcome many design problems with their turbines and centrifugal compressors, and they were well aware of the problems of materials, temperatures and compressor efficiencies.

One trick, however, they missed. Their turbo-superchargers compressed engine gases and cold air between centrifugal compressor and turbine, and then fed the mixture to an air-breathing engine. If they had put a combustion chamber in there, between the wheels, and heated the fuel-air mixture, they would have had the jet engine.

But if anybody did grasp this simple next step, there is no record of it; the final, crucial connection was not made. 'Just dumb, just dumb,' was Moss's reply to those bold enough to ask him why he just missed the point. It was one of the great lost opportunities of twentieth-century America, one which defines the very good from the truly great in the mysterious annals of invention.

America did have men who foresaw the future of the jet engine, but they were ignored. One of them was Vladimir Pavlecka, who, by his mid-thirties, was head of structural research at Douglas Aircraft Corporation in Santa Monica. He had helped build the world's first all-metal dirigible airship and in 1936 he designed the pressurized fuselage for the DC4 airliner. He also introduced Douglas to the use of rolled metal sections in aircraft construction, developed the first tricycle landing gear for a large aircraft and invented a self-sealing fuel tank. He became convinced of the future of the jet engine in 1933. His proposal was for a turboprop, not a pure jet, and it was forwarded by Douglas to the engine manufacturer, Pratt and Whitney, which sent it on to the Massachusetts Institute of Technology. All the engineers agreed that if the engine worked, which was unlikely, it would be vastly overweight and there could be nothing useful which it could do. (How prescient of Whittle and von Ohain to avoid the engine manufacturers.)

Pavlecka persisted in his convictions and, on joining the Northrop Aircraft Company in 1939, started work on a proposal which in 1940 he sent to the power plant section of the Navy's Bureau of Aeronautics, because he knew a senior engineer there who was also convinced. But aircraft carriers in those days had wooden decks and naval officers looked askance at the idea of having hot gases directed on to them. Pavlecka also went to the Army's power plant division at Wright Field, Dayton, which was deep into turbo-superchargers. There, four engineers and a serving officer, Major Donald Keirn, also rejected the idea, though Major Keirn would later be abruptly converted by the sight of Whittle's working jet in England. Pavlecka also took his idea to Lockheed, the Californian aircraft manufacturer, where the atmosphere was more hopeful because they had, in Nathan Price, a brilliant designer who was working on his own very advanced design. The Lockheed L1000 was an axial flow engine which was under way by 1940. The prototype was at least partly built but there were serious early difficulties because it would not turn under its own power. The project was put to Wright Field engineers in 1940, but there was little enthusiasm for it. However, America was now on the eve of initiation.

The US government was well aware of British work by early 1941 and it seems that US intelligence also had some inkling of German work, though the government and the military still had no idea how far down the line their future enemy had progressed. On 25 February General H. H. ('Hap') Arnold, Deputy Chief of Staff for Air (later C-in-C of the US Army Air Force and known as the father of the USAF), wrote to Dr Vannevar Bush, chairman of NACA, urging him to form a jet research group. In March Bush's special committee on jet propulsion was formed under Professor Durand, with representatives from the Army Air Force, the Navy Bureau of Aeronautics, the National Bureau of Standards, Johns Hopkins University and MIT. Three US turbine manufacturers, Allis Chalmers, Westinghouse and GE, were also represented but General Arnold had specifically asked that the US aero-engine manufacturers should *not* be represented because they were wholly committed to the military aircraft build-up using orthodox piston engines. By June the three gas turbine manufacturers all put forward proposals based on axial flow compressors and by July 1941 NACA had decided to go ahead with development work. GE started work at its Schenectady plant on a turboprop engine, claimed to be the world's first. Europe may smile at the Americans' failure to invent the jet but, once they got the message, American developments were very rapid and their progress the most formidable in the world.

A few days after the first flight of the E28/39 General Arnold was invited by the Air Ministry to come and witness the aircraft in flight. If there were any doubts, they cleared there and then, and the General resolved that the United States should press ahead immediately with British designs, impressed by how far Power Jets and Gloster had advanced. Because of GE's turbine and turbo-supercharger work, Arnold selected it to take the initiative in America, asking that a senior company engineer be sent to England at once to work with Colonel Lyon as the US Army Air Corps technical representative in Britain. In fact this engineer was already there. Roy Shoults had been sent by GE in the spring of 1941 to help introduce supercharged B17s to the RAF and he had gradually become aware of Whittle's work. Shoults and Lyon believed that the Army Air Corp's engineers should also be involved, so Arnold despatched Major Keirn from Wright Field. Keirn, the former sceptic, quickly became very highly regarded in British circles.

The American team in Britain had virtually free run of Power Jets. Although the company was uneasy about its position in the USA post-war, there was no question of any but the fullest collaboration.

The Air Ministry, under the Free Crown User provision, had an explicit right to authorize American manufacture, and data and patents flowed from Britain on a no-royalty basis under the Lease-Lend agreement. Three months before America entered the war in December 1941, an agreement was signed between Sir Henry Self of the British Air Commission in Washington and Henry Stimson, US Secretary of State for War, which gave the USA complete details of the Whittle engine, provided full secrecy was maintained and the number of people involved kept to the minimum. Shoults had to have the permission of General Arnold before he could talk with his company vice-president Roy Muir. On 4 September Arnold convened a meeting of officials of the US government and Army Air Corps, and Muir and Shoults, along with two other GE men. In the corner of his office Arnold had a small safe with a combination lock from which he took out a sheaf of Power Jets' drawings and other reports. After some discussion he handed the documents to Muir, saying: 'Gentlemen, I give you the Whittle engine. Consult all you wish and arrive at any conclusion you please – just so long as GE accepts a contract to build fifteen of them.'

Muir committed GE to do this, saying that his company would undertake the project at Lynn without handicapping the turbo-supercharger work that was going on there. (Thus was a site picked for the start of America's jet engine industry: Lynn has produced some of the greatest US aero engines.) After some discussion about a suitable airframe manufacturer, Bell Aircraft of Buffalo was selected and its president, Larry Bell, was called to Washington for a briefing the following day. Secrecy and speed were of, course, the springs of action but it remains remarkable how completely the government ignored the private enterprise principle in its search for what it judged a capable manufacturer. However, after the initial selection, public officials reverted to US practice. Manufacturers were again spurred to compete with one another and the administration severely limited the circulation of British technical information, despite the complete discretion given to them by British officials. The Americans shied away from anything on the lines of the Gas Turbine Collaboration Committee: if companies wanted to enter jet engine manufacture there was to be no cosy collaboration between them.

Despite material shortages, scarcities of skilled manpower and utter lack of experience, Muir committed the company to build and test an engine within six months. An experienced turbine man, Donald ('Truly') Warner, was put in charge of a top secret engineering and drafting building with its own special test cell. Muir personally screened any new employee, and any spread of information was strictly on a 'need to know' basis. All this activity was camouflaged as part of a giant turbo-supercharger project – though supercharger men were kept firmly away from the plant. The revered Sanford Moss was called out of retirement, whence he had gone in 1938, to lend his undoubted brilliance to the work (and there, perhaps, secretly to regret the final step he never took) and the British drawings were examined and modified to US specifications. The engine was known as the Type I (pronounced 'eye') supercharger and the parts were ordered on a hand-crafted basis.

The GE men quickly became puzzled by the British drawings – the engine control system was incomplete, for example – and Truly Warner asked for an English engine to be flown out so that they could study it. There was only one available – this was mid-1941 – but the W1X was willingly broken down into packing cases and taken to Prestwick Airport with an armed guard provided by Power Jets' section of the Home Guard. Three engineers, Dan Walker, G. B. Bozzoni and Flight Sergeant King, were packed, together with the crates, into the bomb bay of a Liberator aircraft and flown on 29 September to Bolling Field at Washington. They were cold and nervous, not least because they feared the pilot might pull the wrong toggle and deposit them all in the Atlantic. Security in the USA was remarkably tight. When the W1X arrived at Lynn, customs officials demanded the right to examine the crates. Major Keirn, who had flown from Washington, flatly refused and in the final compromise one customs man was allowed to count the number of crates.

The British engineers were set to work quickly at Lynn, where they found much enthusiasm, but a slow start because of difficulties with the English drawings. Two of the team stayed until 1 March and helped in the struggles to meet the almost impossible deadline. Undoubtedly the personal British technical help and the opportunity to strip a sample engine helped the US project greatly, but the work of the GE team was phenomenal. By early 1942 the first engine was assembled and installed in the test cell (nicknamed Fort Knox). It was run on 18 March but it stalled far below full speed and the GE engineers had to go back to the drawing board for modifications to key parts. By 18 April, however, the test log read: 'Everybody working to finish Type I so that it can go into Fort Knox. We did a great deal of checking before attempting to start. A great deal of trifling troubles were found and corrected – but after many attempts Type I RAN!' In block letters at the top of the log are the words, 'Type I runs at 11.05 pm. Operator D. Warner.' Truly Warner and his team had handsomely beaten their deadline of 1 May.

Six weeks later Whittle flew to the USA to give GE and Bell the benefit of his advice as the first test flight neared. He flew first from Bristol to Shannon in Eire and his passport made him out to be a civilian (Eire was a wartime neutral). Delayed by bad weather for his transatlantic flight, Whittle fretted that he might be interned and his fears increased when his wife sent him a thirty-seventh birthday telegram addressed with his RAF rank. A case of secret papers and drawings that he was carrying did nothing to help his peace of mind. However, he survived his six-day stay in Limerick and arrived by Pan Am Clipper at La Guardia, New York, on 4 June. Blinded by American hospitality, food and lights, he travelled to Boston, where, at the insistence of security, he registered at his hotel as Frank Whitley, but he was unable to remember the correct spelling of his surname and soon took to signing bills in his proper name. He was transferred with great charm and friendliness to the private home of a GE employee, Reg Standerwick, and given an American secretary, who warned him that the house might be anything but secure because of its intercom system. He decided to do his dictation on the beach, out of earshot, but his secretary's suntan aroused her husband's suspicion until they invented the story that she was a guinea pig for a new type of ultra-violet lamp.

Whittle worked well with Warner and his GE team, and envied them their facilities at Lynn. He also visited Bell, who had the jet fighter, named Airacomet, under construction. Whittle's American counterparts impressed him with a sense of determination, speed and enthusiasm. He had to return home before the Airacomet's first flight on 2 October – incredibly five months ahead of the British Meteor and only thirteen months after the W1X had been flown into the US. While in Washington on his way home he learned that GE planned to build 1,000 engines per month and their test plant would allow for individual testing of compressors and turbines. Although his new plant at Whetstone was coming along, Whittle estimated GE's investment to be about twelve times that of Power Jets.

GE were now almost ready to ship their first two flight engines across America to California for test flying in the Bell Airacomet P59 from Muroc Dry Lake (now Edwards Air Force Base), a site chosen because of its excellent weather and uninterrupted take-off and landing space. Security decreed that the engines should travel in a railroad boxcar, to the discomfort of the three GE engineers who had to travel locked in with them and who had to provide their own mattresses and canned food. The engine bearings and shafts were protected during the trip by turning them continuously, using a gas-driven air compressor. At Muroc a dummy wooden propeller was always attached to the P59 when it was outside its hangar. Bell's chief test pilot, Bob Stanley, started taxiing tests on 29 September and the diary entry of Ted Rogers, one of GE's boxcar travellers, for 2 October reads:

We worked till 1.30 am. Later Stanley climbed into the cockpit. A brief pause and he was off to the far end of the field. He turned at the end of his taxi run and ran the engines alternately at maximum speed. A momentary pause while the pilot released the brakes and the jets began to take hold. The plane rolled ever so slowly at first with us mentally pushing it along. It soon began to pick up speed and just opposite us it lifted gently into the air, gaining altitude it banked and passed directly over our heads . . . dead silence as it passed over, then a low rumbling sound like a blow torch and it was gone, leaving a smell of kerosene in the air.

By 1944 Germany was doomed. That fact above all others colours the introduction into battle of the Messerschmitt Me 262. To be the first jet fighter on so desperate a scene of battle was a dubious form of honour, for it meant that the careful processes by which any new warplane is launched into squadron service were brutally telescoped. The Jumo 004 engine was only 'frozen' for production in June 1944, although the Luftwaffe received its first pre-production aircraft the previous April.

A new aircraft being brought into service should have had the lessons learnt by test pilots on the prototypes and pre-production aircraft fed into the production lines and taught to hand-picked pilots so that they could be applied to the first of the new planes to reach the fighter squadrons. New battle tactics for the use of such a revolutionary aircraft as the Me 262 should have been worked out far behind the battle areas and intensive training should have made sure that the pilots flying into the attack understood their aeroplanes thoroughly. In 1944 those were counsels of perfection which the Germans simply could not afford.

The first sixteen pre-production aircraft with early variants of the Jumo engines were delivered to the Luftwaffe in April 1944, followed by a further score in May. Some went to Rechlin for the official test programme but most were sent to a proving squadron at Lechfeld, near Munich, commanded by Hauptmann Thierfelder. Difficult maintenance problems were encountered with the engines, which led to some tricky handling problems with the engine throttles for the pilots. However, everyone agreed that in most circumstances the Me 262 was easier to fly than the leading piston-engined fighter, the Bf 109, and except in turning it could outfly any aircraft, Allied or German, then in the sky.

The urgent task was to train as many pilots as quickly as possible to fly the Me 262. The men were experienced fighter and bomber pilots, together with a few brand-new officers who had just completed fighter training. All of them had to complete a twenty-hour course of pre-jet flying on Bf 110s and Me 410s to get twin-engine experience. The throttles of these aircraft were fixed in one position to simulate the 262, whose throttles were not supposed to be moved over 20,000 feet. Once allowed into the 262, these pilots, many of whom were to die in their aircraft in the remaining months of war, were given a training that in many ways was pitifully short. They would do two half-hours of 'circuits and bumps' – as many landings and take-offs as were possible in the time; two one-hour flights at height to gain handling experience and to try limited aerobatics; one hour of flying at 30,000 feet; one hour of cross-country at 12,000 to 15,000 feet; two one-hour spells of formation flying in pairs; and finally some gunnery practice on ground targets.

This programme was for the 262 Swallow – the fighter version. For the 262 Stormbird bomber there had to be further training in level flight and dive-bombing from various heights. Despite their hectic training programme, Thierfelder's squadron soon scored their first 'kills' with their four- and six-cannon fighters – two Lockheed Lightnings and a Mosquito. The Allies did not know how these aircraft had been lost – they usually flew too high and fast for Germany's piston-engined interceptors – but the Allied sighting on 25 July 1944 confirmed that the jet fighter, long figured in intelligence reports, was now in service. Hauptmann Thierfelder was killed shortly afterwards when his 262 crashed in flames near Lechfeld after being damaged in combat.

With the death of Thierfelder, his unit was disbanded and re-formed as an interceptor squadron under a famous Luftwaffe ace, Major Walter Nowotny, whose job was the interception of US Air Force bombers. Based near Osnabruk, under the main US route into Germany, the squadron had a strength of forty 262s – such was the pace at which they were now coming off the production line – and it lost the first of its aircraft when a US Mustang attacked and shot down two as they were taking off. This became a favourite Allied tactic. The Me 262 was very vulnerable both at take-off and landing because it required longer runs and British and US commanders instituted standing patrols over German airfields to pounce on the jets at the right moment. In the end the Germans retaliated by ringing their airfields with anti-aircraft guns to provide a canopy of fire above their fighters.

Squadron Nowotny's pilots claimed twenty-two kills by the end of their first four weeks of operations but on 8 November Nowotny himself was killed when his aircraft nose-dived into the ground after being damaged by Allied fighters. Two other pilots were lost that day and the strength was reduced to three flyable aircraft. The squadron was then disbanded, the pilots who had survived becoming the nucleus of a new Luftwaffe group of 262 squadrons. The terrible attrition rate in Nowotny's squadron was due, however, not so much to the Allies as to technical failure and hasty and inadequate training. As many as fifty per cent of 262s may have been lost in accidents which had nothing to do with combat. The Luftwaffe was nevertheless well pleased with the 262 and hastened its pilot training programme still faster.

The fighter squadrons were now working out, almost as they flew into combat, the best tactics with which to pitch their high-speed fighters against the slower flying but well-armed and prickly US Fortress and Liberator bombers. Allied escort fighters were avoided whenever possible so that the 262s could go straight for the bombers, approaching them in three flights of three aircraft each. About 150 yards separated each 262, with 300 yards between each flight. One bomber group would be singled out from the others and the attack would begin from about 5,000 yards astern at a height of about 6,000 feet above. The fighters would dive to 1,500 feet below the bombers, thus gaining great speed, pulling up and flying straight and level for the final attack. (Some pilots slowed down on the final approach so as to aim their guns steadily, but this lost the aircraft its great advantage – speed.) The 262s were equipped with either cannon or missiles and, once they had fired at the first chosen targets in the formation, they would fly over the bombers and select another group to attack before diving away at top speed to avoid fighters and to land to refuel and rearm. If forced to attack Allied fighters, 262 pilots invariably used their speed to climb above their enemy and then dive on them; Allied pilots would almost always turn steeply into the attack, forcing the Germans to miss because their aircraft were less manoeuvrable than their piston-engined opponents.

Clear evidence of the ascendancy provided by speed came from the 262s which were used in Hitler's beloved bomber role. The Stormbird was used to attack difficult strategic targets such as the Remagen Bridge across the Rhine, captured by the Americans as their bridgehead into the German heartlands, and Nijmegen bridge in Holland, held by the British. On daylight raids, solo 262s would fly above 25,000 feet, going into a shallow dive and releasing their bombs at about 18,000 feet. In poor visibility they would attack from 1,000 feet, descending to 500 feet to release bombs, while at night they would dive on their target from 12,000 feet, releasing bombs at 8,000 feet. With these tactics they presented the anti-aircraft defences with near-impossible targets, so rapid were their changes in altitude and course. Allied fighter patrols were little better off because of the 262 pilots' habit of diving and climbing away at speeds greater than those of the USAAF and RAF fighters. While the Allies saw in these raids nothing more than nuisance value, they do indicate the trouble-making possibilities of the 262 had it been around in larger numbers earlier on.

Greater numbers *were* now becoming available and more fighter squadrons were being formed throughout the 1944–45 winter. Even in the indescribable condition of Germany in those last months and days, 1,433 Me 262s were built – 368 to 31 December 1944 and 865 to April 1945. By the end of 1944 Hitler had decided that his bomber version should be converted into fighters to defend the heartland.

The 262 fighter in squadron service had a maximum speed of 540 mph at 20,000 feet and could climb to that altitude in 6.8 minutes, with a range of just over 500 miles. Its wing span was 41 feet, its length 35 feet and its loaded weight was 14,900 lb – 6.25 tons; its armament was four 30 mm cannon and its Jumo 004 engines were rated at 1,980 lb thrust each. The fighter could dive at well over 600 mph and these dives could bring it perilously close to its never-exceed speed, beyond which its aerodynamic behaviour could change rapidly for the worse. Allied fighters were to experience the same problems as they approached the so-called sound barrier.

The Allies devoted much of their bombing effort to those factories where Me 262 production was known to happen, and the German response was to switch component and sub assembly manufacture to small wooden workshops, their roofs painted green, hidden under the leaves and branches of the south German forests. Assembled Me 262s (and the aircraft was designed to be built and assembled easily, by the semi-skilled) could then be flown off the nearest autobahn, leaving few clues to Allied fighters unless they were caught at the moment of take-off (scorch marks on the autobahn were also give-aways to Allied photo-interpreters). By and large the forests kept their secrets well but further back up the production line every kind of scarcity and bottleneck was met by 1945. The flow of pumps, instruments, radios, undercarriages, jigs etc. was always problematic and the number of Me 262s delivered was little short of miraculous, although it has been estimated that as few as 300 completed fighters actually reached the squadrons. Even so, it was a miracle of human tenacity and ingenuity.

Ascendancy was not always with the 262. One squadron based near Wurzburg was 'scrambled' to intercept Allied bombers on 25

February 1945 to find itself confronted by US Mustang fighters with a large height advantage. Despite its performance, seven 262s were shot down and the commanding officer and two other pilots were killed. The squadron never fully recovered from this blow.

The most extraordinary fighter unit formed in the death throes of the Third Reich was JV44, based at Munich from 31 March 1945. It was commanded by Adolf Galland, previously mentioned as a General of Fighters while still in his twenties. In the famous fighter commanders' mutiny of January 1945 a group of veterans had confronted Goering, demanding that he sack all his notorious cronies and focus production on the Me 262 rather than on other new products which he supposed, even then, might win the war – these included the so-called People's Fighter. Goering dispersed the group and sent several to especially unpleasant postings. Galland, who had been banished from Berlin for his continued criticism of the hierarchy, was recalled by Goering to be told that he would not be court-martialled in view of his past services. At Hitler's instigation he was to command a squadron of his chosen plane, the Me 262, and he could pick his comrades from any other units he pleased. Galland collected under him at Munich a team of Luftwaffe veterans, all aces and ten of them holders of the Knight's Cross, the highest bravery award.

Galland's elite unit of fifty pilots seldom had more than twenty-five operational aircraft between them but again and again during Germany's Götterdämmerung, they tore into Allied bomber formations regardless of the cost to themselves. On 26 April Galland led six 262s into an attack on a large formation of American Marauder bombers. He was 'jumped' from on high by a Mustang fighter and his cockpit shattered by cannon fire; hit in the knee, he landed on Riem airfield in the middle of a thunderous attack by US Thunderbolts. He was taken to Munich hospital for treatment, and his part in the war ended there. His squadron fought on, flying off from the Munich-Augsburg autobahn to avoid the strafe-ridden airfields. In the last days of war the squadron transferred to Salzburg, where it was overrun by an American armoured unit on 3 May 1945.

So ended the career of the world's first operational jet aircraft. Rushed into battle too soon, bedevilled in its development by too many 'experts' – including Hitler – both the airframe and its miraculous engine had nevertheless proclaimed the jet age and given some foretaste of its promise and perils. It was the greatest fighter of World War Two, though how many Allied aircraft it shot down will never be known because of the chaos and confusion in which it operated. Most authorities guess around 300 Allied bombers were lost to it; given a more even deal than the last days of war, it would have accounted for many more.

All over western Germany British and US intelligence teams picked over the rubble of the Third Reich to discover what secret developments were under way when the Germans collapsed. The Americans were particularly well briefed about what to look for – their units included engineers, even senior plane makers from the USA; the British effort was under-subscribed and in certain sectors amateurish by comparison. However, both teams scored successes in the secret war and some uncomfortable finds were made, indicating the powerful thrust of Germany's jet and rocket research efforts. The US scoop of von Braun and the rocket men is well known; but the Americans also captured the key men in the German jet effort and provided many of them with useful and important jobs in the US aircraft and aero-engine industry after the war. Some of the circumstances were comic: Dr Helmut Schelp was flown to London for interrogation and, walking across Horse Guards Parade, he encountered the Gloster E28/39 on display, with a plaque proclaiming it to have been the first jet aircraft to have flown. He pointed out the mistake, tactfully, to his captors and the claim was removed the next day.

Of all the special projects under way towards the end of the war the most bizarre was undoubtedly the jet-propelled Heinkel 162 Volksjäger – the People's Fighter. In September 1944 Hitler decreed the formation of a Home Guard of young and old soldiers under the command of Heinrich Himmler. Goering dreamed of the Volksjäger as the aerial equivalent, in which a complete year's intake of the Hitler Youth would be trained on gliders and then convert straight to the He 162, a single-jet fighter with a top speed of 520 mph at 20,000 feet. The idea that sixteen-year-old boys could step into the cockpit of the Volksjäger and immediately fly into combat with the vast wings of American and British fighters now daily invading German airspace is a measure of the hysterical fantasies to which Goering had become prey.

The Volksjäger was the original vision of Albert Speer and Party Leader Otto Saur. It would be very simple to build, carrying two 30 mm cannon as armament. When the idea was mooted, it met the anguished opposition of Willy Messerschmitt and Galland, who suspected that production of this aircraft would detract from production of the Me 262. Nevertheless the project was circulated by the Air Ministry for a fighter powered by a single BMW engine. Its endurance (time in the sky) was to be only half an hour and its weight no more than 4,410 lb. Leading aircraft firms, including Focke Wolf, Arado and Junkers, submitted proposals and out of the shades appeared Ernst Heinkel with his ideas for a Volksjäger. The Air Ministry issued its project on 8 September 1944 and the manufacturers had to submit proposals by 20 September – twelve days! The design had to be ready for mass production by 1 January 1945. In the end the Volksjäger was designed, built and test flown in the incredible space of ninety days.

At first Heinkel's design was rejected by the Air Ministry but then a row broke out among the other manufacturers' representatives which was not settled until there was a further meeting at Goering's headquarters a few days later, at which Heinkel's man partly clinched the deal by producing a mock-up similar to the Volksjäger. It turned out that Heinkel had been working on such an idea since the summer. Such stalwarts as Gunter and Schwarzler, designers of von Ohain's original jet plane, had come up with something very like what the Air Ministry wanted. Its jet was mounted atop the fuselage between the cockpit and the fin, which was highly unorthodox, but after one or two further rows in committee the design was adopted and blessed by Saur and Goering.

Heinkel's designers were to work day and night, sleeping by their drawing boards, and detailed drawings were completed by 29 October. Work started on the prototype long before that – in fact all the stages of development and design started virtually together. The Volksjäger was to be built at Marienehe, Junkers and in the slave caves of Nordhausen. The first production order was for 1,000 planes per month.

The fuselage of the Volksjäger was of metal but the wing was made of wood and plywood; the fin was also wooden but the rest of the tail was metal. The pilot was provided with an ejector seat – baling out of the Volksjäger was highly dangerous because of the top-mounted jet engine. The combat life of the fighter was expected to be no more than ten hours maximum: they were designed virtually as throw-aways. Apart from the manufacturing centres, a vast network of subcontractors, mainly woodworkers and furniture-makers, was set to building the wooden components – rather like the scheme in which the furniture-makers around High Wycombe found themselves building large parts of the Mosquito without realizing they were in aircraft manufacture at all. Much metal subcontracting was located in disused salt mines.

The first Volksjäger prototype flew on 6 December 1944 and the aircraft, already in mass production, reached a top speed of 522 mph at 20,000 feet, before an undercarriage door broke off because of defective bonding. Despite this warning the Luftwaffe and Nazi officials gathered four days later to watch a demonstration flight. During a low-level, high-speed pass in front of the spectators the aircraft disintegrated, again because of bonding defects, and the pilot was killed. However, production was by now rolling and during January 1945, test pilots were committed to a large programme of flight testing of ten prototypes. Production was scheduled into 1946, by which time the Volksjäger would be powered with the engine von Ohain was designing – the 011.

The dream that quickly died was that of the youth groups leading squadrons of Volksjägers into the skies against the Allies. In fact, the plane was proving quite difficult to fly in the hands of experienced Luftwaffe pilots at Rechlin and Munich. The top-mounted engine gave rise to instability and there were other defects which ensured that it was a machine for grown-ups only. One or two squadrons were formed and 120 aircraft were actually delivered to the Luftwaffe, while another 100 were awaiting flight testing and an astonishing 800 were in the final stages of construction, when the final collapse came. Although its performance figures read well – the BMW 003 engine gave 1,760 lb of thrust at take-off, a maximum speed of 490 mph at sea-level rising to 562 mph at 20,000 feet on maximum thrust – the Volksjäger was anything but a people's fighter. In the hands of the inexperienced it would have been lethal to themselves rather than to the Allies, who would clearly have found it easier to deal with than the more formidable Me 262. For all the speed and ingenuity displayed in its conception and execution, the Volksjäger was no more than a dying spasm.

Far more challenging was the concept of the world's first jet reconnaisance-bomber – another German first – the Arado 234. The Arado company, based at Warnemünde, had been an aircraft manufacturer in the First World War and, although shut down in 1921, it had managed to keep active in the years of the Weimar Republic by building some successful training aircraft biplanes and seaplanes. Although never in large-scale production, Arado with its half million square feet of factory space was a prime candidate for Nazi interest when Hitler took power in 1933. Quite soon it was part of the clandestine rearmament programme and from 1935 it was a great builder of other people's aeroplanes under licence, among them Heinkel, Messerschmitt, Junkers and Focke Wulf. Arado spent most of the war years doing this type of work and by 1945 the company was a large user of foreign slave workers in its plants.

Arado's design staff did not have much success with their home-grown projects but by late 1940 the chief engineer, Walter Blume, was asked by the Air Ministry if he would do some studies for a medium-range reconnaisance aircraft which would use the new jet engines being tested by BMW and Junkers. It would have the speed and altitude to carry it well clear of Allied fighters. Blume's response was a single-seat monoplane, high wing, with two jet engines on the wings – a very clean-looking aeroplane to slip through the sky high and fast. The pilot would sit in a pressurized cockpit in a fully glazed nose which gave superb visibility. With thin wing and narrow fuse-lage there was no room to stow an undercarriage, so the Ar 234 was designed to take off from a trolley, which was jettisoned once it was airborne, and to land on skids – one under the fuselage and the other two (retractable) under the wings. The aircraft was designed to have a range of 1,200 miles for a top speed of 460 mph at 20,000 feet (these figures were to vary considerably for different loads).

The first two prototypes of the Arado 234 were completed by the end of 1941 but unfortunately the Jumo 004 engine had got development troubles so the Arados stood about waiting for their engines for some thirteen to fourteen months. They could not be fitted with piston engines because the landing skids gave insufficient clearance from the ground for the propellers. The Jumo engines were not ready until March 1943, when the aircraft were located at an airfield near Munster. The Arado first flew on 15 June 1943 with test pilot Selle in control. The flight was successful but the jettisoned trolley's parachute failed to open and it was wrecked when it hit the ground. A new trolley was provided but on the second flight this, too, was destroyed for the same reason. After that the trolleys were released on the runway as soon as the aircraft reached flying speed. This undercarriage innovation was to plague the aircraft for some time. In the end the designers had to make structural alterations to the wings and fuselage so that a retractable tricycle undercarriage could be fitted. The flight test programme went smoothly but for the death of test pilot Selle, killed when the seventh prototype's port engine caught fire.

By the middle of 1944 pre-production aircraft were being delivered to the Luftwaffe at the flight test centre at Rechlin and the production version, the B1, a pure reconnaisance aircraft, was soon being delivered to squadrons. The B2 followed quickly, a much more versatile reconnaisance bomber designed to carry 3,000 lb of bombs. The top speed of the B2 was 461 mph at 20,000 feet and 435 mph at 33,000 feet. The range was around 1,000 miles but only 680 miles with a full bomb load. The B2 was a good aircraft to fly: it was fitted with an automatic pilot which the pilot would use as he was busy aiming his bombs, and for his defence (though speed and height were to be his main protection) he had two backward-firing cannon which he aimed with a periscope.

In squadron service the Ar 234 was called the Blitz and its first job was to spy out British ports and airfields around the south and east coasts in case the Allies were planning further landings on the Dutch coast. This was September 1944 and the French landings were firmly established. The plane flew a large number of photographic missions over France and Britain, and the Blitz showed itself well able to evade Allied fighters. As a bomber it flew many missions in the closing months of the war, mainly attacking Allied ground forces and airfields in France, and it was also flung into the German counter-attack in the Ardennes. In March 1945 it distinguished itself with the Me 262 in a despairing onslaught on the Remagen bridge, which finally fell into the Rhine, but too late to save Germany.

Just before the end of the war another version of the Blitz was on the production line, with four BMW 003 engines in place of the usual two Jumo 004s. This would have been an even higher performance reconnaisance bomber, with a navigator as well as a pilot. Its speed was increased to a maximum of 540 mph and one of the test aircraft reached a height of 42,000 feet, well above the operational heights of Allied aircraft. The four-engined version was too late to see any action but one of its variants, an experimental Arado, exhibited some of the powers of the Phoenix. It was fitted with a crescent-shaped wing, designed to give a better aerodynamic performance up towards the speed of sound. British troops captured this curious spoil of war and a few years later a similarly shaped wing was fitted to one of Britain's V bombers, the Handley Page Victor.

In all, more than 200 Ar 234s were built and wherever they were used they proved formidable warplanes. They demonstrated once more the strength of the German design teams and their readiness to meet the challenge of new ideas and make them work successfully at previously unknown heights and speeds. It was as well for the Allies that the Blitz bomber came too late to do them any real damage.

Another example of the German's willingness to rethink the aeroplane when the revolutionary jet engine demanded it was the Junkers 287, designed to be a six-engined heavy bomber which could outfly any Allied fighter. It would have a maximum speed of 509 mph at 35,000 feet – again comfortably ahead of any Allied fighter of the time. At such speeds, approaching the speed of sound, some parts of an aircraft's wing will generate shock waves – the compressibility effect – which can lead to difficulties with the controls. One way of delaying these effects is to sweep the wings back quite sharply. Most of today's airliners and all military jets have swept-back wings which, in effect, deceive the surfaces that they are not flying as fast as they are.

By 1944 the Germans were beginning to accumulate quite a lot of evidence about compressibility and the swept wing, which also has some drawbacks because it performs less well at low speeds. The Junkers team reasoned that the poor low-speed performance could be evened out by sweeping the wing *forward* from the fuselage instead of backwards, while other design arrangements would take care of high-speed compressibility. Wind tunnel tests confirmed the theories of the Junkers team and detailed design work on a prototype began. Before building the aircraft, however, they decided to try out the wings on a flying test bed – a monstrous hybrid consisting of a Heinkel 177 fuselage, a Junkers 388 tail, the nosewheel of an American Liberator bomber, main wheels from another Junkers aircraft and four Jumo 004 jet engines, two of them fixed to the fuselage, two to the wings.

Surprisingly, this aircraft flew, not once, but seventeen times from an airfield near Leipzig and it was reputed to have quite good handling qualities. To study its flying characteristics, dozens of wool tufts were stuck all over the wings and fuselage, and a film camera mounted ahead of the fin to record their movements as they responded to the airflow. The visual data tended to confirm the wind tunnel results. The Junkers team were building a full prototype by July 1944 when orders came from Berlin for everyone to stop work on bombers and prepared for an emergency fighter programme. The hybrid was transferred to Rechlin, where it was badly damaged in an Allied bombing raid. Early in 1945 Junkers was allowed to restart work on the full prototype, followed by one more. These aircraft were to have been fitted with the von Ohain 011 engine but the inevitable delays in its development meant that they had to use six B M W 003s, mounted three under each wing, instead.

The Junkers factory and the two aeroplanes were captured intact by the Russian armies and the design team, planes and engines were taken to the Soviet Union, where the Junkers 287 was completed and actually flew, though with what results are not known. English engineers who still fulminate over the sale to the Russians in 1946 of Rolls-Royce Nene and Derwent engines by the Labour government might reflect that the Soviet Union's jet programme was given a good start by what their armies found in Germany.

The Germans were also first in the field to marry the jet engine to the idea of the flying wing, which still has supporters who claim that it is the most efficient low drag airframe design possible. The company finally responsible was Gotha – an ominous name for England because of the Gotha bombers which spread terror by their indiscriminate bombing of London and other cities in World War One. In return, Gotha received special attention in the Treaty of Versailles, one clause of which specified the destruction of the aircraft plant. This clause was evaded and, with the advent of the Nazis, Gotha began to design and make training planes and cabin monoplanes.

Meanwhile, two brothers, Reimar and Walter Horten, became the great proponents of the flying wing in Germany. In the thirties they carried out many experiments with sailplanes, which they designed and built on flying wing principles. The brothers joined the Luftwaffe in 1936 and were encouraged to go on with their design work (in contrast with the RAF attitude to Whittle). By 1939 they were aware of the jet engine and its implications for their flying wings, and they designed the Horton IX glider, to be tested first as a glider before BMW 003 jets were fitted. By 1944 the Luftwaffe became very interested in the concept and the flying wing was now taken up by Goering, who ordered that a jet-powered version should fly as soon as possible. The glider flew well, so well that the design was now taken out of the hands of the Hortens and given to Gotha, where the prototype was named Gotha 229. The fighter version was to carry four 30 mm cannon and two 2,000 lb bombs. Two 004B engines had to be fitted to the prototype (the 003 was not ready in time), which was flight tested at Oranienberg to a speed of 500 mph – the design speed was 600 mph at 40,000 feet. After only two hours flying the Gotha 229 crashed on landing. Goering held a meeting in March 1945 which marked the inclusion of the aircraft in the Luftwaffe's fighter programme but within weeks US troops occupied the factory and seized the prototypes under construction. One of these aeroplanes is now in the Smithsonian National Air and Space Museum in Washington, a monument to one of the most revolutionary jet designs to fly.

The most revolutionary jet design *not* to fly came from Messerschmitt's company. It had about it the sweep of future shapes, and it was called Projekt 1101, a design for a fighter with variable sweep, or swing wings, a patent for which was taken out in 1942 by Professor Alexander Lippisch. (This pre-dates the famous post-war work of Sir Barnes Wallis in England.) As mentioned in a previous chapter Professor Busemann had done work on swept-wing aircraft. His studies were neglected for some time but after he published another paper on the compressibility phenomenon, Dr Albert Betz, another researcher, did more work on compressibility and sweep-back which caught the eye of Messerschmitt's Waldemar Voigt, no longer immersed in the Me 262 design. Voigt proposed further wind tunnel tests on an advanced model aircraft with pronounced wing sweep-back. Lippisch warned him of the disadvantages of this wing form at low speeds, but Voigt did not immediately heed the advice. By July 1942 design work began on the P1101 research aircraft which *might* become a high-speed interceptor fighter some time in the future. A lot was learned from the wind tunnel model and in the autumn of 1944 the Luftwaffe called for something very like the P1101 (which was still on the drawing board), a fighter with a single jet engine; this was another departure because twin jets had always been specified until now because of the unreliability of the early engines.

The Air Ministry jumped at Projekt 1101 and ordered a prototype. Work began at a secret Messerschmitt plant at Oberammergau, which had not been attacked by the Allies because they did not know it was there. The engine was to be von Ohain's 011 and the estimated speed was 610 mph at 23,000 feet. By the end of 1944, however, the Air Ministry outlook on the 1101 cooled for technical reasons, so Messerschmitt decided to continue the project alone for research purposes. It was at this stage that Voigt modified the prototype so that its wings could be adjusted, on the ground, to three different angles of sweep. The idea was to flight test the aircraft in each of the three different positions to see which performed best and at what heights – not quite the original swing-wing aircraft but certainly its precursor. By April 1945 the prototype was three-quarters complete but it was obvious even to the most sanguine that the Allies would arrive before the first flight date in June. In fact, US infantry stumbled across the unknown factory on 29 April. By this time Messerschmitt staff had microfilmed the engineering drawings and hidden them, while they made off to the forests and villages around.

By 7 May an American intelligence unit reached Oberammergau, led, as it happened, by the chief designer of the US Bell Aircraft Corporation, Robert Woods. He organized a round-up of Messerschmitt staff and enough people were collected to restart work on the P1101. The French army meanwhile stumbled on the hidden microfilm and sent it off to Paris. Despite American orders, then entreaties, the French refused to disgorge the material, so work on the prototype could not be checked against drawings and performance calculations. In the end the Americans shipped 1101 to Wright Field, the vast experimental base outside Dayton, Ohio, where scientists and engineers were swamped with German aircraft, designs, data and people – Waldemar Voigt and his team arrived in person a short time after the prototype, leaves in the European gale scooped up by Operation Paperclip. For two years P1101 lay on Wright Field while scientists and engineers assimilated all the German booty now in their hands. In 1948 Robert Woods borrowed the prototype to fit it with the hinge which would allow its wings to swing in flight. Woods and Bell then offered the swing-wing to the USAF as a fighter. Wright Field engineers raised various technical objections to the idea and Woods then argued that two aircraft should be built anyway, to try out swing-wing technology. By 1949–50 this proposal had resulted in two aircraft, one of which became the X5 supersonic experimental aeroplane.

In sum, the German jet programme was often extemporized because of the harsh press of war but by 1945 it presented a formidable array of fighting planes, prototypes, designs and sheer dreams. German designers were taking full advantage of all the pre-war aerodynamic research, which was very advanced indeed (sweep-back, swing-wing) and people like Helmut Schelp were now directing a relatively well-organized engine programme which was led by designs such as von Ohain's 011. Quite simply, Germany was found in 1945 to be leading the world, at any rate in this sphere.

If Britain's entry into the jet age was lacklustre, America's was slightly worse. But unlike the Germans, scientists and technologists of both countries had time on their side and were quickly able to catch up and exceed the brilliance of their late enemy's accomplishments. Neither Britain nor America had the variety of aircraft which the Germans were either flying or studying by 1945, although their needs were not of course so desperate as those of the Germans. The war was won with piston-engined aircraft flying at the limits – up to 450 mph – of which the propeller and airframe were capable in 1945.

The Meteor 1 was the first British jet aircraft into squadron service, and the only Allied jet to see any active service, albeit carefully protected from German eyes by not being allowed to fly beyond the line of the Allied advance into Western Europe. Long before it was ready to fly, this twin-jet fighter had suffered vicissitudes which faithfully reflected the chaos of the national jet engine programme, and it is significant that when the first (Rover) engines were fitted in July 1942 they could only be used for taxiing trials because the W2B gave only 1,000 lb thrust – not enough to lift the Meteor from the ground.

The Meteor first flew on 5 March 1943 with de Havilland–Halford jet engines (the Goblin, as it became) which gave about 1,500 lb thrust. The test pilot, Michael Daunt, reported that when his speed reached 200 mph the aircraft began to yaw violently. Daunt had developed very strong leg muscles playing rugby football, but they could not control the flailing rudder bar at his feet. He quickly reduced speed and regained control, landing in three minutes. This alarming symptom was traced back to an unbalanced rudder, a fault fairly easily rectified on the ground.

This flight was made from Cranwell and for greater security the Meteor was taken to another airfield at Newmarket. However, Whitehall became worried because horse racing took place there every Wednesday fortnight and insisted that the aircraft be grounded on that day lest the enemy was attending the race meeting with binoculars. Whittle-based engines, the W2B/23, later the Welland, were fitted to the aircraft and flown in June 1943. Michael Daunt immediately commented on its poor take-off and climb performance. The Welland gave only 1,400 lb of thrust (as the production engine delivered to the R A F from May 1944 it gave 1,600 lb).

During the late summer of 1943 more prototypes joined the test programme and the E28/39 was fitted with the W2/500, an engine largely built by Power Jets with nickel alloy turbine blades and other refinements. Daunt regarded this as an extremely good engine, proof that Power Jets on their own could build successful engines which flew. The third prototype was fitted with the F2 Metro-Vick axial flow engine, which had been conceived by Hayne Constant and his team at Farnborough. This engine was the founding design for all axial flow engines made by Britain and it led directly to the successful Sapphire, made by Armstrong Siddeley.

Slowly, then, the British jet engine programme was getting some shape as well as finding its feet. The test pilots who had the job of flying the Meteor prototypes into the unknown and assessing the performance of these revolutionary turbojets did not have the advantage of today's wind tunnels, sophisticated computers and airborne telemetry. As they edged their aircraft towards the so-called sound barrier their sole recording method (apart from their memories) was the notepad strapped to the knee on which they wrote down performance details. Their method was to take limited 'bites' at each problem, making as much use of planning and forethought as possible. In exploring the problem of compressibility at high speed they would take the aircraft to the limits of its previous flights and then edge it gently beyond them.

When Michael Daunt first encountered compressibility, he climbed to 35,000 feet and then made a series of shallow dives, each one 10 mph faster than the previous one. The aircraft told him of the problem by excessive vibration and stiffening of the controls. He let the Meteor continue its descent so that it slowed down as the air became thicker around it. Once while flying at high speed Daunt's port engine exploded, debris bursting through the nacelle. With the aircraft out of control he got ready to bail out but, by the time he had jettisoned his hood, the speed had fallen off enough for him to regain some sort of control. Although unable to turn to starboard, he decided to try a landing, which he made in a potato field without injury. Thus, the precious aircraft was saved, together with the evidence.

Daunt also encountered a new terrestrial danger from the jet engine. Early in 1943 a technician was running up a Meteor's engines on the ground, while Daunt looked on from the side of the nacelle. When he stepped back, the collar of his coat was sucked into the intake, together with Daunt inside it – he described the noise as deafening. He was saved because the technician in the cockpit saw what had happened and snapped the throttles shut. Daunt was pulled from the nacelle feet first with nothing more serious than bruises. After this, wire grills were fitted over the intakes of parked Meteors. They were known as Daunt stoppers.

The first Meteor 1s were delivered to 616 Squadron at Manston, Kent, in July 1944. Its pilots had been flying high-altitude, high-speed Spitfires, and the difference in performance was not so great. The early Meteors were fitted with two Rolls-Royce Welland engines (W2B/23s) of 1,700 lb thrust and weighed (loaded) 13,800 lb (6 tons), about the same as the Me 262, but top speed at 30,000 feet was 410 mph, which was slower than some piston-engined fighters and slower than the Me 262 by more than 100 mph. The later mark 4 fighter was fitted with two 3,500 lb thrust Rolls-Royce Derwents and had a speed of 550 mph at 30,000 feet – a vastly different proposition, but one much later into service.

The early mark 1s were used by pilots of 616 Squadron to take on the V1 bombs which flew from occupied France across Kent to fall on and around London. The V1, though pilotless and unarmed, could be a dangerous target because its one-ton warhead could explode under cannon fire and engulf the attacking aircraft. The first sorties were flown almost immediately the squadron was re-equipped, but the 20 mm cannons of the Meteor were constantly jamming, so the pilots had little success. On 4 August Flying Officer T. D. Dean, patrolling at 4,000 feet, saw a V1 below him, overtook it and attacked head on, but again his cannon jammed. He turned his aircraft, caught up with the bomb and cautiously slid his wing tip under its wing tip. By rocking his aircraft he was able to disturb the airstream sufficiently for the V1 to roll over and dive harmlessly into open country. (Using the airstream to topple a V1 was first developed by Tempest piston-engined fighter pilots.) Half an hour later Flying Officer J. K. Roger intercepted another V1 over Kent and shot it down with his cannon.

Attacks on V1s continued through August, thirteen of them being forced down by cannon or destabilization; there was very little action in September because the landing sites in France were being overrun by British ground forces.

By January 1945 the Meteor 3 was delivered to the squadron.

With its improved, but by no means exceptional, performance, the squadron moved to Belgium, where it was under orders not to fly into enemy-held territory. In March it was the victim of a jet attack when two Arado 234 bombers swept in with a low-level strafe which damaged one Meteor on the ground. By April flying restrictions were lifted and the Meteors took part in some attacks on the remaining German airfields, destroying some aircraft on the ground. Thus the war ended without any jet-to-jet combat.

The Meteor had thus made only a token appearance in World War Two, the responsibility for which must lie within the civil service and the Rover company for the appalling muddle into which the British jet programme was allowed to fall. But had the first jets in the air, the Meteor and the Me 262, encountered one another there is little doubt that, with its vastly better performance, the German plane would have outfought and out-gunned the English. British Air Ministry reports comparing German and British programmes prompted *The Times* to say on 12 September 1945:

> The account prepared by the technical experts of the Air Ministry and published today is a short, revealing document. Not only does it show that Germany, not Britain, was the first country in the world to fly a jet aircraft – it had previously been thought that the Whittle-propelled E28/39 Gloster machine was the first to fly – it also shows beyond doubt that in the early development of this revolutionary new form of power, the Germans led the world.

British aerospace projects to this day are bedevilled by a chauvinism which insists, whatever the truth, that British airframes and British engines are the best – always; air correspondents of the popular and not-so-popular press have been peculiarly afflicted with this disease, which is often accompanied by ill-concealed xenophobia. Thus some writers have asserted, despite the official reports, that the Jumo 004 engine and the Messerschmitt airframe of the Me 262 were far inferior in quality and performance to the Rolls-Royce Welland and the Meteor. In fact, technical comparisons show that the axial flow 004 and Welland offer no superiority one above the other in the ratios of thrust to weight. The 004's fuel consumption was inferior to the Welland but the 004 flew a year before the Welland and in the latter part of the war German engine efficiencies were at least as good as the British. German turbine design was poorer than the British because they did not use Whittle-type blading but undoubtedly the greatest German inferiority was in reliability and durability. The Welland had a reliability of 100 hours; the 004 had to be overhauled every twenty-five hours and many engines failed before that time. The brief life of the German engine was not, however, due to poor engineering, but to poor materials. The metals needed for high-temperature alloys were non-existent in Germany, whereas the Welland used nickel and chromium for its combustors. The 004 was incomparably easier to produce than the Welland and gave much higher performance, albeit for a shorter life, in an aircraft that was vastly superior in speed and flight to the Meteor.

German industrial cooperation was poor and they had nothing like the Gas Turbine Collaboration Committee; they would have been better off if they had, as the German Air Ministry foresaw but was unable to bring about because of the independence of the manufacturers. Only late in the war was compulsory exchange of information introduced – too late for effect. The leading authorities on development of aero engines, Robert Schlaifer and S. D. Heron, conclude:

> Almost all the differences between the results of turbojet develop-ment in Britain and Germany are to be explained by differences between the conditions under which the engines were developed in the two countries and the purposes for which they were developed. The difference in purpose was the desperate German need for high performance interceptors from 1943, whereas the British and Amer-icans by that time had little if any need for a fighter of extremely high performance attained at the cost of range.

The Germans had to rush into production with an engine using inferior materials; the British had the time to develop a more reliable engine using better materials, but its performance was poor. As for the Americans, a few more flights of the Bell P59 Airacomet revealed that, although American engineers had done everything in record time, the result was failure. The trouble with the Airacomet was that Bell had not designed an aircraft for the jet age, or more accurately the jet engine age. Apart from the absence of a propeller, it looked like a piston-engined fighter and, worse still, it performed like one – a speed of 404 mph at 25,000 feet from two 1,400 lb thrust General Electric I-A engines. The P59 had too much frontal area, too much wing area and a too conventional aerofoil. In the end only sixty-six Airacomets were completed from an order of 100. However, pilots trained on it and test pilots gained a lot of knowledge which went into the next aeroplane, which was a very different proposition.

The Lockheed P80, designed by the great US engineer, Kelly Johnson, had a top speed of 502 mph at 20,000 feet. The first aircraft was powered by a de Havilland Goblin sent over from Britain for the first flight in 1943. The Shooting Star – as it became – was so promising that the USAAF ordered 5,000 of them but VJ Day cut that back to 1,000. The first idea was to power it with the Goblin built in America under licence but General Electric were working hard on their I series and the I–40 gave 3,800 lb thrust – greater than anything in Britain or Germany at that moment. Some Americans had foreseen the advantages of a larger engine developing much higher thrust and so the I-40 went into the Shooting Star.

By this time Rolls-Royce had the Nene engine in being, if not in production. It produced 5,000 lb thrust for a weight of 1,580 lb – 300 lb lighter than the I-40. The reason for this great leap forward by a British manufacturer was that in 1943, touring the new American jet centres, Stanley Hooker was shocked – no lesser word will do – to discover that General Electric were working on really ambitious engines of 4,000 lb thrust. When he returned to Barnoldswick, now Rolls' jet headquarters, he sought and was given permission to design an engine of 5,000 lb thrust explicitly to get ahead of the Americans. The Nene was designed and built in six months of 1944, proof that British engineers could work just as fast and, more important, just as ambitiously as their American rivals. The only problem with the Nene was that there was no aircraft into which to fit it, and nobody was designing one. The Anglo-American competition epitomized in this story almost ceased with the end of the war, but until then it had a useful function. British manufacturers, with the collaboration committee and wartime circumstances, badly needed an outside stimulus; so did the Americans, whose aero-engine companies were forbidden to do jet work in wartime. The usual stimulus was missing here and this – together with the absence of any collaboration either – was held to be responsible for the American failure to get a really commanding lead once they held the jet engine in the palm of their hand. Ruthless Anglo–US competition soon re- emerged in peace-time and it remains to this day one of the main world driving forces in jet engine work.

America's early days in jet flight were not wholly successful apart from the abortive Airacomet. When peace came, a number of Me 262s were shipped to the USA and one was tested against the P80 Shooting Star in aerial trials. The results were so favourable to the 262 that they were promptly declared secret. The German fighter had better speed and acceleration, and the rate of climb was equal. The Americans believed that both these fighters were much superior to the Meteor, which, at any rate in its earlier days, they considered to be another Airacomet.

Nobody there knew, but for some time Britain had a sensational lead project which held the promise of peace-time leadership in the most dangerous and least known area – beyond the speed of sound. It was a scheme for a single-seat, single-engined experimental aircraft which would breast the 'sound barrier' and fly at 1,000 mph at 36,000 feet. This breathtaking vision was conceived within the Ministry of Aircraft Production by civil servants in 1943 and they awarded it the specification number E24/43. The minister, Sir Stafford Cripps, personally blessed the project and the contract was given to a small but highly innovative company, F. G. Miles, which up to then had produced only trainers and sports competitors made of wood and fabric. Miles was called personally to the Ministry to see the controller of research and development, Ben (later Sir Ben) Lockspeiser, to be told that henceforth he would be working in metal and the jet engine would provide his propulsive force. Frank Whittle had for some time argued for a supersonic flight programme and he had patented engine developments, including the ducted fan and after-burning (or re-heat) to power an aircraft past Mach 1, as long ago as 1936. In 1940 he had applied for patents for an engine with a large front fan – familiar to every jet passenger today – and another with the fan aft – at the back end of the engine. At first, trials were to be held with a Power Jets 2/700 engine of 2,000 lb thrust for subsonic testing. This engine was to be uprated for high-speed flight with modifications to provide for an aft fan and after-burning – burning extra fuel in the jet outlet at the rear of the engine to give the supersonic kick.

Miles was given the help of the RAE at Farnborough and the National Physical Laboratory. He was to find that the research establishments had done no significant work on supersonics and he worked out the basic shape of the M52 – as it was called – from a study of the profiles of shells and bullets, reasoning that if they could attain supersonic speeds, then his aircraft should have the same form. What took shape on the drawing board was very like a winged bullet with the pilot lying semi-prone in the nose cone. The wings were elliptical, rather like the Spitfire, and their tips were clipped. Nothing like this had been wind tunnel tested before – indeed wind tunnels were barely available – so the company built its own to do model tests. The fuselage was five feet in diameter and the cockpit was to be pressurized and sited ahead of a 200-gallon fuel tank, behind which was the engine. The basic 2/700 was flown attached to a Wellington bomber in 1943 and by 1945 the M52 project was looking like a supersonic fighter for the 1950s and 1960s.

By 1946 most of the detail design was finished and materials were available for three prototypes when an almost everyday note from Lockspeiser dropped on Miles' desk, informing him that supersonic work was discontinued and all work on the M52 must stop at once. Miles was unable to believe what he read, still less tell his workforce. He drove to London to see Lockspeiser, who confirmed the cancellation on the grounds of economy. He expressed doubts whether aeroplanes would ever fly supersonically and said that any future research must be done with unmanned robots. Miles fought for his project for a while, proposing to use a captured German rocket motor and an automatic pilot, but Whitehall was adamant and also ordered him to turn over his calculations and drawings to the Americans. Lockspeiser then confirmed his distrust in Miles' design by turning to Dr (later Sir) Barnes Wallis and his famous swing-wing design, which would lead to an equally famous cancellation in the 1950s. Miles was allowed to announce the cancellation publicly late in 1946, amid considerable fruitless public protest. In effect, the lead in supersonic research was passed to the Americans, who obliged in 1947, with Chuck Yeager flying the rocket-propelled Bell XS1 faster than the speed of sound. It would be ten years before a Briton, Peter Twiss, flew beyond 1,000 mph to establish a world speed record of 1,122 mph on 10 March 1956.

Behind the cancellation of the M52 lay the discoveries in the German aeronautical world which had shaken the British intelligence teams when they analysed them. They were especially worried about the wing shape evolved for the M52 because more advanced German work suggested the need for much sharper sweep-back to counter the effects of compressibility. And so it was to be.

By mid-1945 American intelligence had found most of the early German jet pioneers, except for some who opted for – or were captured by – the Russians. Hans von Ohain, perhaps the most valuable German 'catch' of all, was found in southern Germany, where he had been in charge of the design and development of the 011 advanced engine. Five experimental copies of this complex engine were built in 1943 and another five in 1944. By 1945 nine engines had been tested on the ground and one flew attached to a Junkers 88. However, none had flown under its own power and by 1945 von Ohain and Heinkel, the men responsible for the world's first jet plane in 1939, did not have a single jet engine in production. The youthful von Ohain (still only thirty-four) had seen his first project launched into the air with Heinkel's money and ruthless drive, but Heinkel's improvident shortage of good development engineers had ensured that the genius of von Ohain was grounded in 1945, with only a few prototypes on which to work. When American intelligence men reached him they found that his technicians had buried the 011 engines still in existence. They were persuaded to dig them up and reassemble them for analysis by American engineers in the USA.

Hans von Ohain, and engineers such as Anselm Franz and Helmut Schelp, were all offered work in America after the war. The offers were not particularly generous by US standards, and at first the men had to live in Spartan wooden hostels at such centres as Wright-Patterson Air Force base, but compared with a future in the embers of western Germany they looked decidedly enticing, not least because they were the only means of returning to the work which had become their lives as well as their livelihood. Men with families, such as Dr Franz, were allowed to bring them to America after a year. Bachelors such as Dr von Ohain had no such problems; he married later, in the USA, an American girl of impeccable German origins. Her only problem with this charmingly shy and modest man was the realization, dawning first from meeting the guests at their wedding, that she had married a genius with a growing international reputation. Her husband became chief scientist in the Aerospace Research Laboratories at Wright-Patterson.

As war shaded into peace in 1945, so the pioneering days of jet propulsion ended. In Britain, Germany and the USA the nervous testing in laboratories and workshops of crude prototypes had given way to the confident factory production of engines by the thousand. It was clear that the new power plant would quickly usurp the piston engine which, until 1943 at any rate, had been supreme. This was just as the pioneers predicted. There were still doubters who believed that the jet's voracious fuel consumption would prevent its use in civil airliners but their numbers were shrinking as news spread of the design of the de Havilland Comet. The world's first jetliner is remembered today for its tragedies but the vision behind it, born of the Brabazon committee in Whitehall in the middle of the darkest war in history, was a wonderful one and its realization a magnificent achievement.

On such a scene of triumph, Whitehall's savage foreclosure on the inventor of the jet engine, Frank Whittle, looks all the more dark, not least because it happened at the very moment when the horizons for jet travel were opening world wide. Frank Whittle, not any of his German competitors, was to be the major victim of the peace, and his executioners were to be the civil servants and engine-makers who were beginning to reap the rewards of his originality, courage and insistence on the validity of his concept. His company's position had always seemed anomalous to Whitehall: if only he had worked through the Royal Aircraft Establishment, or a private company like Rolls-Royce, there would have been no problems (and most probably no British jet engine either!). Instead, because of the indifference shown to his ideas by the orthodox, Power Jets had been set up as a private company through which to prove the merit of his ideas by making the first jet engine and flying it. By 1943, through the genius of its founder and the help of his team, Power Jets was in a position to make and test jet engines as well as design them. But the official historian unerringly points to the problem which exercised Whitehall: Power Jets was 'halfway between a research establishment and a commercial firm. There had also been criticism of its attitude of prickly independence.' The British bureaucracy could not work out what to do with a private company whose moving spirit was a serving RAF officer and which had been built up largely by public money.

To this day there are survivors like Lord King Norton (formerly Dr Roxbee Cox) who hold that Power Jets could have survived as an independent R&D company. Certainly, in the present climate and with the experience of the last forty years behind it, government could have devised a tidier and more humane solution which would have left Whittle as an entrepreneur free to compete with the rest of the world. Whittle's solution in 1943 was to suggest to the minister, Sir Stafford Cripps, the nationalization of the entire gas turbine industry as a way of securing Power Jets' future. (Nationalization did happen, only thirty years later.) In May 1943 Cripps replied that, while he personally agreed with Whittle's suggestion, the government was not socialist and the law allowed him to take over Power Jets only if it was found to be inefficient. Later in 1943 Cripps stated that he intended Power Jets alone to be taken over by the state – not the rest of the industry as suggested by Whittle. The terms to the shareholders, who had risked their money since 1936 and could now reasonably expect a good return, were ungenerous: the price to be paid for the shares was to be between £100,000 and £200,000. Cripps pointed out ruthlessly that the takeover might be done in such a way that Power Jets would be left with only its paper assets.

While talks were going on, Whittle's personal position became most unhappy. He was never far away from mental illness and he could see only a confused future in which the government was hell-bent on the destruction of his company without any commercial safeguarding of his own position. Between the Gas Turbine Collaboration Committee in this country and the disclosure of his invention to companies in the United States, there was precious little left of his work to safeguard anyway: it was fully available to anyone the government chose to let in on the secret. And the secret itself was now made public. On 6 January 1944 the British and American governments disclosed to the press for the first time the existence of jet propulsion and the existence of Whittle – to whom all due credit was given. Whittle, now a Group Captain, blinked in the limelight. He became a public hero overnight, a role for which he had not asked and to which he was completely foreign. He was to grow to enjoy fame but at that moment he was conscious only of the shortcomings of the British jet programme and the emasculation of his company, which had brought about jet propulsion in this country and the USA. He was confused by the need to behave as a public figure after years of secrecy and anonymity, and at the same time to dissemble his real feelings about government treatment and what was in store for Power Jets and for his gifted team.

Power Jets' nationalization was announced a few weeks after the publication of its existence, an event which attracted not the slightest public comment. Cripps had made a last offer of £135,000 for the shares, which Tinling accepted on behalf of the company, noting that the offer was unfair and accepted only under duress. A government letter to shareholders pointed out that the plant at Whetstone cost £350,000 to build and the government had spent a further £950,000 in development work by Power Jets. The government's standpoint was that Britain needed a national centre for gas turbine technology and they set up Power Jets (Research & Development) as a public body to answer this need. Dr Roxbee Cox, Williams and Tinling were on the board, Cox as chairman. The shareholders were hardly amply rewarded by the nation and Whittle himself got nothing: he had offered his shares and rights to the government because he felt that a serving officer should not profit from commercial work even though it was done in the national interest. He surrendered some £47,000 in this way, although government feeling, of which he was aware, was moving strongly in favour of some kind of national *ex gratia* payment as a reward for his work. If Whittle thought by now that his problems were solved he was wrong. And he was once more in hospital at RAF Halton with nervous trouble.

The new Power Jets (R&D) was an ill-fitting alliance between the old company and the turbine section of the Royal Aircraft Establishment at Pyestock. The government felt that Hayne Constant and his

RAE team, which had specialized in axial flow turbines and done the work leading up to the Metro-Vick F2 aero engine, could not be left out of the new set-up. So when Roxbee Cox was made chairman, Constant became head of engineering and Whittle was appointed chief technical advisor. But Constant and his team regarded themselves as dedicated research scientists, while the old Power Jets' men regarded themselves as engineers who could design, construct and test jet engines. The fusion of these teams is still regarded by some of the survivors as a disaster – 'in my view a great tragedy' said Sir William Hawthorne many years later. In the end the difficulties were overcome and the teams did manage to produce results, but it was not a propitious start for the state's spearhead into the jet age and there were major convulsions before the teams settled down. The new body had within it ample seeds for its own destruction, not to mention the uncertain appetite of the wolf at the door, the aero-engine manufacturers.

The official brief of Power Jets (R&D), as outlined to the House of Lords on 14 June, 1944, was to design, construct and develop engines; devise methods of manufacture; manufacture small batches of engines: test engines; and make available the knowledge so obtained. Such a brief looked as though it might have satisfied Whittle, since it meant that his old Power Jets functions were left virtually intact, but no sooner had the announcement been made than Lord Hives and Mr A. F. Sidgreaves of Rolls-Royce, though representing the whole of the industry, sought a meeting with the chief executive of the Ministry of Aircraft Production, Sir Edwin Plowden, and asked him for an assurance that there would be no competition in the quantity production of aero engines. Plowden gave this assurance and, to reassure them still further, he set up a small committee under the chairmanship of Roxbee Cox on which all the manufacturers were to be represented, to monitor the activities of Power Jets. At its first meeting the chairman went out of his way to reassure the companies that there was no threat from Power Jets (R&D), that it was not a competitor and that much good could accrue to the engine companies if they would use the fruits of the company's work. 'The firms' fears were temporarily quieted but remained very near the surface,' noted the official historian.

Despite the warning shots from the manufacturers, Whittle, backed by his engineering team and by Roxbee Cox, stuck to the view that Power Jets should have the right and the freedom to build engines up to production standard. In March 1945 Power Jets (R&D) formally asked the Ministry for 100,000 extra square feet of factory floor space and 400 machine tools. Whittle and Roxbee Cox were called upon to explain the request to Sir Edwin Plowden. They told him that it was their understanding that Power Jets (R & D) would be free to build an engine up to contemporary standards and, after making a trial batch, standardize production and hand over the results to one manufacturer or another to mass produce. Any further development would be under the direction of Power Jets (R & D). Plowden sounded out the manufacturers on this interpretation and they at once flatly refuted it, stating that they would not collaborate at all with the new company if this sort of thing was to happen. Since such a system would give the leading engineers (Whittle and his colleagues) a commanding competitive position, it is hardly surprising that the manufacturers would have none of it. They no doubt also sensed that the Ministry was sensitive to their claims – more so than they were sensitive to those of Power Jets.

Thus Whittle fought to the end to preserve and, if possible, extend something like his original relationship with Rover in the short time before it went sour. If it was hard to see this sort of agreement ever working out in peace-time, it was equally hard to see what else Whittle could do to try to preserve his position and that of his company. He had, after all, been forced to set up the company because of the sloth of government and private enterprise: why should he not, now that Power Jets had successfully pioneered jet propulsion, enjoy the fruits after the years of disappointment, strife and penury?

However, the civil service was more afraid of offending the established engine companies, especially Hives and Rolls-Royce, than they were of preserving Whittle and his team intact. If, at this point, Whitehall had cast Power Jets loose as an independent consultancy bound to earn its own living by selling its services, it is quite likely that the company, with worldwide markets opening up as the Western nations turned to the jet engine, would have succeeded. In today's terms it would have been known as a management buy-out, but nobody had then invented the concept. Moreover, if Whittle had been allowed to go it alone, the manufacturers may not have liked it but they could not have legitimately objected to the stimulus of independent competition. In any case, they now adopted a line of attack which argued that Rolls-Royce and other companies had made such strides that Power Jets was really not needed in any form any more. The Ministry allowed itself to be swayed to the extent, not of bolstering Power Jets, but of refusing its demands for space and tools.

Throughout 1945 Whittle, now an Air Commodore, and Roxbee

Cox fought a losing battle with the Ministry. As the official historian wrote:

> Not only was the opposition of the firms too strong to overcome, but for other reasons as well, the basis upon which the status of the firm had been built was crumbling away. Long before this particular issue arose, critics had repeatedly assailed the independence of the management of Power Jets. But in the past the usefulness of Power Jets won them enough support in influential quarters to enable them to resist attempts to reduce their status to that of a government research institution. In addition, the war had always provided an overwhelming argument against major disturbances which might be caused by turning a large number of important scientists and engineers into civil servants. These arguments however had in the meantime lost much of their strength. Opinion in [the ministry], especially from the administrative and contracts branches, hardened into the dilemma of public financial backing without public administrative control.

Whittle now had to witness the end of his company, his influence and all his aspirations. The government achieved this by the device of turning Power Jets into a pure research establishment under their direct control. It was called the National Gas Turbine Establishment and there was to be no design or making of engines, no testing, no development. The new body came into being early in 1946 and Air Commodore Whittle resigned immediately, the victim of supine government and jealous industry. The entire senior team of engineers which he had built up resigned soon afterwards. They were snapped up by industry and some became distinguished national figures. None took jobs with aero-engine manufacturers. The faithful Williams and Tinling were also dispossessed of their jobs. Whittle wrote of them: 'There is not a shadow of doubt that but for their initiative in 1935 my work would never have taken practical shape. . . . They carried the greater part of the administration throughout the time during which Power Jets expanded from nothing to an organization of about 1,300 strong.'

Throughout 1945–46 Whittle led a busy if unfulfilled life as a public figure and lecturer. In April 1946 he received £10,000 from the Ministry pending the hearing of his case by the Royal Commission on Awards to Inventors, set up after the war to reward people for inventions which had contributed to victory. Whittle also received some overtures from industry, including Rolls-Royce, but he could not agree on terms. He was a very difficult figure to place, since he could reasonably expect to be offered a status senior to men who would not consider themselves in any way his junior.

Following his resignation Whittle also retired from the RAF after his third and most severe mental breakdown. He was made financially secure with an RAF pension and a salary as temporary civil servant which together equalled his service pay. In 1948 the Royal Commission awarded him £100,000, the largest sum given to any inventor under this scheme. In the same year he was awarded his knighthood. In financial terms he was treated well by the standards of those times; in every other respect he was allowed to go to waste.

Whittle's surest champion, Harold Roxbee Cox, Lord Kings Norton, wrote an appraisal of him for the Royal Commission which included these words:

> It is one thing to have an idea. It is another to have the technical and executive ability to give it flesh. It is still another to have the tenacity of purpose to drive through to success unshaken in confidence, in the face of discouraging opposition. Whittle, whose name in the annals of engineering comes after those of Watt, Stephenson and Parsons only for reasons of chronology or alphabetical order, had these things.

Such was the man whom Britain compelled to retire at forty-one, believing that a successful jet revolution could be wrought without his genius.

Sir Frank Whittle now lives near Baltimore, in a terrace house on three floors with a split-level living room that looks across a placid lake. The rooms are heavy with trophies – pictures, models, shields, which remind you that he has five British orders, nine honorary doctorates from British universities and nineteen medals of British and American learned societies. After he left the RAF he also took on various consultancies in Britain and the USA. In the long run, it may be thought that he did not suffer unduly. But he never worked on jet engines again and that must have been an agonizing amputation. 'I do not know even now why we were treated so harshly', he stated over forty years later.

But the loss was more than Whittle's: Britain lost too. When Whittle patented the by-pass engine in 1936 he was on the road to the turbofan engine, which came into service in airlines only in the 1960s. This engine was then an American innovation. With its greatly improved fuel consumption it was the engine for which airlines were looking in their quest for an economic transport – a people-carrier by the million and a great leap forward. Had Whittle been at or near the top of Rolls-Royce it is inconceivable that he would not have driven his original concept through to a practical working engine ahead of the USA, making Rolls a more secure company. It is also possible that his knowledge of materials and engineering design would have saved Rolls from its financial collapse caused by technical mistakes with the RB211 engine, in 1971. As it was, Sir Stanley Hooker was called out of retirement to save the engine.

Hans von Ohain, too, has his trophies. They fill two studies of his ranch-style house outside Dayton, Ohio; most of them are American. Although the collapse of Germany must have been traumatic for him, he was at least able to continue his career in the USA and he has about him an air of contentment that seems to elude Whittle and tells you something of the different lives these men have led.

Images, not of a pair of retired gentlemen, heaped with public honours, secure in the history books, come to mind: of Whittle the student fishing out his plans from the back of his desk, then building a contraption – no more – in a hovel of a workshop in the Midlands; and of Hans von Ohain pacing the Baltic shore at night, wondering how to reconcile Heinkel's clamour for results and his own conception of what should be done. They are images to recall when watching Concorde or a 747 climb into the sky. The power behind such jets is descended from the work of these two men who had the vision to see, not what is, but what might be.

Bailey, A. Harvey, *Hives, the Quiet Tiger* (Sir Henry Royce Memorial Foundation)

Bower, Tom, *The Paperclip Conspiracy* (Michael Joseph, London, 1987)

Boyne, Walter, *Messerschmitt 262: Arrow to the Future* (Smithsonian Institute, Washington, 1980)

Boyne, Walter and Lopez, Donald (eds), *The Jet Age: 40 Years of Jet Aviation* (Smithsonian Institute, Washington, 1979)

Brabazon, Lord, of Tara, *The Brabazon Story* (Heinemann, 1956)

Constant, Edward W., *The Origins of the Turbojet Revolution* (Johns Hopkins University Press, 1980)

Deighton, Len, *Fighter* (Jonathan Cape, London, 1977)

Golley, John, *Whittle, the true story* (Airlife Publishing, 1987)

Green, William, *Warplanes of the Third Reich* (Macdonald and Janes, London, 1970)

Heinkel, Ernst, *He 1000* (Hutchinson, London)

Hooker, Sir Stanley, *Not Much of an Engineer* (Airlife Publishing, 1986)

Postan, M. M., Hay, D and Scott, J. D., *Design and Development of Weapons* (HMSO & Longmans, 1964)

Schlaifer, Robert and Heron, S. D., *Development of Aircraft Engines* (Harvard University, 1950)

Smith, J. R. and Kay, Anthony, *German Aircraft of the Second World War* (Putnam, 1972)

Smith, Richard and Creek, Eddie, *Jet Planes of the Third Reich* (Monogram, Massachusetts)

Speer, Albert, *Inside the Third Reich* (Weidenfeld and Nicolson, London, 1970)

Tedder, Lord, *With Prejudice* (Cassell, London, 1966)

Terraine, John, *The Right of the Line* (Hodder & Stoughton, London, 1985)

Tizard, Sir Henry, *Ronald W. Clark* (Methuen, London, 1965)

Whittle, Sir Frank, *Jet: the Story of a Pioneer* (Frederick Mueller, 1954)